THE DIARY OF
SAMUEL PEPYS

THE DIARY
OF
SAMUEL PEPYS

A new and complete
transcription edited by

ROBERT LATHAM
AND
WILLIAM MATTHEWS

CONTRIBUTING EDITORS
WILLIAM A. ARMSTRONG · MACDONALD EMSLIE
OLIVER MILLAR · T. F. REDDAWAY

VOLUME II · 1661

HarperCollins*Publishers*

University of California Press
Berkeley and Los Angeles

Published in the UK by
HarperCollins*Publishers*
77–85 Fulham Palace Road
Hammersmith, London W6 8JB
www.**fire**and**water**.com

UK paperback edition 1995
Reissued 2000

Published in the USA by
University of California Press
Berkeley and Los Angeles, California

First US paperback edition 2000

1 3 5 7 9 8 6 4 2

First published by Bell & Hyman Limited 1971

ISBN 0 00 499022 6 (UK)
ISBN 0 520 22580 5 (USA)

Printed and bound in Great Britain by
Clays Ltd, St Ives plc

CONTENTS

LIST OF ILLUSTRATIONS

READER'S GUIDE

This section is meant for quick reference.   More detailed information about the editorial methods used in this edition will be found in the Introduction and in the section 'Methods of the Commentary' in vol. I, and also in the statement preceding the Select Glossary at the end of each text volume.

I. THE TEXT

The fact that the MS. is mostly in shorthand makes exact reproduction (e.g. of spelling, capitalisation and punctuation) impossible.

Spelling is in modern British style, except for those longhand words which Pepys spelt differently, and words for which the shorthand indicates a variant pronunciation which is also shown by Pepys's longhand elsewhere.   These latter are given in spellings which reflect Pepys's pronunciations.

Pepys's capitalisation is indicated only in his longhand.

Punctuation is almost all editorial, except for certain full-stops, colons, dashes and parentheses.   Punctuation is almost non-existent in the original since the marks could be confused with shorthand.

Italics are all editorial, but (in e.g. headings to entries) often follow indications given in the MS. (by e.g. the use of larger writing).

The **paragraphing** is that of the MS.

Abbreviations of surnames, titles, place names and ordinary words are expanded.

Single **hyphens** are editorial, and represent Pepys's habit of disjoining the elements of compound words (e.g. Wh. hall/White-hall).   Double hyphens represent Pepys's hyphens.

Single **angle-brackets** mark additions made by Pepys in the body of the MS.; double angle-brackets those made in the margins.

Light **asterisks** are editorial (see below, Section II); heavy asterisks are Pepys's own.

Pepys's **alterations** are indicated by the word 'replacing' ('repl.') in the textual footnotes.

II. THE COMMENTARY

1. Footnotes deal mainly with events and transactions.   They also identify MSS, books, plays, music and quotations, but give only occasional and minimal information about persons and places, words and phrases. The initials which follow certain notes indicate the work of the contributing editors. Light asterisks in the text direct the reader to the Select Glossary for the definition of words whose meanings have changed since the time of the diary. References to the diary are given by volume and page where the text is in page-proof at the time of going to press; in other cases, by entry-dates. In notes to the Introduction, since almost all the references there are to the text, a simpler form of reference (by entry-date only) is used.

2. The **Select List of Persons** is printed unchanged in each text volume. It covers the whole diary and identifies the principal persons, together with those who are described in the MS. by titles or in other ways that make for obscurity.

3. The **Select Glossary** is printed at the end of each text volume. It gives definitions of most recurrent English words and phrases, and identifications of certain recurrent places.

4. The **Companion** (vol. X) is a collection of reference material. It contains maps, genealogical tables, and a Large Glossary, but consists mainly of articles, printed for ease of reference in a single alphabetical series. These give information about matters which are dealt with briefly or not at all in the footnotes and the Select Glossary: i.e. persons, places, words and phrases, food, drink, clothes, the weather etc. They also treat systematically the principal subjects with which the diary is concerned: Pepys's work, interests, health etc. References to the *Companion* are given only rarely in the footnotes.

III. DATES

In Pepys's time two reckonings of the calendar year were in use in Western Europe. Most countries had adopted the New Style – the revised calendar of Gregory XIII (1582); Britain until 1752 retained the Old Style – the ancient Roman, or Julian, calendar, which meant that its dates were ten days behind those of the rest of Western Europe in the seventeenth century. 1 January in England was therefore 11 January by the New Style abroad. On the single occasion during the period of the diary when Pepys was abroad (in Holland in May 1660) he continued to use the Old Style, thus avoiding a break in the run of his dates. In the editorial material of the present work dates relating to countries which had adopted the new reckoning are given in both styles (e.g. '1/11 January') in order to prevent confusion.

It will be noticed that the shortest and longest days of the year occur in the diary ten days earlier than in the modern calendar. So, too, does Lord Mayor's Day in London – on 29 October instead of 9 November.

For most legal purposes (from medieval times until 1752) the new year in England was held to begin on Lady Day, 25 March. But in accordance with the general custom, Pepys took it to begin on 1 January, as in the Julian calendar. He gives to all dates within the overlapping period between 1 January and 24 March a year-date which comprehends both styles – e.g. 'January 1 16$\frac{59}{60}$.' In the present commentary a single year-date, that of the New Style, has been used: e.g. '1 January 1660'.

THE DIARY
1661

$$16\frac{60.}{61.}$$

At the end of the last and the beginning of this year I do live in one of the houses belonging to the Navy office as one of the principall officers – and have done now about half a year.   After much trouble with workmen, I am now almost settled – my family being, myself, my wife, Jane, Will Ewre, and Wayneman, my girl's brother.

Myself in a constant good health – and in a most handsome and thriving condition.   Blessed be Almighty God for it.   I am now taking of my sister Paulina to come and live with me.   As to things of State – the King settled and loved of all.   The Duke of Yorke lately matched to my Lord Chancellor's daughter, which doth not please many.   The Queene upon her return to France – with the Princesse Henrietta.   The Princesse of Orange lately dead, and we into new mourning for her.

We have been lately frighted with a great plot, and many taken*a* upon it and the fright of it not quite over.[1]   The parliament, which hath done all this great good to the King, beginning to grow factious, the King did dissolve it December 29. last – and another likely to be chosen speedily.[2]

I take myself now to be worth 300*l* clear in money.   And all my goods and all manner of debts paid, which are none at all.

a   repl. 'taking'

---

1. This was Overton's Plot: see above, i. 319, n. 1.   The Privy Council was still busy taking counter-measures: R. S. Bosher, *Making of Restoration settlement*, pp. 205 6.
2. Elections were held in the following spring, and the new parlia-ment met on 8 May.   The old parliament's offence was not its factiousness (which the Government mostly controlled) but its illegal origin as a convention summoned before the return of the King.

JANUARY. 16$\frac{60}{61}$.

1. Called up this morning by Mr. Moore, who brought me the last things for me to sign for the last month; and to my great comfort tells me that my fees will come to 80*l* clear to myself and about 25*l* for him, which he hath got out of the pardons, though there be no fee due to me at all out of them.[1]

Then comes in my Brother Tho., and after him my father, Dr. Tho. Pepys, my uncle Fenner and his two sons[2] (Anthonys only child dying this morning, yet he was so civil to come and was pretty merry) to breakefast. And I have for them a barrel of oysters, a dish of neat's tongues, and a dish of Anchoves – wine of all sorts, and Northdown*a* ale.[3] We were very merry till about 11 a-clock, and then they went away.

At noon I carried my wife by Coach to my Cosen Tho. Pepys; where we, with my father, Dr. Tho., Cozen Stradwick, Scott, and their wifes dined. Here I saw first his Second wife, which is a very respectful* woman.[4] But his dinner a sorry, poor dinner for a man of his estate – there being nothing but ordinary meat in it. Today the King dined at a Lord's two doors from us.[5] After dinner I took my wife to White-hall; I sent her to Mrs. Pierces (where we should have dined today) and I to the Privy Seale, where Mr. Moore took out all his money; and he and I went to Mr. Pierces (in our way seeing the Duke of Yorke bring his Lady this day to wait upon the Queene, the first time that

---

a word blotted

---

1. Pepys and Moore acted as Sandwich's deputies at the Privy Seal: for their fees, see above, i. 213, n. 1. In December 1660 Pepys had signed 'a deadly number' of free pardons: above, i. 312.

2. Sons-in-law: Anthony and William Joyce.

3. Margate ale: see above, i. 232, n. 1.

4. Thomas Pepys, a well-to-do business man of Westminster, had

married Ursula Stapelton at Kensington in March 1660.

5. He had just attended the christening of the Duke of York's child (Charles, Duke of Cambridge) at Worcester House in the Strand: *Kingd. Intell.*, 7 January, p. 2. In the first few months of his restoration the King often dined or supped at the London houses of the nobility. See Rugge, i, passim.

2

ever she did since that great business;[1] and the Queene is said to receive [her] now with much respect and love); and there he cast up the fees and I told the money. By the same token, one 100*l* bag, after I had told it, fell all about the room, and I fear I have lost some of it that we told.*a*

That done, I left my friends and went to my Lord's; but he being not come in, I lodged the money with Mr. Sheply; and I bade good-night to Mr. Moore and so returned to Mr. Pierces and there supped with them and Mr. Pierce the purser, and his wife and mine – where we have a calfes head carbonadoed, but it was [so] raw we could not eat it, and a good hen. But she is such a slut that I do not love her victualls.

After supper I sent them home by Coach and I went to my Lord's and there played till 12 at night at cards at Best[2] with J. Goods and N. Osgood.[3]

And then to bed with Mr. Sheply.

2. Up earely; and being called up to my Lord, he did give me many commands in his business. As, about taking care to write to my uncle that Mr. Barnewells papers should be locked up, in case he should die, he being now suspected to be very ill.[4] Also, about consulting with Mr. W. Mountagu for the settling of the 4000*l* a year that*b* the King hath promised my Lord.[5] As also about getting of Mr. George Mountagu to be chosen at Huntington this next parliament, &c.[6]

That done, he to White-hall stairs with much company, and I with him; where he took water for Lambeth; and there, coach for Portsmouth.

The Queenes things were all in White-hall court, ready to be sent away, and her Majesty ready to be gone an houre after to

---

a MS. 'could'   *b* repl. 'upon him'

---

1. Their secret marriage: see above, i. 261 & n. 1. For the Queen Mother's attitude to it, see Lister, ii. 79.
2. 'Beast'; a card-game.
3. Servants.
4. Robert Barnwell was Sandwich's steward at Hinchingbrooke. He died on 4 June 1662, heavily in debt to his employer.
5. See above, i. 285 & n. 4. Mountagu wrote to Sandwich on this subject on the following day: Carte 73, ff. 341r, 345r.
6. He was returned for Dover on 6 May.

Hampton-court tonight, and so to be at Pourtsmouth on Saturday next.

I by water to my office, and there all the morning; and so home to dinner – where I found Pall (my sister) was come; but I do not let her sit down at table with me; which I do at first, that she may not expect it hereafter from me. After dinner I to Westminster by water – and there found my Brother Spicer at the Legg with all the rest of the Exchequer men (most of whom I now do not know) at dinner. Here I stayed and drank with them; and then to Mr. George Mountagu about the business of eleccion; and he did give me a piece in gold. So to my Lord's and got the chest of plate brought to the Exchequer, and my Brother Spicer put it into his Treasury. So to Wills with him to a pot of ale; and so parted.

I took a turne in the hall, and bought the King and Chancellors speeches at the dissolving the parliament last Saturday.[1]

So to my Lord's and took my money I brought thither last night and the Silver Candlesticks; and by Coach left the latter at Alderman Backwells, I having no use for them, and the former home. There stood a man at our door when I carried it in, and saw me; which made me a little afeared.

Up to my chamber and wrote letters to Huntington and did other business.

This day I lent Sir W. Batten and Captain Rider my chine of beef for to serve at dinner tomorrow at Trinity-house, the Duke of Albemarle being to be there and all the rest of the Bretheren, it being a great day for the reading over of their new Charter which the King hath newly given them.[2]

3. Early in the morning to the Exchequer, where I told over what money I have of my Lord's and my own there, which I find to be 970*l*: thence to Will's, where Spicer and I eat our dinner of a roasted leg of porke which Will did give us. And

1. *His Majestie's gracious speech, together with the Lord Chancellor's, to both houses of parliament; on . . . the 29th day of December 1660 . . .;* published according to Thomason on this day; reprinted *Parl. Hist.,* iv. 169–77; not in the PL.

2. The charter of 27 November 1660; a copy was kept by Pepys in his Miscellanies, xi. 665: PL 2879.

after that, I to the Theatre, where was acted *Beggars bush*[1] - it being very well done; and here the first time that ever I saw Women come upon the stage.[2] From thence to my father's, where I find my mother gone by Bird the carrier to Brampton, upon my uncles great desire, my aunt being now in despair of life. So home.

4. Office all the morning (my wife and Pall being gone to my father's to dress dinner for Mr. Honiwood,[3] my mother being gone out of town); dined at home, and Mr. Moore with me – with whom I had been early this morning at White-hall at the Jewell-Office, to choose of a piece of gilt plate for my Lord in returne of his offering to the King (which it seems is usuall at this time of the year, and an Earle gives 20 pieces in gold in a purse to the King);[4] I chose a gilt tankard weighing 31 ounces and a half, and he is allowed 30; so I paid 12s for the ounce and a half over what he is to have. But strange it was to me to see what a company of small Fees I was called upon by a great many to pay there; which I perceive is the manner that courtiers do get their estates.[5]

1. See above, i. 297, n. 2; now produced at the TR, Vere St. (A).
2. These were not the first professional actresses to appear on the English stage. In 1629 actresses in a French troupe performed at the Blackfriars, Red Bull and Fortune theatres, but were hooted off the boards. In 1656, Mrs Edward Coleman, who visited Pepys on 31 October 1665, sang the part of Ianthe in Sir William Davenant's opera, *The siege of Rhodes*, at Rutland House in Charterhouse Yard. The articles of agreement which Davenant made when he formed the Duke of York's company on 5 November 1660 show that he had decided to employ actresses. But the King's company, under the management of Thomas Killigrew, probably preceded him in the use of actresses. A woman evidently played the part of Desdemona in Killigrew's production of *Othello*

at the TR, Vere St on 8 December 1660, for Thomas Jordan wrote a special prologue for it 'to introduce the first Woman that came to act on the Stage'. Her identity is not known; Anne Marshall, Margaret Hughes and Katherine Coreyhave been suggested: J. H. Wilson, *All the King's ladies*, pp. 6–8; id. in *Theatre Notebook*, 18/no. 2. (A).
3. Peter Honywood of West Hawkes, Kent, lodged at John Pepys's house in Salisbury Court until *c*. 1666.
4. New Year gifts were regularly exchanged between the King, on the one hand, and peers and office holders, on the other, their value being nicely graded by status. At this time the King spent c. £2000 p.a. on them: BM, Egerton 2543, f.129v.
5. Cf. Sandwich's remark to Pepys about the importance of fees: above, i. 223 & n. 1.

After dinner Mr. Moore and I to the Theatre, where was *The Scornefull Lady*[1] acted very well – it being the first play that ever he saw. Thence with him to drink a cup of ale at Hercules pillars, and so parted. I called to see my father, who told me by the way how Will and Mary Joyce do live a strange life together, nothing but fighting, &c., so that sometimes her father hath a mind to have them divorced.[2] Thence home.

5. Home all the morning. Several people came to me about business; among others, the great Tom: Fuller, who came to me to desire a kindness for a friend of his who hath a mind to go to Jamaica with these two ships that are going, which I promised to do.[3]

So to White-hall to my Lady, whom I found at dinner, and dined with her and stayed with her talking all the afternoon. And thence walked to Westminster-hall; so to Wills and drank with Spicer; and thence by Coach home, staying a little in Pauls churchyard to bespeak Ogilby's *Æsop's fables* and Tullys *officys* to be bound for me.[4] So home and to bed.

6. *Lords day. and Twelfeday.*

My wife and I to church this morning; and so home to dinner to a boiled leg of mutton – all alone.

To church again; where before Sermon,[a] a long Psalm was set that lasted an houre while the Sexton gathered his year's contribucion through the whole church.[5]

a l.h. repl. s.h. 'com'-

---

1. See above, i. 303, n. 3; now produced at the TR, Vere St. (A).

2. Sc. by a decree obtained in an ecclesiastical court, which (except in cases of nullity) gave no rights of remarriage.

3. The ships sailed in February with settlers and stores – an important step in the colonisation of Jamaica. The 'great Tom: Fuller' was the divine and author. His friend may have been Peter Beckford, his parishioner at Cranford, Middlesex, who founded a prominent dynasty of Jamaican planters.

4. He retained neither in his library, but kept later editions of both (1665 and 1695 respectively): PL 2832, 856. John Ogilby's verse paraphrase of Aesop had been published in 1651 and again in 1658: for its purchase, see below, vii. 48 & n. 1. The Cicero was possibly the Cambridge edition of 1660.

5. To set a long psalm for this purpose was a common practice: cf. below, ix. 21 & n. 1. The sexton was Fleetwood Duell, appointed in 1644.

After sermon home; and there I went to my chamber and wrote a letter to send to Mr. Coventry with a piece of plate along with it – which I do preserve among my other letters.[1]

So to supper; and then after prayers to bed.

7. This morning news was brought to me to my bedside that there hath been a great stirr in the City this night by the Fanatiques, who have been up and killed six or seven men, but all are fled.[2] My Lord Mayor and the whole City have been in armes, above 40000.[3] To the office; and after that to dinner, where my brother Tom came and dined with me; and after dinner (leaveing 12*d* with my servants to buy a cake with at night, this day being kept as Twelfeday), Tom and I and my wife to the Theatre and there saw *The Silent Woman*,[4] the first time that ever I did see it and it is an excellent play. Among other things here, Kinaston the boy hath the good turn to appear in three shapes:[5] 1, as a poor woman in ordinary clothes to please Morose; then in fine clothes as a gallant, and in them was clearly the prettiest woman in the whole house – and lastly, as a man; and then likewise did appear the handsomest man in the house. From thence by link to my Cosen Stradwickes, where my father and we and Dr. Pepys – Scott and his wife, and one Mr. Ward and his. And after a good supper we have an excellent cake, where the mark for the Queene was cut;[6] and so there was two queenes, my wife and Mrs. Ward; and the King being lost, they chose the Doctor to be King, so we made him send for some wine;

---

1. In a book of drafts or copies: see below, p. 10. Neither the book nor the letter has been traced.

2. This was the rising of the Fifth-Monarchists, led by Thomas Venner, begun on the previous evening. After a service at their meeting-house off Coleman St, c. 60 had come out in arms to conquer the world in the name of Christ the King (Charles II being away at Portsmouth). Despite their numbers, they were to strike terror into London and Westminster for the next three days. After a skirmish with the trained bands, they had now fled into hiding in Kenwood,

near Highgate.

3. A slip for 4000.

4. By Jonson; see above, i. 171, n. 2. (A).

5. Epicœne, one of Kynaston's chief roles at this time, is the boy who masquerades as a woman before his identity is revealed at the end of the play. (A).

6. For the method by which the King and Queen of Twelfth Night festivities were chosen, see above, i. 10, n. 3. Thomas Strudwick was a provision-dealer – hence the excellence of the food.

and then home: and in our way were in many places strictly examined, more then in the worst of times, there being great fears of these fanatiques rising again. For the present I do not hear that any of them are taken.

Home, it being a clear Mooneshine and after 12 a-clock at night. Being come home, we find that my people have been very merry, and my wife tells me afterward that she hath heard that they had got young Davis and some other neighbours with them to be merry; but no harme.

8. My wife and I lie very long in bed today, talking and pleasing one another in discourse. Being up, Mr. Warren came and he and I agree for the deales that my Lord is to have.[1] Then Will and I to Westminster, where I dined with my Lady. After dinner I took my Lord Hinchingbrooke and Mr. Sidny to the Theatre and showed them *The Widdow*, an indifferent good play, but wronged by the womens being much to seek in their parts.[2] That being done, my Lord's coach*a* waited for us; and so back to my Lady, where she made me drink of some Florence wine and did give me two bottles for my wife. From thence walked to my Cosen Stradwickes and there chose a small banquett* and some other things against our entertainment on Thursday next. Thence to Tom. Pepys and bought a dozen of trenchers,[3] and so home.

Some talk*b* today of a head of Fanatiques that doth appear about Barnett, but I do not believe it.[4]

However, my Lord Mayor, Sir Rich. Brown, hath carried himself very honourably, and hath caused one of their meeting-houses in London to be pulled downe.[5]

a MS. l.h. 'coached'   *b* MS. 'talks'

1. See above, i. 324 & n. 1.
2. The play was a comedy by Thomas Middleton, written c. 1616 and published in 1652. The faulty memorising of parts was not un-common in the Restoration theatre because of its repertory system and the frequent changes of programme. (A).
3. Tom (the turner) was son of

Thomas, elder brother of Pepys's father. His shop was on the e. side of St Paul's churchyard.
4. This rumour was possibly started by the rebels taking to the woods near Highgate.
5. Probably Venner's meeting-house in Swan Ailey, off Coleman St; but there appears to be no trace of this order in the city records.

9. waked in the morning about 6 a-clock by people running up and down in Mr. Davis's house, talking that the Fanatiques were up in armes in the City,[1] and so I rise and went forth, where in the street I find everybody in arms at the doors; so I returned (though with no good courage at all, but that I might not seem to be afeared) and got my sword and pistol, which however I have no powder to charge, and went to the door, where I found Sir R. Ford; and with him I walked up and down as far as the Exchange, and there I left him. In our way, the streets full of trainebands, and great stories what mischief these rogues have done; and I think near a dozen have been killed this morning on both sides. Seeing the city in this condition, the shops shut and all things in trouble, I went home and sat, it being office day, till noon. So home and dined at home, my father with me. And after dinner he would needs have me go to my uncle Wights (where I have been so long absent that I am ashamed to go): I found him at home and his[a] wife; I can see they have taken my absence ill, but all things are past and we good friends; and here I sat with my aunt till it was late, my uncle going forth about business – my aunt being very fearful to be alone. So home to my lute till late, and then to bed – there being strict guards all night in the City, though most of the enemy they say are killed or taken.

10. This morning my wife and Pall went forth early. I stayed[b] within and there comes Mr. Hawly to me and brings me my money for the Quarter of a year's salary of my place under Downing[2] that I was at Sea. So I did give him half,[3] whereof he did in his noblesse give the odd 5s. to my Jane. So we both went forth (calling first to see how Sir W. Pen doth, who I find very ill); and at the hoope by the bridge we drank two pints of Woremoode and sack – talking of his wooing afresh of Mrs. Lane and of his going to serve the Bishop of London.

a MS. 'my' *b* MS. 'state'

---

1. Driven from the woods by hunger, Venner's band had under the cover of darkness slipped past the regulars sent after them and had returned to the city in the early morning of this day. They were now being hunted down by large forces of militia, and by regulars under York and Albemarle.

2. Pepys's clerkship in the Exchequer.

3. See above, i. 83, 238.

Thence by water to White-hall and found my wife at Mrs. Hunts; and leaving her to dine there, I went and dined with my Lady, and stayed to talk a while with her.

After dinner Will comes to tell me that he hath presented my piece of plate to Mr. Coventry, who takes it very kindly and sends me a very kind letter, and the plate back again[1] – of which my heart is very glad. So to Mrs. Hunts, where I find a French-man, a lodger of hers, at dinner; and just as I came in was kissing my wife, which I did not like, though there could not be any hurt in it.

Thence by Coach to my uncle Wights with my wife; but they being both out of doors, we went home.   Where after I had put some papers in order and entered some letters in my book which I have a mind to keep,[2] I went with my wife to see Sir W. Pen,*a* who we find ill still – but he doth make very much of it.   Here we sat a great while; at last comes in Mr. Davis and his lady (who takes it very ill that my wife never did go to see her)[3] and so we fell to talk: among other things, Mr. Davis told us the perticular examinations of these Fanatiques that are taken.   And in short it is this –

Of all these Fanatiques that have done all this, *viz.*, routed all the train-bands that they met with – put the King's lifeguard to the run – killed about 20 men – broke through the City gates twice – and all this in the daytime, when all the City was in armes – are not in all above*b* 31.[4]   Whereas we did believe them (because they were seen up and down in every place almost in the City, and have been about Highgate two or three dayes, and in several other places) to be at least 500.   A thing that never was heard of, that so few men should dare and do so much mischief.

a repl. 'Batten'   *b* MS. 'about'

---

1. As Pepys had hoped: above, i. 322.

2. See above, p. 7. This book has not been traced.

3. John Davis (Navy Office clerk) had a very proud wife: cf. above, i. 277, 278.

4. Davis was perhaps referring to the number arrested earlier in the rising, which was about 30: *State Trials* (ed. Howell), vi. 105, n. Contemporary accounts agree in placing the total number of the rebels at 40–60: ib., vi. 106, n.; *CSPD 1660–1*, p. 470; *EHR*, 25/741; Sir Richard Baker, *Chronicle* (1679), p. 735. But it is certain that these fanatics fought with a wild courage.

Their word was "King Jesus, and the heads[1] upon the gates!" Few of them would receive any Quarter but such as were taken by force and kept alive, expecting Jesus to come and reign here in the world presently,* and will not believe yet but their work will be carried on, though they do die.

The King this day came to towne.

11. *office day.* This day comes news by letters from Portsmouth that the Princesse Henriette is fallen sick of the meazells on board the *London*, after the Queene and she was under sail – and so was forced to come back again into Portsmouth harbour. And in their way, was by negligence of the Pilott run upon the Horsesand. The Queene and she continues aboard, and do not entend to come on shore till she sees what will become of the young Princesse. This newes doth make people think something endeed; that three of them should fall sick of the same disease one after another. This morning likewise, we have order to see guards set in all the King's yards; and so we do appoint who and who shall go to them. Sir Wm Batten to Chatham – Collonell Slingsby and I to Deptford and Woolwich[2] – Portsmouth, being a garrison, needs none.

Dined at home – discontented that my wife doth not go neater, now she hath two maids. After dinner comes in Kate Sterpin (whom we have not seen a great while) and her husband to see us – with whom I stayed a while; and then to the office and left them with my wife.

At night walked to Pauls churchyard and bespoke some books against next week; and from thence to the Coffee-house – where I met Captain Morrice the upholster. Who would fain have lent me a horse tonight to have rid with him upon the City-guard with the Lord Mayor – there being some new expectations of these rogues; but I refused by reason of my going out of town tomorrow. So home and to bed.

---

1. The regicides' heads: see above, i. 269.

2. Cf. Duke of York to Sir W. Compton, 11 January, ordering the delivery of arms for this purpose: PRO, Adm. 2/1745, f.23*v*. The Duke mentioned Slingsby, but not Pepys, as responsible for Deptford and Woolwich.

12.   **Saturday.**^a

With Collonell Slingsby and a friend of his, Major Waters (a
deafe and most amorous melancholy gentleman, who is under a
despayre in love as the Collonell told me, which makes him bad
company, though a most good-natured man), by water to
Redriffe; and so on foot to Deptford – our servants by water.
Where we fell to choosing four Captains to command the guards,
and choosing the places where to keep them and other things in
order thereunto.   We dined at the globe, having our messenger
with us to take care for us.   Never till now did I see the great
authority of my place, all the Captains of the fleet coming cap in
hand to us.

Having stayed very late there talking with the Collonell, I went
home with Mr. Davis, storekeeper (whose wife is ill and so I could
not see her), and was there most princlike lodged, with so much
respect and honour that I was almost at a loss how to behave
myself.

13.   In the morning we all went to church[1] and sat in the pew
belonging to us.   Where a cold sermon of a young [man] that
never hath preached before.   Here Comissioner Pett came with
his wife and daughters – the eldest, being his wife's daughter,
is a very comely black woman.   So to the globe to dinner.
And then with Comissioner Pett to his lodgings there (which he
hath for the present while he is in building the King's yacht,
which will be a very pretty thing and much beyond the Duch-
man's);[2] and^b from thence with him and his wife and daughter-
in-law* by Coach to Greenwich church,[3] where a good sermon, a
fine church, and a great company of handsome women.   After
sermon to Deptford again; where at the Comissioners and the
globe we stayed long.   And so I to Mr. Davis's to bed again.

a blot in upper margin   *b* repl. 'where'

---

1. St Nicholas's, Deptford.
2. Peter Pett's yacht was the
Catherine. For the Dutch yacht
(given to the King by the city of
Amsterdam and commanded by Jan
de Gens), see above, i. 222 & n. 1.
Yachts were a Dutch invention, and

at 8 November 1660 Pepys had not
believed it possible that the English
could build anything comparable.
3. St Alfege's, a medieval building
of various periods, replaced in 1718
by the present church.

But no sooner in bed but we have an alarme and so we rise. And the Comptroller comes into the yard to us – and seamen of all the ships present repair to us; and there we armed, with every-one a handspike, with which they were as fierce as could be. At last we hear that it was only five or six men that did ride through the guard in the towne without stopping to the guard that was there and some say shot at them. But all being quiett there, we caused the seamen to go on board again; and so we all to bed (after I had sat awhile with Mr. Davis in his study, which is filled with good books and some very good song=bookes): I likewise to bed.

14. The armes being come this morning from the tower, we caused them to be distributed. I spent much time walking with Lieutenant Lambert, walking up and down the yards, who did give me much light into things there. And so went along with me and dined with us. After dinner Mrs. Pett (her husband being gone this morning with Sir Wm. Batten this morning to Chatham) lent us her coach and carried us to Woolwich – where we did also dispose of the armes there and settle the guards. So to Mr. Pett's the shipwright[1] and there supped; where he did treat us very handsomely (and strange it is to see what neat houses all the officers of the King's yards have),[2] his wife a proper woman and hath been handsome, and yet hath a very pretty hand.

Thence I with Mr. Ackworth to his house, where he hath a very pretty house and a very proper lovely woman to his wife,[3] who both sat with me in my chamber; and they being gone, I went to bed – which was also most neat and fine.

15. Up and down the yard all the morning, and seeing the seamen exercize, which they do already very handsomely.

Then to dinner at Mr. Ackworths, where there also dined with us one Captain Bethell, a friend of the Comptrollers. A good dinner and very handsome. After that and taking our leaves of

---

1. Christopher Pett was Master-Shipwright at Deptford and Woolwich yards, and youngest brother of Commissioner Peter Pett.

2. It was often remarked that the officers of the yards used the King's

workmen and materials to embellish their houses: e.g. John Hollond, *Discourses* (ed. Tanner), pp. 150–1.

3. William Ackworth was Storekeeper at Woolwich; his wife was a sister of Christopher Pett.

the officers of the yard, we walked to the waterside and in our way walked into the Ropeyard, where I do look into the tarr-houses and other places, and took great notice of all the several works belonging to the making of a Cable.[1]

So after a cup of burnt wine at the taverne there, we took barge and went to blackwall and viewed the dock and the new wett=dock which is newly made there,[2] and a brave new merchant-man which is to be launched shortly, and they say to be called the Royall=oake.[3]

Hence we walked to dick=shoare, and thence to the towre, and so home – where I found my wife and pall abroad; so I went to see Sir Wm. Pen, and there found Mr. Coventry come to see him and now have an opportunity to thank him and he did express much kindness to me. I sat a great while with Sir Wm after he was gone, and have much talk with him. I perceive none of our officers care much for one another, but I do keep in with them all as much as I can. Sir Wm. Pen is still very ill, as when I went. Home, where my wife not yet come home. So I went up to put my papers in order. And then was much troubled my wife was not come, it being ten a-clock just now striking as I write[a] this last line.

This day I hear the Princesse is recoverd again. The King hath been this afternoon at Deptford[b] to see the yacht that Commissioner Pett is building, which will be very pretty; as also that that his Brother at Woolwich is in making.[4]

By and by comes in my boy and tells me that his mistress doth

a   repl. 'make'　　　　b   repl. 'Woolwich'

---

1. For cable making, see below, vi. 34 & n. 3.
2. The largest wet dock in England; used by the E. India Company: H. Green and R. Wigram, *Chron. Blackwall Yard*, p. 16; Sir W. Foster, *John Company*, p. 149. 'The first recorded wet dock with gates on the Thames': Sir J. G. Broodbank, *Hist. port London*, p. 64. Description in Mundy, v. 159–60. Henry Johnson had bought the yard in 1656 from the

E. India Company: Foster, op. cit., p. 149.
3. An E. Indiaman, to be distinguished from the royal ship of the same name. The symbol of the oak-tree (associated with royalty for many centuries) had now been given new vitality by Charles II's hiding in the Boscobel oak after the battle of Worcester, 1651.
4. The *Anne*; now being built for the Duke of York by Christopher Pett.

lie this night at Mrs. Hunts, who is very ill. With which being something satisfyed, I went to bed.

16. This morning I went early to the Comptroller's; and so with him by coach to White-hall to wait upon Mr. Coventry to give him an account of what we have done. Which having done, I went away to wait upon my Lady; but coming to her lodgings, I hear that she is gone this morning to Chatham by coach, thinking to meet me there. Which did trouble me exceedingly and did not know what to do, being loath to fallow her and yet could not imagine what she would do when she found me not there. In this trouble, I went to take a walking in Westminster-hall and by chance met with Mr. Childe, who went forth with my Lady today; but his horse being bad, he came back again – which then did trouble me more, so that I did resolve to go to her. And so by boate home and put on my boots; and so over to Southworke to the posthouse and there took horse and guide to Dartford;[1] and thence to Rochester*a* (I having good horses and good way, came thither about half an houre after daylight, which was before*b* 6 a-clock, and I set forth after 2); where I found my Lady and her daughter Jem and Mrs. Browne and five servants, all at a great loss not finding me here. But at my coming, she was overjoyed. The sport was how she had entended to have kept herself unknown and how the Captaine (whom she had sent for) of the *Charles*[2] had forsoothed her, though he knew her well enough, and she him. In fine, we supped merry; and so to bed – there coming several of the *Charles* men to see me before I got to bed. The page lay with me.

17. Up; and breakefast with my Lady. Then came Captain Cuttance and Blake to carry her in the barge on board. And so we went through Ham Creeke to the *Soverayne*[3] (a goodly sight

a repl. 'Uxbridge' *b* l.h. repl. s.h. 'about'

---

1. For riding post with a guide (postboy), see *Comp.*: 'Travel; By road'. The Southwark posthouse was frequently used by the Navy Office: cf. below, p. 231 & n. 2.

2. Roger Cuttance.

3. The *Royal Sovereign*; the largest and best-known warship of the fleet (some said the most useless); one of the first of the three-deckers; built from ship-money in 1637, burnt by accident in 1696. See below, iv. 29, n. 4.

all the way to see the brave ships that lie here) first, which is a most noble ship I never saw before – my Lady Sandwich – my Lady Jemimah – Mrs. Browne – Mrs. Grace, and Mary and the page, my lady's servants – and myself, all went into the Lanthorne together.[1]   From thence to the *Charles*, where my Lady took great pleasure to see all the rooms and to hear me tell her how things are when my Lord is there.   After we had seen all, then the officers of the ship have prepared a handsome breakefast for her; and while she was pledging[a] my Lord's health, they gave her five guns.[2]   That done, we went off; and then they gave us thirteen guns more.   I confess it was a great pleasure to myself to see the ship that I begun my good fortune in.[3]   From thence on board the *Newcastle* to show my Lady the difference between a great and a small ship.   Among these ships I did give away 7*l*. So back again and went on shore at Chatham-yard, where I had ordered the Coach to wait for us.   Here I heard that Sir Wm. Batten and his lady (who I knew were here, and did endeavour to avoyd)[b] were now gone this morning to London.   So we took coach; and I went into the Coach and went through the towne without making stop at our Inn, but left J. Goods to pay the reckoning.   So I rode with my Lady in the Coach, and the page on the horse that I should have rid on, he desiring it.   It begun to be darke before we could come to Dartford and to rain hard and the horses to fayle; which was our great care to prevent, for fear of my Lord's displeasure.   So here we set up for tonight – as also Captain Cuttance and Blake, who came along with us. We sat and talked till Supper; and at supper my Lady and I entered into a great dispute concerning what were best for a man to do with his estate; whether to make the elder son heire,

a l.h. repl. s.h. 'drink'-   *b* accidental ink strokes above word

1. There were seven lanterns at the stern; when in use they were lit by huge candles: *Mar. Mirr.*, 42/233-4. According to Magalotti (p. 358), the largest held six people; James Howell says ten: *Epist. Ho-Elianae* (ed. Jacobs), i. 338.   There were nine on this occasion.

2. For the Admiral's orders on the subject of salutes (4 December 1660), see PRO, Adm. 2/1725, f.34r.

3. In the Dutch voyage of the spring of 1660.   The *Charles* was then the *Naseby*.

which my Lady is for and I against*a* but rather to make all equall.[1] This discourse took us much time, till it was time to go to bed. But we being merry, we bade my Lady good-night and entended to have gone to the post-house to drink and hear a pretty girl play of the Gitterne (and endeed, we should have lain there, but by a mistake we did not); but it was late and we could not hear her, and the guard came to examine what we were. So we returned to our Inn and to bed – the page and I in one bed and the two Captains in another, all in one chamber – where we had very good mirth with our most abominable lodging.

18. The Captains went with me to the post-house about 9 a-clock; and after a morning draught I took horse and guide for London – and though some rain and a great wind in my face, I got to London at 11 a-clock. At home found all well, but the Monkey loose, which did anger me; and so I did strike her till she was almost dead, that they might make her faste again – which did still trouble me more. In the afternoon we met at the office and sat till night. And then I to see my father, who I found well, and took him to Standings to drink a cup of ale. He told me my aunt[2] at Brampton is yet alive, and my mother well there. In comes Will. Joyce to us, drunk and in a talking vapouring humour, of his state and I know not what – which did vex me cruelly. After him Mr. Hollier [who] had learned at my father's that I was here (where I had appointed to meet*b* him); and so he did give me something to take for prevention.[3] Will. Joyce not letting us talk as I would, I left my father and him and took Mr. Hollier to the Greyhound – where he did advise me above all things both as to the Stone and the decay of my memory (of which I now complain to him), to avoyd drinking often; which I am resolved, if I can, to leave off.

a s.h. repl. badly formed s.h.   *b* MS. 'me'

---

1. The latter method ('gavelkind'; applying to all male heirs) was prevalent in several parts of England, but particularly in Kent (the county in which this conversation took place), and, although by 1661 less widespread than in the Middle Ages, was not abolished until 1922. Pepys had heard Capt. Silas Taylor discourse about it on 21 February 1660: above, i. 63.

2. Anne, wife of Robert Pepys.

3. Thomas Hollier was the surgeon who (it seems) had operated on Pepys for the stone in 1658.

Hence home; and took home with me from the bookesellers Ogilbys *Æsop*, which he hath bound*ª* for me;[1] and endeed, I am very much pleased with the book.

Home and to bed.

19. To the Comptrollers; and with him by Coach to White-hall (in our way meeting Venner and Prichard upon a sledge, who with two more fifth Monarchy=men were hanged today, and the two first drawn and quartered):[2] where we walked up and down and at last found Sir. G. Carteret (whom I have not seen a great while) and did discourse with him about our assisting the Comissioners in paying off the Fleete – which we think to decline.[3] Here the Treasurer did tell me that he did suspect Tho. Hater to be an informer of them in this work, which we do take to be a diminucion of us. Which doth trouble me, and I doe entend to find out the truth.

Hence to my Lady, who told me how Mr. Hetly[4] is dead of the small-pox going to Portsmouth with my Lord. My Lady went forth to dinner to her father's – and so I went to the Legg in King-street and had a Rabbit for myself and my Will. And after dinner I sent him home and myself went to the Theatre, where I saw *The Lost lady*,[5] which doth not please me much. Here I was troubled to be seen by four of our office Clerkes, which sat in the half-Crowne box and I in the 1s-6d.[6]

a repl. 'not'

---

1. Cf. above, p. 6 & n. 4.
2. Thomas Venner and Roger Hodgkin were the only two hanged, drawn and quartered: *Somers Tracts* (ed. Scott), vii. 470. The other two referred to were William Oxman and Giles Pritchard, hanged and beheaded in Wood St: ib., p. 472. Nine others met the same fate on the 21st. Pepys kept a drawing of one of the sledges used on such occasions: PL 2973, p. 316 (a).
3. See below, p. 19. The parliamentary commissioners (provided since 29 December 1660 with additional funds by 12 Car. II c. 27) had held their first meeting (as the statute

required) on 12 January. Local commissioners had been appointed to assist them to pay off 65 ships. The Navy Board (normally in charge of pay) was required by the act to supply information, but not to assist in the paying-off. *CJ*, viii. 217, 220–1; *LJ*, xi. 235.
4. William Hetley of Brampton.
5. A tragicomedy by Sir William Berkeley, acted and published in 1638; now at the TR, Vere St. (A).
6. Above the pit there were usually three tiers of seats: the boxes, where a seat cost 4s., the middle gallery, and the top gallery. Pepys was in the middle gallery; the clerks probably in a special box in the same tier. (A).

From hence by Linke, and bought two mousetrapps of Tho Pepys the Turner; and so went and drank a cup of ale with him; and so home and wrote by post to Portsmouth to my Lord, and so to bed.

20. *Lords day.*

To church in the morning. Dined at home. Wife and I to church in the afternoon. And that being done, we went to see my Uncle and aunt White. There I left my wife and came back and sat with Sir Wm. Pen, who is not yet well again. Thence back again to my wife and supped there and were very merry; and so home – and after prayers, to write down my journall for the five last days; and so to bed.

21. This morning, Sir Wm. Batten, the Comptroller, and I to Westminster-hall, to the Comissioners for paying off the Army and Navy, where the Duke of Albemarle was – and we sat with our hatts on[1] – and did discourse about paying off the ships. And do find that they do entend to undertake it without our help; and we are glad of it, for it is a work that will much displease the poor seamen, and so we are glad to have no hand in it.[2]

From thence to the Exchequer and took 200*l* and carried it home. And so to the office till night. And then to see Sir Wm. Pen, whither came my Lady Batten and her daughter; and then I sent for my wife, and so we sat talking till it was late. So home to supper. And then to bed – having eat no dinner today.

It is strange what weather we have had all this winter; no cold at all, but the ways are dusty and the flyes fly up and down, and the rosebushes are full of leaves; such a time of the year as never

1. A sign of equality of status among the members of the meeting; the parliamentary commissioners would (as M.P.'s) normally be in the habit of wearing their hats when at work, either in committee or in the House.

2. See below, p. 45 & n. 1. The commissioners finished paying off the army on 26 January. The standing army of the revolution was thus peacefully disbanded. *Merc. Pub.*, 31 January, p. 53.

was known in this world before here.¹   This day, many more of the fith monarchy men were hanged.²

22.   To the Controller's house, where I read over his proposalls to the Lord-Admirall for the regulating of the officers of the navy*³ – in which he hath taken much pains – only, he doth seem to have too good an opinion of them himself.   From thence in his coach to Mercer's Chappell.   And so up to the great hall, where we met with the King's Councell for trade⁴ upon some proposalls of theirs for settling convoys for the whole English trade – and that by having 33 ships (4 fourth-rates, 19 fifth, 10 sixth) settled by the King for that purpose – which endeed was argued very finely by many persons of Honour and merchants that were there.⁵

It pleased me much now to come in this condition to this place, where I was once a*a* peticioner for my exhibicion in Pauls school.⁶ And also where Sir G. Downing (my late master) was chaireman, and so but equally concerned with me.

From thence home; and after a little dinner – my wife and I by coach into London and bought some glasses; and then to

a MS. 'was a'

---

1. Dr D. J. Schove writes: 'This and to a less extent the following winter were the mildest in England between at least those of 1647–8 and 1675–6.'

2. Nine were now hanged in addition to the four executed on the 19th: *Kingd. Intell.*, 21 January, p. 46; ib., 28 January, pp. 57–8.

3. Sir Robert Slingsby, 'A discourse upon the past and present state of his Majesty's navy' (1660); printed in John Hollond, *Discourses* (ed. Tanner, pp. 327+) from the MS. which Pepys preserved (PL 2193). BM, Add. 9335 seems to be a later version; so, more certainly, are PL 2871, pp. 683+ and BM, Harl. 6003, ff. 160+.

4. The Council of Trade had been established as a separate body in November 1660.   It met on Tuesdays and Thursdays: *Merc. Pub.*, 6 December, p. 60.   Its resolutions of 14 March 1661 about convoys are in *CTB*, i. 245–7.   For its various places of meeting, see C. M. Andrews, *Brit. Committees of Trade, 1622–75*, pp. 74–5; for its work, see W. R. Scott, *Joint stock companies*, i. 266–7.

5. Since 1649 convoys had been provided at the state's charge: Oppenheim, p. 313.

6. The Robinson exhibition awarded him in 1650.

White-hall to see Mrs. Fox – but she not within, my ⟨wife⟩ went to my mother Bowyer and I met with Dr. Tho. Fuller and took him to the Dogg, where he tells me of his last and great book that is coming out: that is, his history of all the families of England – and could tell me more of my owne then I knew myself.[1]   And also to what perfection he hath now brought the art of memory; that he did lately to four eminently great Schollars dictate together in Latin upon different Subjects of their proposing, faster then they were able to write, till they were tired.[2]

And by the way, in discourse tells me that the best way of beginning a sentence, if a man should be out and forget his last sentence (which he never was), that then his last refuge is to begin with an *Utcunque*.[3]

From thence I to Mr. Bowyers and there sat a while.   And so to Mr. Foxes and sat with them a very little while; and then by coach home.   And so to see Sir Wm. Pen, where we find Mrs. Martha Batten and two handsome ladies more, and so we stayed supper and were very merry; and so home to bed.

23.   I to the office all the morning.   My wife and people at home busy, to get things ready for tomorrow dinner.   At noon, without dinner, went into the City; and there meeting with Greatorex, we went and drank a pot of ale.   He told me that he was upon a design to go to Tenariffe to try experiments there.[4]   With him to Gresham Colledge (where I never was before)

---

1. Fuller's *History of the worthies of England* (1662) did not pretend to cover all families.   To Pepys's chagrin it contained nothing about his own: below, iii. 26.

2. Fuller was reputed to have the most remarkable memory of anyone of his generation.   He could repeat 500 random words after one hearing; he could recite, in any order, the shop-signs in a series of London streets after walking once through them.   As a preacher he rarely used notes.   See *The life of . . . Dr Thomas Fuller* (1661),

pp. 75+.   He always denied that he used mnemonics.

3. However.

4. The peak of Tenerife (in the Canaries: 12,162 ft) was often reckoned the highest in the world: cf. James Yonge, *Journal* (ed. Poynter), p. 61. On 2 January the 'Royal Society' (q.v. below, p. 22, n. 1) had arranged to enquire about air pressure on the mountain: Birch, i. 8–10.   Nothing seems to be known of any visit by Ralph Greatorex.

and saw the manner of the house, and find great company of persons of Honour there.[1]

Thence to my bookseller's and for books; and to Stevens the silversmith to make clean some plate against tomorrow. And so home, by the way paying many little debts for wine and pictures, &c., which is my great pleasure.

Home and find all things in a hurry of business, Slater our messenger being here as my Cooke – till very late.

I in my chamber all the evening, looking over my Osborns works[2] and new Emanuel Thesaurus's *Patriarchae*.[3]

So late to bed – having eat nothing today but a piece of bread and cheese at the ale-house with Greatrex – and some bread and butter at home.

24. At home all day. There dined with me Sir Wm. Batten and his Lady and daughter – Sir W. Pen – Mr. Fox (his lady being ill could not come) and Captain Cuttance.

The first dinner I have made since I came hither. This cost me above 5*l.* And merry we were – only, my chimny smokes.

In the afternoon Mr. Hater brings me my last Quarter salary[4] – which I received of him. And so I have now Mr. Barlow's money[5] in my hand.

1. A meeting of the society which became known after its first charter (15 July 1662) as the Royal Society. Since November 1660 it had regularly held meetings on Wednesdays from 3 p.m. to 6 p.m. The 'persons of Honour' present on this occasion (listed in Birch, i. 12–13) included Lord Brouncker, William Petty, Sir Kenelm Digby and John Evelyn. Greatorex attended these early meetings, but does not appear to have been a fellow of the Society after its incorporation.

2. Francis Osborne (d. 1658) wrote moralising tracts for the guidance of young men. Pepys was very fond of his *Advice to a son* (1656 etc.), and called him 'my father Osborne': below, p. 199. The reference here is to separate works: the first collected edition appears to be what was called the 'seventh' (1673), of which Pepys retained a copy: PL 941. Cf. F. F. Madan, *Some notes on bibliog. of F. Osborne* (Oxf. Bibliog. Soc. Pub., n.s. iv), p. 60.

3. *Patriarchae, sive Christi servatoris genealogia, per mundi aetates traducta* (1657; PL 736); a book of Latin verses on the patriarchs by Emanuele Tesauro (d. 1675), a fertile and forgotten Italian litterateur and historian; first published at Milan in 1645.

4. See Navy Treasurer's warrants (25 December): PRO, Adm. 20/1, nos 1287, 1289 (£87 10s. for Pepys, £15 for his two clerks).

5. Money payable to Pepys's predecessor: above, i. 202 & n. 1.

The company all go away. And by and by Sir Wms. both, and my Lady Batten and his daughter came again and supped with me and talked till late; and so to bed, being glad that that trouble is over.

25. At the office all the morning. Dined at home and Mr. Hater with me; and so I did make even with him for the last Quarter. After dinner he and I begin to look upon the Instruccions of my Lord Northumberlands,[1] but we were interupted by Mr. Salsbury's[2] coming in – who came to See*ᵃ* me – and to show me my Lord's picture in little of his doing.[3] And truly, it is strange to what a perfection he is come in a year's time. From thence to Pauls churchyard about books. And so back again home. This night comes two cages which I bought this evening for my Canary birds which Captain Rooth this day sent me. So to bed.

26. Within all the morning. About noon comes one that hath formerly known me and I him, but I know not his name, to borrow 5*l* of me; but I have the wit to deny him.

There dined with me this day both the Pierces and their wifes and Captain Cuttance and Lieutenant Lambert (with whom we made ourselfs very merry by taking away his ribbans and garters,[4] having made him to confess that he is lately married).

The company being gone, I went to my lute till night; and so to bed.

27. *Lords day.* Before I rose, letters came to me from Portsmouth, telling me that the Princesse is now well and my Lord Sandwich set sail with the Queene and her yesterday from thence

a l.h. repl. s.h. 'see'

---

1. The 10th Earl, appointed Lord Admiral (as the Duke of York's substitute) in 1638. His Instructions (14 November 1640) set out, *inter alia*, the duties of the Principal Officers of the Navy Board. (Pepys's copy in Rawl. C 679; Penn's in BM, Sloane 3232, ff. 87–138.) They were replaced by the Duke of York's Instructions of 1662: see below, iii. 24 & n. 1.

2. 'Salisburye', a 'platter' of St John's St, was Quartermaster to a troop of Mountagu's regiment in the 1650s: Carte 74, f.253r.

3. Untraced. (OM).

4. Cf. above, i. 27, n. 2.

for France.[1] To church, leaving*a* my wife now sick of her *menses* at home. A poor dull sermon, of a stranger. Home; and at dinner was very angry at my people's eating a fine pudding (made me by Slater the Cooke last Thursday) without my wife's leave.

To church again; and a good sermon of Mr. Mills. And after sermon Sir Wm. Pen and I an houre in the garden, talking – and he did answer me to many things I asked*b* – Mr. Coventry's opinion of me and Sir Wm. Batten's of my Lord Sandwich – which do both please me. Then to Sir Wm. Battens, where very merry; and here I met the Comptroller and his lady and daughter (the first time I ever saw them) and Mrs. Turner, who and her husband supped with us here (I having fetched my wife thither); and after supper we fell to oysters, and then Mr. Turner went and fetched some strong waters. And so, being very merry, we parted and home*b* and to bed.

This day the parson read a proclamacion at church for the keeping of Wednesday next, the 30th of January, a fast for the murther of the late King.[2]

28. At the offic? all the morning. Dined at home. And after dinner to Fleetstreete with my sword to Mr. Brigden (lately made Captain of the Auxiliarys) to be refreshed. And with him to an alehouse, where I met Mr. Damport; and after some talk of Cromwell, Ireton and Bradshaws bodies being taken out of their graves today,[3] I went to Mr. Crews and thence

a repl. 'all' or 'al'-   *b* MS. 'asked by'   *c* repl. 'we'

---

1. Cf. the two letters to the Navy Board, sent from Portsmouth, 26 January: PRO, SP 29/29, nos 32, 33; summaries in *CSPD 1660–1*, pp. 487–8.

2. *A proclamation for observation of the thirtieth day of January as a day of fast and humiliation according to the late act of parliament for that purpose*; published on 25 January 1661, and ordered to be read in all churches each year on the Sunday before the fast-day: Steele, no. 3283.

3. See above, i. 309, n. 4; below, p. 27 & n. 1. The work of exhumation had begun on the 26th; on the 28th the coffins were taken to the Red Lion in Holborn. Pride's body seems to have escaped the fate of the others: M. Noble, *Lives Engl. regicides* (1798), ii. 132–3. For the story that Cromwell's corpse had been exchanged for that of a king, see below, v. 297 & n. 2.

to the Theatre, wher[...] [la]*dy*, which doth
now please me better [...] I sitting behind
in a dark place, a lad[...] [b]y a mistake, not
seeing me. But afte[...] [p]retty lady, I was
not troubled at it at [...]s; and there met
Mr. Moore, who cam[...] [we]nt with me to my
father's and with hi[...] came to us Dr:
Fairebrother,[2] who I [...] Beare and gave a
pint of sack and a [...] still continue his
expressions of respec[...] [te]lls me my brother
John will make a g[...]

    Thence to see th[...] at Mr. Holden's,
where I bought a ha[...] [b]y mooneshine and
by the way was ov[...] [l]er's coach; and so
home to his house [...] to bed. This noon
I had my presse set [...] [pa]pers to be put in.

    29. Mr. Moore [...] me all this morning
till Lieutenant Lam[...] [t]hem over the water
to Southwark and s[...] [?]th, and there drank –
it being a most gl[...] [?]n to amazement for
this time of the year. Thence to my Lord's, where we find my
Lady gone with some company to see Hampton Court; so we
three went to blackfryers (the first time that ever I was there
since plays begun);[3] and there, after great patience and little
expectacions from so poor beginnings, I saw three acts of *The Mayd
in the Mill*[4] acted, to my great content. But it being late, I left
the play and them, and by water through bridge home. And so
to Mr. Turner's house, where the Comptroller, Sir Wm. Baten,

a l.h. repl. s.h. 'yesterday'

1. See above, p. 18 & n. 5; at the TR, Vere St. (A).

2. Fellow of King's College, Cambridge.

3. Pepys cannot be referring to the famous Blackfriars Theatre used by the King's Men from c. 1608 until 1642, because it had been pulled down on 5 August 1655. His 'Blackfryers' is an error for 'Whitefriars', i.e. the Salisbury Court Theatre, at which the Duke of York's company was performing at this time under the management of Davenant: Hazelton Spencer in *Mod. Philol.*, 24/173+. Cf. below, p. 34, where Pepys again makes the error but corrects it. (A).

4. A comedy by Fletcher and Rowley, acted in 1623 and published in 1647. (A).

and Mr. Davis and their[a] ladies; and here we have a most neat little, but costly and genteele supper. And after that, a great deal of impertinent mirth by Mr. Davis and some catches, and so broke up. And going away, Mr Davis's eldest son took up my old Lady Slingsby in his armes and carried her to the Coach, and is said to be able to carry three [of] the biggest men that were in the company – which I wonder at. So home and to bed.

30th. *Fast day.*

The first time that this day hath been yet observed.[1] And Mr. Mills made a most excellent sermon – upon "Lord, forgive us our former iniquitys."[2] Speaking excellently of the justice of God in punishing man for the sins of his ancesters.

Home, and John Goods comes; and after dinner I did pay him 30*l* for my Lady. And after that, Sir Wm. Pen and I into Moorefields and have a rare walk, it being a most pleasant day. And besides much discourse, did please ourselfs to see young Davis and Whitton, two of our clerks, going by us in the field – who we observe to take much pleasure together; and I did most often see them at plays together.

Back to the old James[3] in Bishops-gate-street, where Sir Wm. Batten and Sir Wm. Rider met him[4] about business of the Trinity-house: so I went away home, and there understand that my mother is come home well from[b] Brampton. And have a letter from my brother John – a very ingenious one; and he therein begs to have leave to come to town at the Coronacion.[5]

Then to my Lady Batten's, where my wife and she are lately come back again from being abroad and seeing of Cromwell,

---

a 'and their' repeated   *b* repl. 'in'

---

1. Cf. above, p. 24 & n. 2. The fast-day commemorating the execution of Charles I had been established by an act of December 1660. A form of service was drawn up in 1662 and incorporated in the Prayer Book. It was not removed until 1859.

2. A loose recollection of Ps. lxxix. 8.

3. The Great James. (R).

4. I.e. Penn, who with Rider was an Elder Brother of Trinity House; Batten was Deputy-Master.

5. According to the diary, his request does not appear to have been granted. Penn's son William (later the Quaker leader, now an undergraduate at Oxford) seems to have been luckier: below, p. 82.

Ireton, and Bradshaw hanged and buried at Tiburne.[1] Then I home.

31. This morning with Mr. Coventree at White-hall about getting a ship to carry my Lord's Deales to Lynne,[2] and we have chosen the *Guift*. Thence at noon to my Lord's – where my Lady not well; so I eat a mouthful of dinner there, and thence to the Theatre and there sat in the pitt among the company of fine Ladys, &c.; and the house was exceeding full to see *Argalus and Parthenia*, the first time that it hath been acted;[3] and endeed, it is good, though wronged by my over-great expectacions, as all things elsc are. Thence to my father's to see my mother, who is pretty well after her journy from Brampton. She tells me my aunt is pretty well, yet cannot live long. My uncle pretty well too, and she believes would marry again were my aunt dead, which God forbid.[4] So home.

1. The shrouded and embalmed corpses of the regicides were hanged in public from morning until sundown, then cut down, the heads removed and the 'loathsome trunks' buried under the gallows. Descriptions in Evelyn; Rugge, i, f.154*v*.

2. The timber would travel from King's Lynn to Hinchingbrooke by the Ouse. For the building works at Hinchingbrooke, see below, p. 49, & n. 1.

3. A romantic pastoral play by Henry Glapthorne, written between 1632 and 1638, published in 1639. Now presented (at the TR, Vere St) for the first time since the Restoration. (A).

4. Pepys was his heir. The aunt, however, outlived the uncle (Robert Pepys) by three months.

FEBRUARY.

1. *Friday.* A full office all this morning; and busy about answering the Comissioners of Parliament to their letter, wherein they desire to borrow two Clerkes of ours – which we will not grant them.[1]

After dinner into London and bought some books – a belt – and have my sword new-furbished. To the alehouse with Mr. Brigden and Wll. Symons and drank together. At night home. So after a little musique, to bed, leaving my people up getting things ready against tomorrow's dinner.

2. early to Mr. Moore; and with him to Sir Peter Ball, who proffers my uncle Robt. much civility in letting him continue in the grounds which he had hired of Heately, who is now dead.[2]

Thence home – where all things in a hurry for dinner – a strange Cooke being come in the room of Slater, who could not come.

There dined here my Uncle Wight and my aunt – my father and mother and my brother Tom – Dr. Fairebrother and Mr. Mills the parson and his wife, who is a neighbour's daughter of my uncle Robts. and knows my aunt Wight and all her and my friends there. And so we have excellent company today.

After dinner I was sent for to Sir G. Carterets, where he was and I find the Comptroller; who are upon writing a letter to the Comissioners of parliament; in some things a rougher style then our last, because they seem to speak high to us.[3]

---

1. See above, p. 18 & n. 3.

2. Ball was Attorney-General to the Queen Mother and one of the trustees administering her property, which included Brampton manor. William Hetley (who had died in January) had until 1653 owned Brampton Park: VCH, *Hunts.*, iii. 16.

3. An undated draft of the new letter, in Pepys's hand, is in PRO, SP 29/30, no. 43. In it the Board, after asserting that they have already done what is required by the act of disbandment, ask the commissioners that 'you will not impose upon us what wee cannot possibly performe or justifie by Law . . .'. See below, p. 33 & n. 3.

So the Comptroller and I thence to a tavern hard by, and there did agree upon drawing up some letters to be sent to all the pursers and clerks of the Cheques[1] to make up their accounts. Then home, where I find the parson and his wife gone – and by and by the rest of the company, very well pleased, and I too – it being the last dinner I entend to make a great while. It having now cost me almost 15*l* in three dinners within this fortnight. In the evening comes Sir Wm. Pen, pretty merry, to sit with me and talk, which we did for an houre or two; and so good-night – and I to bed.

3. *Lordsday.* This day I first begun to go forth in my coate and sword, as the manner now among gentlemen is.[2] To White-hall. In my way heard Mr. Tho. Fuller preach at the Savoy upon our forgiving of other men's trespasses – showing, among [other] things, that we are to go to law never to Revenge, but only to repayre – which I think a good distinction. So to White-hall, where I stayed to hear the trumpets and kettle-drums – and then the other drums; which is much cried up, though I think it dull, vulgar music. So to Mr. Foxes unbidd, where I have a good dinner and special company. Among other discourse, I observed one story, how my Lord of Norwich*ᵃ* at a public audience before the King of France made the Duke of Anjou cry by making ugly faces as he was stepping to the King, but undiscovered.[3] And how Sir Phillip Warwickes lady did wonder to have Mr. Darcy send for several dozen bottles of Rhenish wine to her house, not knowing that the wine was his.

a MS. 'Northwich'

1. The latter were the principal clerical officers of the dockyards. These letters have not been traced; they may have been prompted by requests sent to the Board on 21 January and 1 February by the parliamentary commissioners for disbanding the forces: PRO, Adm. 106/3, ff. 17*r*, 59*r*.

2. A French mode, which now displaced the old cloak and rapier. The sword may have been a short one, as the fashion demanded; it was apparently an old one recently refurbished: see above, p. 28. On 4 May 1662 Pepys equipped his manservant with a sword. See Cunnington, pp. 142, 168–9; J. D. Aylward, *Small-sword in Engl.*; *Country Life*, 1961, p. 876.

3. In 1643–4 the Earl of Norwich (then Lord Goring) had negotiated the Treaty of Rueil (23 June/3 July 1644) between the English and French crowns. Louis XIV was then only five and his brother Anjou three.

Thence to my Lord's – where I am told how Sir Tho. Crew's Pedro, with two of his countrymen more, did last night kill one soldier of four that quarrelled with them in the street about 10 a-clock. The other two are taken; but he is now hid at my Lord's till night, that he doth entend to make his escape away.

So up to my Lady and sat and talked with her long. And so to Westminster-stairs and there took boat to the bridge, and so home – where I met with letters to call us all up tomorrow morning to Whitehall – about office business.

4. earely up to Court with Sir Wm. Pen; where at Mr. Coventry's chamber we met with all our fellow-officers; and there, after a hot debate about the business of paying off the fleet and how far we should joyne with the Commissioners of Parliament (which is now the great business of this month and more to determine, and about which there is a great deal of difference between us and them how far we shall be assistant to them) therein. That being done, he and I back again home – where I met with my father and mother going to my Cozen Snowes to Blackwall, and have promised to bring me and my wife along with them – which we could not do because we are to go to the Dolphin today to a dinner of Captain Taylors.[1] So at last I let my wife go with them; and I to the tavern, where Sir Wm. Pen and the Comptroller and several others were, men and women; and we had a very great and merry dinner. And after dinner the Comptroller begun some sports; among others, the Nameing of people round, and afterward demanding Questions of them that they are forced to answer*a* their names to;[2] which doth make very good sport. And here I took pleasure to take the forfeits of the ladies who could not do their duty, by kissing of them – among others, a pretty lady who I found afterward to be wife to Sir W. Battens son.[3]

Home. And then with my wife to see Sir W. Batten, who could not be with us this day, being ill – but we found him at

a   or 'swear' (same symbol)

---

1. John Taylor, shipbuilder, of Chatham.

2. A game presumably akin to 'Questions and Commands', which was common at this time.

3. William, eldest son of Sir William Batten, was a barrister of Lincoln's Inn. Pepys often admired his wife's looks.

Cards. And here we sot late, talking with my Lady and others and Dr. Whistler,[1] who I found good company and a very ingenious*a* man. So home and to bed.

5. *washing day*. My wife and I by water to Westminster. She to her mother's and I to Westminster-hall, where I find a full terme; and here I went to Will's and there found Shaw and Ashwell and another, Brograve (who knew my mother washmaid to my Lady Veere);[2] who by cursing and swearing made me weary of his company, and so I went away. Into the Hall and there saw my Lord Treasurer (who was sworn today at the Exchequer, with a very great company of Lords and persons of Honour to attend him) go up to the Treasury Offices and take possession thereof.[3] And also saw the heads of Cromwell, Bradshaw, and Ireton set up upon the further end of the hall.[4]

Then at Mrs. Michells in the hall, met my wife and Shaw; and she and I and Captain Murford to the Dogg, and there I give them some wine; and after some mirth and talk (Mr. Langly coming in afterwards), I went by Coach to the playhouse at the Theatre – our Coach in King-street breaking, and so took another. Here we saw *Argalus and Parthenia* – which I lately saw.[5] But though pleasant for the dancing and singing, I do not find good for any wit or design therein.

That done, home by coach. And to supper, being very hungry for want of dinner; and so to bed.

a or 'ingenuous' (abbrev. l.h.)

---

1. Daniel Whistler, physician.

2. Wife of the 1st Baron Vere of Tilbury; she had lived in Clapton, Middlesex. Pepys's mother had come from a humble family (the Kites, of Newington Green, Middlesex) and had married John Pepys in 1626.

3. The Earl of Southampton had acted as Lord Treasurer since 24 August 1660 (*CTB*, i. 18), but did not take the oaths of office until now. For the ceremony, see *Merc. Pub.*, 7 February, p. 80. Cf. S. B. Baxter,

Devel. of Treasury 1660–1702, pp. 6, 259.

4. Cf. above, p. 24 & n. 3, for the exhumation of the bodies. The heads were now set on poles on top of the s. end with Bradshaw's in the middle, above the very part of the hall where he had presided in 1649 over the regicide court: *Merc. Pub.*, 7 February, p. 80. They remained there as late as 1684 or 1688. See below, v. 297 & n. 2.

5. See above, p. 27 & n. 3. (A).

6.   Called up by my Cosen Snow, who sat by me while I was trimmed, and then I drank with him – he desiring a courtesy for a friend, which I have done for him.[1]   Then to the office and there sat long; then to dinner – Captain Murford with me. I had a dish of fish and a good Hare, which was sent me the other day by Goodenough the plaisterer.[2]

So to the office again, where Sir W. Pen and I sat all alone answering of peticions and nothing else.   And so to Sir W. Batten's, where comes Mr. Jessop (one whom I could not formerly have looked upon; and now he comes cap in hand to us from the Commissioners of the Navy, though endeed he is a man of a great estate and of good report)[3] about some business from them to us, which we answered by letter.

Here I sat long with Sir W., who is not well.   And then home and to my chamber and some little Musique; and so to bed.

7.   With Sir Wm. Batten and Pen to White-hall to Mr. Coventry's chamber to debate upon the business we were upon the other morning;[a] and thence to Westminster-hall and after a walk or two, to my Lord's; where, while I and my Lady was in her chamber in talk, in comes my Lord from Sea, to our great wonder.   He had dined at Havre de Grace on Monday last and came to the Downe[s] the next day and lay at Canterbury that night;   and so to Dartford, and thence this morning to White-hall.   All my friends, his servants, well.   Among other, Mr. Creed and Captain Ferrers tell me the story of my Lord Duke of Buckingam's and my Lords falling out at Havre de Grace at Cards – they two, and my Lord St. Albans, playing.

The Duke did, to my Lord's dishonour, often say that he did in his conscience know the contrary to what he then said about the difference at Cards;   and so did take up the money that hee should have lost to my Lord.   Which my Lord resenting, said nothing then;   but that he doubted not but there was ways enough to get his money of him.   So they parted that night,

a   MS. 'day morning'

---

1. Cf. above, i. 242.
2. Edward Goodenough, a neighbour; he had done some recent work at Pepys's lodgings: above, i. 254 etc.
3. William Jessop had been Clerk to the Council of State, 1654-60, and Clerk to the House of Commons in 1660.   The 'Commissioners of the Navy' were the parliamentary commissioners appointed to pay off the ships, to whom he was now secretary.

and my Lord sent for Sir R. Stayner and sent him the next morning to the Duke to know whether he did remember what he said last night and whether he would owne them with his sword and a second; which he said he would, and so both sides agreed. But my Lord St. Albans and the Queene and Abbot Mountagu[1] did waylay them at their lodgings till the difference was made up, much to my Lord's honour, who hath got great reputation thereby.[2]

I dined with my Lord and then with Mr. Sheply and Creed (who talk very high of France for a fine country) to the tavern; and then I home. To the office, where the two Sir Wms. had stayed for me; and there we drow up a letter to the Commissioners of Parliament again;[3] and so to Sir W. Battens, where I stayed*a* late in talk; and so home. And after writing the letter fayre, then I went to bed.

8. At the office all the morning. At noon to the Exchange to meet Mr. Warren the timber-Merchant, but could not meet with him. Here I met with many sea-commanders; and among others, Captain Cuttle, and Curtis and Mootham; and I went to the Fleece tavern to drink and there we spent till 4 a-clock telling stories of Algier and the manner of the life of Slaves there;[4]

---

a MS. 'state'

1. Walter Mountagu, Abbot of St Martin, near Pontoise; Sandwich's cousin; a prominent convert to Roman Catholicism; Almoner to the Queen Mother and a friend of Princess Henrietta.

2. This is confirmed by the statement of a newsletter-writer (5 February) in HMC, *Sutherland*, p. 159. Cf. also Marvell, ii. 18.

3. PRO, SP 29/30, no. 44; summary in *CSPD 1660–1*, p. 505. The letter argued that the parliamentary commissioners were making demands of naval officials which could properly be addressed only by the King to the Admiral himself. Cf. above, p. 28 & n. 3.

4. Many such stories are collected in E. de Aranda, *Relation de la captivité et liberté du sieur Emanuel d'Aranda . . .* (Brussels, 1662), of which Pepys retained John Davies's translation: *The history of Algiers and it's slavery* (1666; PL 754). According to Sir Godfrey Fisher's *Barbary Legend* (esp. pp. 103+), Algiers had a good reputation in this respect, and treated its captives rather better than Christian countries treated their slaves or jailbirds. He points out that, although slaves under Muslim law, they were regarded as prisoners-of-war, and had well-established rights. There is, however, much evidence besides Pepys's to controvert this view. See esp. Sir George Clark, *War and society in 17th cent.*, ch. v.

and truly, Captain Mootham and Mr. Dawes (who have been both slaves there) did make me full acquainted with their condition there. As, how they eat nothing but bread and water. At their redempcion, they pay so much for the water that they drink at the public fountaynes during their being slaves. How they are beat upon the soles of the feet and bellies at the Liberty of their *Padron.* How they are all at night called into their master's Bagnard, and there they lie. How the poorest men do use their slaves best. How some rogues do live well, if they do endent to bring their masters in so much a week by their industry or theft; and then they are put to no other work at all. And theft there is counted no great crime at all.

Thence to Mr. Rawlinsons, having met my old friend Dick Scobell, and there I drank a great deal with him; and so home and to bed betimes, my head akeing.

9. To my Lord's with Mr. Creed (who was come to me this morning to get a bill of imprest signed); and my Lord being gone out, he and I to the Rhenish wine-house with Mr. Blackburne – to whom I did make known my fears of Will's losing of his time, which he will take care to give him good advice about.[1]

Afterward to my Lord's and Mr. Sheply; and I did make even his accounts and mine. And then with Mr. Creed and two friends of his (my late lord Jones's son one of them)[2] to an ordinary to dinner. And then Creed and I to White*a*friers to the playhouse and saw *The Mad Lover*, the first time I ever saw it acted[3] – which I like pretty well.

Then home.

a   repl. 'Black'-

---

1. Will Hewer, Pepys's clerk, was Blackborne's nephew.
2. Col. Philip Jones (Comptroller of the Protector's Household under Oliver and Richard Cromwell, and member of the Upper House, 1657–8) had three sons.
3. The playhouse was not the Whitefriars Theatre opened c. 1605, but the Salisbury Court Theatre (opened in 1629), situated in the Whitefriars district east of the Temple and south of Fleet St. The Duke of York's Company, managed by Sir William Davenant, played here before he transferred it to a new theatre in Lincoln's Inn Fields in June 1661. See above, p. 25, n. 3. The play, a tragicomedy by John Fletcher, was first acted in 1617, and published in 1647. (A).

10. *Lord's day*. Took Phisique all day. And God forgive me, did spend it in reading of some little French Romances. At night my wife and I did please ourselfs talking of our going into France, which I hope to effect this summer.[1] At noon one came to aske for Mrs. Hunt that was here yesterday and it seems is not come home yet, which makes us afeared of her. At night to bed.

11. At the office all the morning. Dined at home. And then to the Exchange and took Mr. Warren with me to Mr. Kennard the Maister-Joyner at White-hall, who was at a tavern; and there he and I to him and agreed about getting some of my Lord's Deales on board tomorrow.[2]

Then with young Mr. Reeve[3] home to his house, who did there show me many pretty pleasures in perspectives that I have not seen before; and I did buy a little glass of him, cost me 5*s*. And so to Mr. Crews; and with Mr. Moore to see how my father and mother did. And so with him to Mr. Adam Chards[4] (the first time I ever was at his house since he was married) to drink. Then we parted, and I home to my study and set some papers and money in order; and so to bed.

12. To my Lord's and there with him all the morning; and then (he going out to dinner) I and Mr. Pickering, Creed, and Captain Ferrers to the Leg in the Palace to dinner – where strange, Pickering's impertinency's. Thence the two others and I, after a great dispute whether to go, we went by water to Salsbury*ᵃ*-court Play-house; where not liking to sit, we went out again and by coach to the Theatre[5] and there saw *The Scorneful Lady*, now done by a woman, which makes the play appear much better then ever it did to me.[6]

a repl. 'Wh'-

---

1. They did not go there until the autumn of 1669.
2. Cf. above, p. 27 & n. 2.
3. John, son of Richard Reeves, optical instrument maker, Long Acre.
4. Shopkeeper in Pope's Head Alley.
5. The TR, Vere St. (A).

6. Pepys had seen this play, a comedy by Beaumont and Fletcher, on 27 November 1660 and again on 4 January 1661, when the title-role was evidently played by a boy-actor. Anne Marshall may have been the actress; Downes (p. 6) lists her as 'the Lady' in his cast. (A).

Then Creed and I (the other being lost in the Croud) to drink a cup of ale at Temple-bar. And there we parted – and I (seeing my father and mother by the way) went home.

13. At the office all the morning. Dined at home; and poor Mr. Wood with me – who after dinner would have borrowed money of me, but I would lend none. Then to White-hall by coach with Sir W. Pen, where we did very little business; and so back to Mr. Rawlinson's, where I took him in and gave him a cup of wine – he having formerly known Mr. Rawlinson. And here I met my uncle Wight and he drank with us. Then with him to Sir W. Batten's; whither I sent for my wife and we chose*a* Valentines against tomorrow. My wife chose me, which did much please me. My Lady Batten, Sir W. Pen &c. Here we sat late; and so home to bed – having got my Lady Batten to give me a spoonful of hony for my cold.

14. *Valentine's day.* Up earely and to Sir W. Battens. But would not go in till I had asked whether they that opened the doore was a man or a woman. And Mingo,[1] who was there, answered "a Woman;" which, with his tone, made me laugh.

So up I went and took Mrs. Martha[2] for my Valentine (which I do only for complacency), and Sir W. Batten, he go in the same manner to my wife. And so we were very merry.

About 10 a-clock we with a great deal of company went down by our barge to Deptford; and there only went to see how forward Mr. Pett's yacht is. And so all into the barge again, and so to Woolwich on board the *Rosebush*, Captain Brown's ship,[3] that is brother-in-law to Sir W. Batten – where we had a very fine dinner dressed on shoare. And great mirth and all things successfull – the first time I ever carried my wife a-shipboard – as also my boy Waineman, who hath all this day been called "young Pepys", as Sir W. Pen's boy "young Pen".

a MS. 'chosen'

---

1. Batten's black servant.

2. Batten's unmarried daughter, aged about 24. Pepys had her as his Valentine again the next year and again with a marked lack of enthu-

siasm. On 2 March 1662 he had to be 'jogged' by Penn before he offered to lead Martha out of church.

3. About to sail for Jamaica: Duke of York, *Mem. (naval)*, p. 9.

So home by barge again; good weather, but pretty cold.

I to my study and begun to make up my accounts for my Lord, which I entend to end tomorrow.

To bed.

The talk of the towne now is, who the King is like to have for his Queene – and whether Lent shall be kept with the strictnesse of the King's proclamacion;[1] which it is thought cannot be, because of the poor, who cannot buy fish – and also the great preparacion for the King's crowning is now much thought upon and talked of.

15. At the office all the morning. And in the afternoon at making up my accounts for my Lord tomorrow. And that being done, I find myself to be clear (as I think) 350*l* in the world, besides my goods in my house, and all things paid for.

16. To my Lord in the morning, who looked over my accounts – and agreed to them. I did also get him to sign a bill (which doth make my heart merry) for 60*l* to me, in consideration of my work extraordinary at sea this last voyage – which I hope to get paid.[2]

I dined with my Lord. And then to the Theatre, where I saw *The Virgin=Martyr*[3] – a good but too sober a play for the company. Then home.

17. *Lords day*. A most tedious, unseasonable, and impertinent* sermon by an Irish Doctor. His text was "Scatter them, O Lord, that delight in warr."[4] Sir Wm. Batten and I very much angry with the parson. And so I to Westminster as soon as I came home. To my Lord's – where I dined with Mr. Sheply and Howe. After dinner (without speaking to my Lord), Mr. Sheply and I into the City. And so I home and took my wife to my Uncle Wights and there did Supp with them; and so home again – and to bed.

1. Issued on 29 January and repeating the substance of a proclamation of 6 February 1640: Steele, no. 3287.

2. See below, pp. 61, 62. He had already received £50 as pay for 90 days' service: PRO, Adm. 20/1, p. 84.

3. A tragedy by Dekker and Massinger, acted c. 1620 and published in 1622. For the text of this production (at the TR, Vere St), see J. G. McManaway in *ELH*, 1/287. (A).

4. A loose recollection of Ps. lxviii. 30.

18.   At the office all the morning.   Dined at home with a very good dinner; only my wife and I, which is not yet very usuall.   In the afternoon my wife and I and Mrs. Martha Batten, my Valentine, to the Exchange; and there, upon a payre of embroydered and six payre of plain white gloves, I laid out 40s upon her.   Then we went to a Mercers at the end of Lombard-streete and there she bought a suit of Lutestring for herself.   And so home.   And at night I got the whole company and Sir Wm. Pen home to my house; and there I did give them Rhenish wine and sugar and continued together till it was late; and so to bed.

It is much talked that the King is already marryed to the neece of the Prince de Ligne and that he hath two sons already by her[1] – which I am sorry to hear, but yet am gladder that it should be so then that the Duke of Yorke and his family should come to the Crowne – he being a professed friend to the Catholiques.[2]

19.   By coach to White-hall with Collonell Slingsby (carrying Mrs. Turner with us); and there he and I up into the House, where we met with Sir G. Cartret – who afterward, with the Duke of Yorke, my Lord Sandwich, and others, went into a private room to consult.   And we were a little troubled that we were not called in with the rest.   But I do believe it was upon something very private.   We stayed walking in the galery, where we met with Mr. Slingsby, that was formerly a great friend of Monsieur Blondeau's – who showed me the stamps of the King's new coyne; which is strange to see how good they are in the

1. This story concerned the Prince de Ligne's sister: he had no niece. For a similar report of the rumour (16 February), see HMC, *Sutherland*, p. 159. It was also reported (as baseless) by the Venetian resident in a despatch dated this day, and by the Florentine envoy five days later: *CSPVen. 1659–61*, p. 248; BM, Add. 27962 Q, f.26r. It was the departure of the Earl of Bristol to the continent on a supposedly secret matrimonial mission – in fact to Parma – which seems to have given

rise to these rumours. Cf. below, p. 52, n. 1.
2. He did not become a Roman Catholic until c. 1669, but already employed Catholics in his service: see esp. Morley to Hyde, 24 April 1659, in *Clar. State Papers*, iii (1786), pp. 458–9; de Vecchii to Sec. of State, Brussels, 7 August 1660, in C. Gilbin, *Collectanea Hib.*, no. 1, p. 107.   Catholics at court had been active since the Restoration in attempts to obtain some relaxation of the penal laws.

stamp and bad in the mony, for lack of skill to make them.[1] But he says Blondeau will shortly come over and then we shall have it better, and the best in the world.

The Controller and I to the Comissioners of Parliament; and after some talk, away again – and to drink a cup of ale. He tells me he is sure that the King is not yet married, as it is said; nor that it is known who he will have. To my Lord's and found him dined; and so I lost my dinner. But I stayed and played with him and Mr. Childe &c., some things of four partes; and so it raining hard and bitter cold (the first winter day we have yet had this winter),[2] I took coach home and spent the evening in reading of a Latin play, the *Naufragium joculare*.[3] And so to bed.

20. All the morning at the office. Dined at home, and my Brother Tom with me – who brought me a payre of fine slippers, which he gives me. By and by comes little Luellin and a friend to see me; and then my he-Cozen Stradwick, who was never here before. With them I drank a bottle of wine or two; and so to the office again – and there stayed about business late. And then all of us to Sir Wm. Pens, where we have, and my[a] Lady Batten, Mrs. Martha, and my wife, and other company, a good supper. And sat playing at cards and talking till 12 at night; and so all to our lodgeings.

21. To Westminster by coach with Sir W. Pen. And in our way saw the City begin to build scaffolds against the Coronacion.[4] To my Lord and there find him out of doors. So to the Hall and called for some capps that I have a-making there. And here

a repl. 'our'

---

1. Cf. C. Oman, *Coinage of Engl.*, pp. 329–30; below, iii. 265. They were made hurriedly and by methods known to be obsolescent. Henry Slingsby (brother of Sir Robert, Comptroller of the Navy) was now Deputy-Master of the Mint. Pierre Blondeau, engineer to Cromwell's mint, returned to take office there again in 1662, and was responsible for the production, though not the design, of the milled money which from that year onwards replaced the older type struck by hammering.

2. Cf. above, p. 20, n. 1.

3. A comedy by Abraham Cowley, acted at Trinity College, Cambridge, and published in 1638; PL 217(2). (A).

4. See below, pp. 81–8.

met with Mr. Hawly and with him to Wills and drank. And
then by coach with Mr. Langly,*a* our old friend, into the City.
Set him down by the way; and I home and there stayed all day
within – having found Mr. Moore, who stayed with me till late
at night, talking and reading some good books. Then he went
away, and I to bed.

22. All the morning at the office. At noon with my wife
and Pall to my father's to dinner, where Dr. Tho. Pepys and my
Cosen Snow and Joyce Norton. After dinner came The.
Turner; and so I home with her to her mother, good woman –
whom I have not seen, through my great neglect, this half year –
but she could not be angry with me. Here I stayed all the afternoon, talking of the King's being married, which is now the
towne talk but I believe false.

In the evening Mrs. The and Joyce took us all into the coach
home, calling in Bishop's-gate street, thinking to have seen a new
Harpsicon that she hath a-making there; but it was not done,
and so we did not see it. Then to my house, where I made very
much of her; and then she went home. Then my wife to Sir
W. Batten's and there sat a while – he having yesterday sent my
wife half-a-dozen pair of gloves and a pair of silk stockings and
garters, for her Valentine's gift.

Then home and to bed.

23. This my *Birth day, 28 yeeres.*

This morning Sir W. Batten, Pen, and I did some business;
and then I by water to White-hall – having met Mr. Hartlibb[1]
by the way at Alderman Backwells: so he did give me a glass of
Rhenish wine at the Steeleyard.[2] And so to White-hall by water.
He continues of the same bold impertinent Humour that he was
alway of and will ever be. He told me how my Lord Chancellor hath lately got the Duke of Yorke and Duchesse, and her
woman, my Lord Ossery, and a Doctor, to make oath before most
of the Judges of the kingdom concerning all the circumstances of

a   repl. 'H'-

----

1. Samuel Hartlib, jun.; underclerk   2. The Rhenish wine-house at the
to the Council.   entrance to the Steelyard.

their marriage.[1]   And in fine, it is confessed that they were not fully married till about a month or two before she was brought to bed; but that they were contracted long before, and time enough for the child to be legitimate; but I do not hear that it was put to the Judges to determine whether it was so or no.

To my Lord and there spoke to him about his opinion of the Light, the Sea-marke that Captain Murford is about and doth offer me an eighth part to concern myself with it.[2]   And my Lord doth give me some incouragement in it – and I shall go on. I dined here with Mr. Sheply and Howe.   After dinner to White-hall chappell with Mr. Childe; and there did hear Captain Cooke and his boy make a tryall of an Anthemne against to-morrow, which was rare Musique.

Then by water to White-fryers to the play-house, and there saw *The Changeling*,[3] the first time it hath been acted these 20 yeeres – and it takes exceedingly.   Besides, I see the gallants do begin to be tyred with the Vanity and pride of the Theatre=actors, who are endeed grown very proud and rich.[4]

1. At a special meeting of Council on 18 February the Duke had brought evidence to prove that he had been contracted in marriage to Anne Hyde at Breda on 24 November 1659 and had thereafter lived with her in clandestine marriage until the religious ceremony at Worcester House on 3 September 1660: PRO, PC 2/55, pp. 131+. (Pepys's shorthand copy of the entry in the council register, made later – ? after 1688 – was sold at Sotheby's in 1919: *Catalogue*, 11 April, no. 940.) Besides the Duke and Duchess, the deponents mentioned above were: Ellen Strode (servant), the Earl of Ossory (both witnesses); and Joseph Crowther, D.D. (the 'Doctor'), who performed the ceremony according to Anglican rites.   The judges do not appear to have been asked to pronounce on the question of legitimacy.

2. This was probably the scheme for the erection of a lighthouse at the mouth of the Humber, in which William Murford (a timber merchant)

went half-shares with Sir Philip Frowde: PCC, Mico, 101. The right to erect lights and other sea-marks was often farmed out by Trinity House, which had general charge of them.   Pepys later condemned the practice: *Naval Minutes*, p. 202.   As for the profits, cf. Batten's patent for a Harwich light: below, vi. 3 & n. 4.

3. A tragedy by Thomas Middleton and William Rowley, first acted in 1622, and published in 1653. Downes notes (pp. 18–19) that Sheppey played Antonio and that Betterton was much praised for his acting of De Flores in this play. Now at the S. Ct, Whitefriars.   (A).

4. Pepys exaggerates the wealth of the actors.   At this time Charles Hart, the leading actor of the King's company, was receiving £3 per week; after their marriage in 1662 Betterton and his wife, the leading players in the Duke of York's Company, jointly received £5 per week.   (A).

Then by linke home – and there to my book awhile and to bed.

I met today with Mr. Townsend, who tells me that the old man is yet alive in whose place in the Wardrobe he hopes to get my father – which I do resolve to put for.[1]

I also met with the Comptroller, who told me how it was easy for us all, the principall officers, and proper for us, to labour to get into the next parliament – and would have me to aske the Dukes letter.[2]   But I shall not endeavour it – because it will spend much money, though I am sure I could well obtaine it.   This is now 28 years that I am born.   And blessed be God, and a state of full content and great hopes to be a happy man in all respects, both to myself and friends.

24.   *Sunday.*   Mr. Mills made an excellent sermon in the morning against Drunkennesse that ever I heard in my life.   I dined at home.   Another good one of his in the afternoon.   My Valentine[3] had her fine gloves on at church today that I did give her.

After sermon my wife and I into Sir W. Batten's and sat awhile.   Then home – I to read.   Then to supper and to bed.

25.   Sir W. Pen and I to my Lord Sandwichs by coach in the morning to see him; but he takes physic today and so we could not see him.   So he went away; and I with Luellin to Mr. Mounts chamber at the Cockpitt, where he did lie of old,[4] and

1. Thomas Townshend, sen., was Clerk of the Great Wardrobe. The place was that of John Young, sen., yeoman tailor.   On Young's belated death in 1667 Pepys decided not to promote his father's interest (below, viii. 508), and the place fell to Capt. Robert Ferrer, whose claims are first mentioned at v. 168.

2. I.e. the Lord Admiral's recommendation to the electors of an Admiralty borough.   Writs of summons had just been issued on 18 February. In the Cavalier Parliament, which met on 8 May, Batten, Penn and Carteret of the Navy Office, together with William Coventry, the Duke's secretary, all sat for dockyard or seaboard constituencies.   Pepys did not at-

tempt to stand, but later he had the Duke's letters in support of his unsuccessful candidature at Aldeburgh in 1669 and in his election for Castle Rising in 1673 and for Portsmouth in 1679: *Priv. Corr.*, i. 243, 273, 335–6. There are copies of eighteen letters of recommendation from the Duke during these elections of 1661 in PRO, Adm. 2/1745, ff. 29+.

3. Martha Batten.

4. Mount was Gentleman-Usher to the Duchess of Albemarle, whose husband had a residence in the Cockpit, Whitehall.   Peter Luellin (Llewellyn) had probably occupied the room (as a junior clerk to the council) before the Moncks came to London in February 1660.

there we drank; and from thence to W. Symons, where we find
him abroad but she, like a good lady, within; and there we did
eat some nettle-porrige, which was made on purpose today for
some of their [friends] coming and was very good.   With her we
sat a good while, merry in discourse; and so away.   Luellin and
I to my Lord's and there dined.   He told me one of the prettiest
stories; how Mr. Blurton, his friend that was with him at my
house three or four days ago, did go with him the same*ᵃ* day from
my house to the Fleece taverne by Guild hall, and there (by some
pretence) got the mistress of the house, a very pretty woman,
into their company.   And by the by, Luellin calling him Doctor,
she thought that he really was so, and did privately discover her
disease to him – which was only some ordinary infirmity belonging to women.   And he proffering her physic – she desired him
to come some day and bring it, which he did; and withal hath the
sight of her thing below, and did handle it – and he swears the
next time that he will do more.

After dinner by water to the office and there Sir W. Pen and
I met and did business all the afternoon.   And then I got him to
my house and eat a Lobster together; and so to bed.

26.   *Shrovetuesday.*   I left my wife in bed, being indisposed by
reason of *ceux=là* – and I to Mrs. Turners, who I find busy with
The and Joyce making of things ready for Fritters.   So I to
Mr. Crews and there delivered Cottgraves dictionary[1] – to my
Lady Jemimah.   And then with Mr. Moore to my Cozen Tom
Pepys's; but he being out of town, I spoke with his lady –
though not of the business I went about, which was to borrow
1000*l* for my Lord.[2]

Back to Mrs. Turners, where several friends, all strangers to me
but Mr. Armiger, din'd.   Very merry, and the best fritters that

a   MS. 'other'

1. Randle Cotgrave, *A French and*
English dictionary; probably the best
of its day; first published in 1611;
issued in a revised and enlarged form
in 1660: not in the PL.

2. For the later history of this
transaction, see, e.g., below, pp. 62–
63 & n.; vii. 32.

ever I eat in my life.   After that look out at Window; saw the
flinging at Cocks.[1]

Then Mrs. The and I, and a Gentleman that dined there and his
daughter, a perfect handsome young and very tall lady, but lately
come out of the country (and Mr. Thatcher the Virginall-maister)
to Bishopsgate-street and there saw the new Harpsicon made for
Mrs. The.   We offered 12*l* – they demand 14*l*.   The master not
being at home, we could make no bargain; so parted for tonight.
So all by coach to my house, where I found my Valentine with
my wife; and here they drank and then went away.   Then I
sat and talked with my Valentine – and my wife a good while;
and then saw her home and went to Sir W. Batten to the
Dolphin, where Mr. Newborne &c. were and there after a
Quart or two of wine, we home and I to bed – where (God forgive me) I did please myself by strength of fancy with the young
country *Segnora* that was at dinner with us today.

27.   At the office all the morning.   That done, I walked in
the garden with little Captain Murford, where he and I have
some discourse concerning the Lighthouse again; and I think I
shall appear in the business, he promising me that if I can bring
it about, it will be worth 100*l* per annum.

Then came into the garden to me young Mr. Powell and Mr.
Hooke, that I once knew at Cambrige,[2] and I took them in and
gave them a bottle of wine and so parted.   Then I called for a
dish of fish, which we had for dinner – this being the first day of
Lent; and I do entend to try whether I can keep it or no.   My
father dined with me – and did show me a letter from my brother
John, wherein he tells us[a] that he is chosen Schollar of the house,[3]
which doth please me much, because I perceive now it must
chiefly come from his merit and not the power of his tutor Dr:
Widrington, who is now quite out of interest there and hath put
over his pupills to Mr. Pepper, a young Fellow of the College.[4]

a   repl. 'me'

---

1. A   Shrove-Tuesday   custom.
Commonly sticks were thrown at a
tied bird, the cock being won by who-
ever knocked it down and caught it
before it got up again.

2. Both were now clergymen.
3. Christ's College, Cambridge.
4. Cf. above, i. 63-4 & n.

With my father to Mr. Rawlinson's, where we met my Uncle Wight – and after a pint or two, away. I walked with my father (who gave me an account of the great falling-out between my Uncle Fenner and his son Will.) as far as Paul's churchyard, and so left him. And I home.

This day the Comissioners of Parliament begin to pay off the Fleet, beginning with the *Hampshire* – and do it at Guildhall for fear of going out of the town into the power of the seamen, who are highly incensed against them.[1]

28. earely to wait on my Lord. And after a little talk with him I took boat at White-hall for Redriffe; but in my way overtook Captain Cuttance and Teddiman in a boat; and so I ashore with them at Queenehithe and so to a tavern with them to a barrel of oysters, and so away.

Captain Cuttance and I walked from Redriffe to Deptford, where I find both Sir Wms. and Sir George Cartrite at Mr. Uthwaytes[2] and there we dined. And notwithstanding my resolution, yet for want of other victualls, I did eat flesh this Lent; but am resolved to eat as little as I can.

After dinner we went to Captain Bodilaws and there made sale of many old stoares by the candle; and good sport it was to see how, from a small matter bid at first, they would come to double and treble the price of things.[3]

After that, Sir Wm. Pen and I and my Lady Batten and her daughter by land to Redriffe, staying a little at Halfway-house. And when we came to take boat, find Sir George, &c, to have stayed with the barge a great while for us, which troubled us.

Home and to bed.

This month ends with two great Secrets under dispute, but yet known to very few. First, who the King will marry. And what the meaning of this fleet is which we are now sheathing to

---

1. For this pay, see *Merc. Pub.*, 7 March, p. 131; for its unpopularity, see above, p. 19.

2. Clerk of the Survey, Deptford.

3. For sales 'by inch of candle', see above, i. 284 & n. 2. This sale was held between noon and 2 p.m., hav-

ing been announced on the Exchange a fortnight before: PRO, Adm. 106/3520, f.3*v*. 'Captain Bodilaw' was William Baddiley, Master-Attendant at Deptford. For another sale at his premises, see below, iv. 319.

set out for the Southward. Most think against Argier against the Turke, or to the East Indys against the Dutch – who we hear are setting out a great fleet thither.[1]

1. The fleet in fact went in June to Algiers under Sandwich's command, and then brought back Charles II's bride, Catherine of Braganza, from Portugal. The match was not publicly announced until 8 May.

MARCH.

1. All the morning at the office. Dined at home, only upon fish, and Mr. Sheply and Tom. Hater with me. After dinner Mr. Sheply and I in private talking about my Lord's ententions to go speedily into the country; but to what end we know not. We fear he is to go to sea with this fleet now preparing. But we wish that he could get his 4000*l* per annum[1] settled before that he doth go.

Then he and I walked into London. He to the Wardrobe and I to White-fryers and saw *The Bondman* acted – an*a* excellent play and well done – but above all that ever I saw, Baterton doth the Bondman the best.[2]

Then to my father's and find my mother ill. After staying a while with them, then I went home – and sat up late, spending my thoughts how to get money to bear me out in my great expense at the Coronacion, against which all provide – and Scaffolds setting up in every street.

I have many designs in my head to get some, but know not which will take.

To bed.

2. early with Mr. Moore about Sir Paul Neale's business with my Uncle[3] and other things, all the morning.

a MS. 'and'

---

1. Granted by the King; see above, i. 285 & n. 4.
2. Thomas Betterton was Pepys's favourite actor (below, p. 207), and is generally considered the greatest actor of the Restoration period. *The Bondman*, a tragicomedy by Philip Massinger, was first acted in 1623, and published in 1624; for the text of this production (at the S. Ct, Whitefriars), see J. G. McManaway in *ELH*, 1/287. During the period of the diary, Pepys records that he saw *The Bondman*, in whole or in part, no fewer than seven times. On this occasion, Betterton played the part of Pisander, who is disguised as the bondman, Marullo. (A).

3. No more appears to be known of this. Neile (son of Richard Neile, late Archbishop of York) was a land-hungry courtier; he may have been negotiating for Robert Pepys's lands in Brampton, the manor of which was held by the Queen Mother in reversion. If so, nothing appears to have come of it.

Dined with him at Mr. Crewes. And after dinner I went to the Theatre,[1] where I find so few people (which is strange, and the reason I did not know) that I went out again; and so to Salsbury Court – where the house as full as could be; and it seems it was a new play – *The Queenes Maske*. Wherein there is some good humours. Among others, a good jeere to the old story of the Siege of Troy, making it to be a common country tale.[2] But above all, it was strange to see so little a boy as that was to act Cupid, which is one of the greatest parts in it. Then home and to bed.

3. *Lords day*. Mr. Woodcocke preached at our church; a very good sermon upon the Imaginacions of the thoughts of man's heart being only evil.[3] So home; where being told that my Lord hath sent for me, I went and got there to dine with my Lord – who is to go into the country tomorrow. I did give up the mortgage made to me by Sir R. Parkhurst for 2000*l*.[4]

In the Abbey all the afternoon. Then at Mr. Pierces the surgeon, where Sheply and I supped. So to my Lord's, who comes in late and tells us how news is come today of Mazarins being dead – which is very great news and of great consequence.[5]

I lay tonight with Mr. Sheply here, because of my Lord's going tomorrow.

4. My Lord went this morning on his journy to Hinchingbrooke, Mr. Packer with him; the chief business being to look

---

1. The TR, Vere St. (A).

2. *Love's Mistress, or The Queen's masque*, was an allegorical drama by Thomas Heywood, first acted in 1634, and published in 1636. In Act II, sc. 1, there is a dialogue between the Clown and certain swains in which Troy is described as a village of 'some twenty houses', Agamemnon as 'high Cunstable of the hundred', Ajax as a butcher, and Hector as a baker. (A).

3. Cf. Gen., vi. 5, viii. 21.

4. See above, i. 310.

5. Cardinal Mazarin, virtual ruler of France since 1643 during Louis XIV's minority, had died at Vincennes on 28 February/9 March. The news did not appear in the newsbooks until 11 March: *Kingd. Intell.*, 11 March, p. 149.

over and determine how and in what manner his great work of building shall be done.[1]

Before his going,[a] he did give me some jewells to keep for him; *viz.*, that that the King of Sweden did give him, with the King's owne picture in it, most excellently[b] done; and a rare George, all of diamonds.[2] And this with the greatest expressions of love and confidence that I could imagine or hope for, which is a very great joy to me.

To the office all the forenoon. Then to dinner and so to White-hall to Mr. Coventry about several businesses. And then with Mr. Moore, who was with me to drink a cup of ale; and after some good discourse, then home and sat late talking with Sir W. Batten. So home and to bed.

5. With Mr. Pierce, purser, to Westminster-hall; and there met with Captain Cuttance, Lieutenant Lambert, and Pierce, surgeon – thinking to have met with the Comissioners of Parliament; but they not sitting, we went to the Swan, where I did give them a barrel of oysters; and so I to my Lady's and there dined and have very much talk and pleasant discourse with my Lady[c] – my esteem growing every day higher and higher in her and my Lord.

So to my father Bowyers, where my wife was. And to the Comissioners of Parliament and there did take some course about having my Lord's Salary paid tomorrow, when the *Charles* is paid off. But I was troubled to see how high they carry themselfs, when in good truth, nobody cares for them.

a followed by blot   *b* MS. 'extently'   *c* MS. 'Lord'

---

1. Hinchingbrooke was mainly Elizabethan–Jacobean in date. Parts, however, survived from the original medieval nunnery. The new work consisted mostly of the addition of two storeys to the w. range, a new n.-w. corner, a kitchen in the n. wing and a new staircase. No plans of the rebuilding appear to have survived. Harris, i. 226+, and VCH, *Hunts.*, ii. 135–9: both reproduce a view of c. 1730. Description [1697] in C. Fiennes, *Journeys* (ed. Morris), pp. 66–7. Philip Packer, Deputy-Paymaster of the King's Works and a kinsman of Sandwich by marriage, was the contractor and possibly the architect, but Sandwich himself probably had a hand in the design – certainly in that of the grounds and waterworks. For his interest in architectural drawing, see below, iii. 206 & n. 1.

2. See above, i. 238 & n. 1.

So home by coach, and my wife. I then to the office; where Sir Wms both and I sat about making an estimate of all the officers Salarys in ordinary in the navy,[1] till 10 a-clock at night. So home; and I, with my head full of thoughts how to get a little present money, I eat a bit of bread and cheese and so to bed.

6. At the office all the morning. At dinner Sir W. Batten came and took me and my wife to his house to dinner, my Lady being in the country – where we had a good Lenten dinner.

Then to White-hall with Captain Cuttle. And there I did some business with Mr. Coventry – and after that home, thinking to have had Sir Wm. Batten, &c, to have eat a wigg at my house at night. But my Lady being come home out of the country, ill by reason of much rayne that hath fallen lately, and the waters being very high – we could not; and so I home and to bed.

7. This morning Sir Wms. both went to Woolwich to sell some old provisions there.[2]

I to White-hall and up and down about many businesses. Dined at my Lord's. Then to Mr. Crew to Mr. Moore and he and I to London to Guildhall to see the seamen paid off; but could not without trouble. And so I took him to the Fleece tavern, where the pretty woman that Luellin lately told me the story of dwells;[3] but I could not see her.

Then towards home; and met Spicer, D. Vines, Ruddiard and a company more of my old acquaintances and went into a place to drink some ale; and there we stayed playing the fools till late; and so I home.

At home I met with ill newes that my hopes of getting some money for the *Charles* were spoiled through Mr. Waith's perverse-

---

1. The Admiral, in a letter of 18 February to the Board, had asked for an estimate of the ordinary charge of the navy in harbour for the whole year: PRO, Adm. 106/3, f.100r. Cf. the estimate (24 June 1660–24 June 1661) in BM, Add. 9312, ff. 3–6. Orders of the commissioners for the payment of salaries of the officers of the yards (17 May, 5 June) are registered in BM, Add. 9314, f.2r.

2. In pursuance of a council order of 13 February, old provisions were to be sold at all principal dockyards: PRO, Adm. 106/3520, f.3v. Cf. also below, pp. 68–9, 93.

3. Above, p. 43.

nesse[1] – which did so vex [me] that I could not sleep at night. But I wrote a letter to him to send tomorrow morning for him to take my money for me; and so, with good words, I thought to cog with him. To bed.

8. All the morning at the office. At noon Sir W. Batten, Collonell Slingsby and I by coach to the tower, to Sir John Robinson's[2] to dinner.

Where great good cheer. High company; among others, the Duchesse of Albemerle, who is ever a plain, homely dowdy.

After dinner, then to drink all the afternoon. Towards night the Duchess and ladies went away. Then we set to it again till it was very late. And at last in came Sir Wm. Wale,[3] almost fuddled; and because I was set between him and another, only to keep them from talking and spoiling the company (as we did to others), he fell out with the Lieutenant of the Towre; but with much ado we made him understand his errour. And then all quiet. And so he Carried Sir W. Batten and I home again in his coach. And so I, almost overcome with drink, went to bed.

I was much contented to ride in such state into the towre and be received among such high company – while Mr. Mount, my Lady Duchesses gentleman-usher, stood waiting at table, whom I ever thought a man so much above me in all respects.

Also, to hear the discourse of so many high Cavaleers of things past – it was of great content and joy to me.

9. To White-hall; and there with Mr. Creed took a most pleasant walk for two houres in the parke, which is now a very fine place.[4]

Here we had a long and candid discourse one to another, of one another's conditions. And he giving me an occasion, I told him of my intentions to get 60*l.* paid me by him for a gratuity for my labour-extraordinary at sea[5] – which he did not seem unwilling to; and therefore I am very glad it is out.

1. Robert Waith was Paymaster to the Navy Treasurer; 'a very rogue': below, iii. 30.

2. Lieutenant of the Tower.

3. Alderman and wine merchant; friend of Albemarle and one of the city representatives sent to the King at Breda.

4. For the reconstruction of St James's Park, see above, i. 246 & n. 2.

5. See above, p. 37 & n. 2.

To my Lord's, where we find him newly come from Hinching-brooke, where he left my uncle very well, but my aunt not likely to live.

I stayed and dined with him. He took me asside[a] and asked me what the world spoke of the King's marriage. Which I answering as one that knew nothing, he enquired no further of me. But I do perceive by it that there is something in it that is ready to come out, that the world knows not of yet.[1]

After dinner into London to Mrs. Turners and my fathers; made visits and then home, where I sat late making of my journall for four days past; and so to bed.

10. *Lords day.* Heard Mr. Mills in the morning, a good sermon. Dined at home on a poor Lenten dinner of Coleworts and bacon. In the afternoon again to church and there heard one Castle,[2] whom I knew of my year in Cambrige: he made a dull sermon.

After sermon came my Uncle and Aunt Wight to see us and we sat together a great while. Then to reading and at night to bed.

11. At the office all the morning. Dined at home and my father and Dr. Tho. Pepys with him, upon a poor dinner – my wife being abroad. After dinner I went to the Theatre and there saw *Loves Mistress* done by them, which I do not like in some things so well as their acting in Salsbury-court.[3]

At night home and find my wife come home; and among

a   word smudged

***

1. The Portuguese match had been in secret negotiation since shortly before the Restoration, and the envoy sent to conclude arrangements had been in England since 9 February: *CSPD 1660–1*, p. 511; *CSPVen. 1659–61*, p. 246. By this time, Sandwich presumably knew officially of it. Pepys does not mention it as an established fact in the diary until 3 April: below, p. 65. It was publicly announced by the King when the new parliament met on 8 May. There had also been proposals for a marriage with a French, a Spanish, and an Imperial bride. The King was married to Catherine of Braganza on 21 May 1662.

2. John Castell had been a scholar of Trinity College. In 1661 he was appointed Rector of Great Greenford, Mdx.

3. See above, p. 48 & n. 2. (A).

other things, she hath got her teeth new done by La Roche;[1] and are endeed now pretty handsome, and I was much pleased with it. So to bed.

12. At the office about business all the morning. So to the Exchange and there met with Nick Osborne, lately married; and with him to the Fleece, where we drank a glass of wine. So home, where I found Mrs. Hunt in great trouble about her husbands losing of his place in the Excize.[2] From thence to Guildhall and there set my hand to the book before Collonell King for my sea-pay. And blessed be God, they have cast me at Midship=man's pay[3] – which doth make my heart very glad. So home and there have Sir W. Batten and my Lady and all their company, and Captain Browne and his wife, to a Collacion at my house till it was late; and then to bed.

13. earley up in the morning to read the *Seamens grammar and dictionary*[4] I lately have got, which doth please me exceeding well.

At the office all the morning. Dined at home; and Mrs. Turner, The, Joyce, and Mr. Armiger, and my father and mother with me – where they stayed till I was weary of their company, and so away.

Then up to my chamber and there set papers and things in order; and so to bed.

---

1. She had much trouble with her teeth and gums. This operation was probably scaling, done by means of a scraper or 'graver'. The dentist was Peter de la Roche, one of the two 'operators for the teeth' to the royal household, who lived near Strand Bridge. Cf. A. W. Lufkin, *Hist. Dentistry*, p. 137.

2. New Commissioners of the Excise had been appointed on 24 February. John Hunt was serving as a sub-commissioner for Oxfordshire and Buckinghamshire in December 1661 (*CTB*, i. 175), and later (below, vii. 92). Pepys had apparently helped him to obtain his original appointment: above, i. 257.

3. Something between £1 10s. and £2 5s. per month according to the rate of the ship: Oppenheim, p. 314; *Cat.*, i. 150. Edward King was one of the commissioners appointed to pay off the fleet.

4. ? John Smith's *The sea-mans grammar* (first published in 1627), or Sir Henry Manwayring's *The sea-mans dictionary* (first published in 1644). Pepys kept both – the Smith in the edition of 1653 and the Manwayring in that of 1667 – bound together in one volume: PL 1142.

14. With Sir W. Batten and Pen to Mr. Coventry's and there had a dispute about my claime to the place of Pourveyor for Petty=provisions. And at last, to my content did conclude to have my hand to all the bills for those provisions and Mr. Turner to purvey them, because I would not have him to lose the place.[1] Then to my Lord's; and so with Mr. Creed to an alehouse, where he told me a long story of his amours at Portsmouth to one of one Mrs. Boates daughters – which was very pleasant.

Dined with my Lord and Lady; and so with Mr. Creed to the Theatre, and there saw *King and no King*, well acted.[2]

Thence with him to the Cock=alehouse at Temple barr, where he did aske my advice about his amours and I did give it him; which was to enquire into the condition of his competitor, which is a son of Mr. Gawdens; and that I promised to do for him – and he to make [what] use he can of it to his advantage.

Home and to bed.

15. At the office all the morning. At noon, Sir Wms. both and I at a great fish dinner at the Dolphin given us by two Tarr=merchants. And very merry we were till night; and so home. This day my wife and Pall went to see my Lady Kingston her brother's Lady.[3]

16. early at Sir Wm. Pen's; and there before Mr. Turner did reconcile the business of the purveyance between us two. Then to White-hall to my Lord's and dined with him; and so to White-fryers and saw *The Spanish Curate*,[4] in which I have no great content.

So home; and was very much troubled that Will stayed out late. And went to bed angry, entending not to let him come in.

1. Cf. above, i. 228 & n. 2. The Clerk of the Acts had once performed these functions, but they had been delegated to others as the business grew in volume. The Admiral's Instructions of 1662 gave the Clerk powers of supervision over the work: cf. below, iii. 25.

2. A tragicomedy by Beaumont and Fletcher, licensed in 1611, published in 1619. Now at the TR, Vere St. The cast may have been the same as that of a later production listed in Downes, p. 5. (A).

3. I.e. Lady Kingston's brother's lady; Elizabeth, wife of Maurice Fenton.

4. A comedy by Fletcher and Massinger, first acted in 1622, published in 1647, and now performed at the S. Ct, Whitefriars. (A).

But by and by he comes and I did let him in; and he did tell me that he was at Guild hall helping to pay off the seamen and cast the books so late – which since I find to be true. So to sleep, being in bed when he came.

17. At church in the morning, a[a] stranger preached a good, honest, and painful sermon. My wife and I dined upon a chine of beef at Sir W. Battens. So to church again. Then home and put some papers in order. Then to supper to Sir W. Batten again – where my wife by chance fell down and hurt her knees exceedingly. So home and to bed.

18. This morning earely, Sir W. Batten went to Rochester, where he expects to be chosen parliament man.[1]

At the office all the morning. Dined at home; and with my wife to Westminster, where I have business with the Commissioners for paying the seamen, about my Lord's pay. And my wife at Mrs. Hunts.

I called* her home; and made enquiry at Greatorex's and in other places to hear of Mr. Barlow (thinking to hear that he is dead); but I cannot find it so, but the contrary.[2] Home; and called at my Lady Battens and supped there. And so home.

This day an Embassador from Florence was brought into the Towne – in state.[3]

Good hopes given me today that Mrs. Davis is going away from us, her husband going shortly to Ireland.[4] Yesterday it was

a MS. 'he'

1. He was returned on 21 March.
2. Thomas Barlow was Pepys's predecessor as Clerk of the Acts and Pepys had agreed in 1660 to pay him a life-annuity of £100, when he struck Pepys as 'old' and 'consumptive': above, i. 202. Presumably as a result of hearing of his present illness, Pepys wrote on the 21st offering to buy him out, but Barlow refused: Rawl. A 174, ff. 322r, 324r. He did not die until early in 1665.
3. Marchese Giovanni Vincenzo Salviati, Ambassador-Extraordinary

from Tuscany, sent to congratulate Charles II on his restoration. The state entry, as always, was made from the Tower to Whitehall Palace, the ambassador travelling in a coach provided by the King, and in the company of a retinue of courtiers and diplomats. Description in *Merc. Pub.*, 21 March, p. 176.
4. John Davis, clerk to Lord Berkeley in the Navy Office, occupied the house next door to Pepys, and his wife ('my lady Davis') was particularly obnoxious to the Pepyses.

said was to be the day that the Princesse Henriette was to marry the Duke D'anjou in France.[1]

This day I find in the news–Booke that Rogr. Pepys is chosen at Cambrige for the towne, the first place that we hear of to have made their choice yet.[2]

To bed with my head and mind full of business, which doth a little put me out of order. And I do find myself to become more and more thoughtful about getting of money then ever heretofore.

19. We met at the office this morning about some perticular business. And then I to White-hall and there dined with my Lord; and after dinner Mr. Creed and I to White-friers, where we saw *The Bondman*[3] acted most excellently; and though I have seen it often, yet I am every time more and more pleased with Batterton's action. From thence with him and young Mr. Jones to Penells in Fleetestreete and there we drank and talked a good while; and so I home and to bed.

20. At the office all the morning. Dined at home and Mr. Creed and Mr. Sheply with me; and after dinner we did a good deal of business in my study, about my Lord's accounts to be made up and presented to our office. That done, to White-hall to Mr. Coventry, where I did some business with him; and so with Sir Wm. Pen (who I find with Mr. Coventry, teaching of him upon the mapp to understand Jamaica)[4] by water, in the dark, home. And so to my Lady Battens, where my wife was;

1. The marriage was not celebrated until 21/31 March, the postponement being due partly to the death of Mazarin and partly to the delay in obtaining a papal dispensation (necessary for the union of first cousins). Anjou (later Orléans) was the brother of Louis XIV, Henrietta the sister of Charles II.

2. *The Kingdomes Intelligencer* of 18 March announced the first of the election results – those of Cambridge University and borough – and pointed out that they were 'good

Precedents to the rest of the Kingdom' (p. 176). Roger Pepys, Recorder of Cambridge and son of Talbot Pepys of Impington, was the diarist's cousin.

3. By Philip Massinger; see above, p. 47 & n. 2. Betterton played Pisander, who is disguised as the bondman, Marullo. (A).

4. Penn had captured Jamaica from the Spaniards in 1655; Coventry had just taken part in the despatch of a squadron there: above, p. 6 & n. 3

and there we sat and eat and drank till very late and so home to bed.

The great talk of the towne is the strange eleccion that the City of London made yesterday for Parliament men – *viz.*, Fowke, Love, Jones, and   ,[1] men that are so far from being episcopall that they are thought to be anabaptistes; and chosen with a great deal of zeale, in spite of the other party that thought themselfs very strong – crying out in the hall, "noe bishops! noe Lord Bishops!".[2] It doth make people to fear it may come to worse, by being an example to the countries to do the same. And endeed, the bishops are so high,* that very few do love them.

21. Up very earely and to work and study in my chamber. And then to White-hall to my Lord, and there did stay with him a good while discoursing upon his accounts. Here I stayed with Mr. Creed all the morning. And at noon dined with my Lord, who was very merry; and after dinner we sang and fiddled a great while. Then I by water (Mr. sheply, pinkny, and others going part of the way) home and there hard at work setting my papers in order and writing letters till night. And so to bed.

This day I saw the Florence Embassador go to his audience, the weather very foule and yet he and his company very gallant.[3] After I was abed, Sir W. Pen sent to desire me to go with him tomorrow morning to meet Sir W. Batten coming from Rochester.

22. This morning I rose early; and my Lady Batten knocked at her door that comes into one of my chambers and called me to know whether I and my wife was ready to go. So my wife got her ready; and about 8 a-clock I got a-horseback and my Lady and her two daughters and Sir W. Pen into coach; and so over London Bridge and thence to Dartford – the day very pleasant,

---

1. Supply '[Ald. Sir William] Thompson': the others were Ald. John Fowke, Ald. William Love and John Jones, common councilman. Thompson and Love were Presbyterians and the others Independents.

2. Coming so soon after Venner's rising, this triumph of the Puritans was disturbing. Other descriptions of the scene in Guildhall are in *CSPD 1660–1*, pp. 536–9; ib., *1670*, p. 660. But the rest of the elections went overwhelmingly against the Puritans.

3. Cf. *Kingd. Intell.*, 25 March, p. 192; *CSPVen. 1659–61*, p. 273.

though the way bad. Here we met with Sir W. Batten and
some company along with him, who have assisted him in his
eleccion at Rochester. And so we dined and was very merry. At
5 a-clock we set out again, I in a coach home, and were very
merry all the way. At Deptford we met with Mr. Newborne
and some other friends and their wifes in a coach to meet us;
and so they went home with us and at Sir W. Batten's we
supped; and thence to bed – my head akeing mightily through
the wine that I drank today.

23. All the morning at home putting papers in order. Dined
at home. And then out to the Red bull[1] (where I have not been
since plays came up again); but coming too soon, I went out
again and walked all up and down the Charter=house yard and
Aldersgate-street. At last came back again and went in, where
I was led by a seaman that knew me, that is here as a servant, up
to the tireing-room; where strange the confusion and disorder
that there is among them in fitting themselfs; especially here,
where the clothes are very poore and the actors but common
fellows.[2] At last into the pitt, where I think there was not above
ten more then myself, and not 100 in the whole house – and the
play (which is called *All's lost by Lust*)[3] poorly done – and with
so much disorder; among others, that in the Musique-room,[4]
the boy that was to sing a song not singing it right, his master
fell about his eares and beat him so, that put the whole house into
an uprore.

Thence homewards and at the Miter met my uncle Wight,
and with him Lieutenant-Collonell Baron,[5] who told us how
Crofton, the great presbyterian minister that hath lately preached so

1. An old open-air playhouse in
St John's St, Clerkenwell; probably used on this occasion by a
minor company, probably George
Jolly's, despite the *de jure* monopoly
of dramatic performances in London
which the King granted to Killigrew
and Davenant in 1660. See Nicoll, p.
309. (A).

2. The best actors had been re-
cruited for the Theatre Royal and
Duke of York's Theatre by Killigrew
and Davenant respectively. (A).

3. A tragedy by William Rowley,
written c. 1619; published in 1633.
(A).

4. Probably a small gallery above
the stage. (A).

5. Benjamin Baron, of the city
militia.

highly against Bishops, is clapped up this day into the tower[1] – which doth please some and displease others exceedingly.

Home and to bed.

24. *Lords day.* My wife and I to church. And then home with Sir W. Batten and my Lady to dinner – where very merry. And then to church again, where Mr. Mills made a good sermon. Home again. And after a walk in the garden, Sir W. Battens two daughters came and sat with us a while. And I then up to my chamber to read.

25. *Lady=day.* This morning came workmen to begin the making of me a new pair of stairs up out of my parlour, which, with other work that I have to do, I doubt will keep me this two months;[2] and so long I shall be all in dirt – but the work doth please me very well. To the office then. And there all the morning. Dined at home; and after dinner came Mr. Salsbury to see me and showed me a face or two of his paynting; and endeed, I perceive that he will be a great master.[3]

I took him to White-hall with me by water; but he would not by any means be wooed to go through bridge[4] and so we were fain to go round to the old swan.

To my Lord's and there I showed him the King's picture,[5] which he entends to copy out in little. After that, I and Captain Ferrers to Salsbury-court by water and saw part of *The Queenes maske.*[6] Then I to Mrs. Turners and there stayed talking late – The. Turner being in a great chafe about being disappointed of a room to stand in at the coronation.

---

1. Zachary Crofton, a leader of the strict Presbyterians, held that episcopacy led straight to Rome, and had written two books supporting armed defence of the Covenant: *CSPD 1660–1*, pp. 539, 546. He was in custody until June 1662: ib., *1661–2*, p. 399. His arrest may have been provoked by the Puritans' victory in the London parliamentary elections three days before. Pepys's reference to his preaching probably relates to a sermon of the 19th, which had come to the

notice of the government: ib., p. 537. Crofton later boasted that he had 'written one bishop silent who could not speak, and spoken another [Dr Morley] dumb who could not write': ib., *1663–4*, p. 357.

2. The joiners finished by 16 May, the painters a month later.

3. Cf. above, p. 23, n. 2. (OM).

4. For the perils of negotiating London Bridge, see *Comp.*, s.n.

5. See above, i. 292–3 & n.

6. See above, p. 48 & n. 2. (A).

Then to my father's and there stayed talking with my mother and him late about my dinner tomorrow.

So homewards and took up a boy that had a lanthorn, that was picking up of rags, and got him to light me home. And had great discourse with him how he could get sometimes three or four bushels of rags in a day, and gat 3*d* a bushel for them. And many other discourses, what and how many ways there are for poor children to get their livings honestly.

So home and to bed – at 12 a-clock at night, being pleased well with the work that my workmen have begun today.

26. Up early to do business in my study.

This is my great day, that three year ago I was cut of the stone[1] – and blessed be God, I do yet find myself very free from pain again. All this morning I stayed at home looking after my workmen, to my great content, about my stairs. And at noon by coach to my father's, where Mrs. Turner, The, Joyce, Mr. Morrice, Mr. Armiger, Mr.*a* Pierce the surgeon and his wife – my father and mother and myself and my wife.

Very merry at dinner. Among other*b* things, because Mrs. Turner and her company eate no flesh at all this Lent and I had a great deal of good flesh, which made their mouths water.

After dinner, Mrs. Pierce and her husband and I and my wife to Salisbury-Court; where coming late, he and she light of Collonell Boone, that made room for them; and I and my wife sat in the pit and there met with Mr. Lewes and Tom. Whitton – and saw *The Bondman*[2] done to admiration. So home by coach – and after a view of what the workmen have done today, I went to bed.

27. Up earely – to see my workmen at*c* work. My brother Tom comes to me, and among other things, I looked over my old clothes and did give him a suit of black stuff clothes and a hat and some shooes.

a MS. 'Mrs.'   *b* repl. 'thing'   *c* accidental ink stroke in upper margin

---

1. The feast was held this year at his father's house, his own being disarranged by workmen. The Turners were always guests of honour, since it was in their house that the operation had been performed.
2. See above, p. 47 & n. 2. (A).

At the office all the morning – where Sir G. Carteret comes; and there I did get*a* him to promise me some money upon a bill of exchange. Whereby I shall secure myself of 60*l*[1] – which otherwise I should not know how to get.

At noon I find my stairs quite broke down, that I could not get up but by a lather. And my wife not being well, she kept her chamber all this day.

Then to the Dolphin to a dinner of Mr. Harris's,[2] where Sir Wms. both and my Lady Batten and her two daughters and other company – where a great deal of mirth. And there stayed till 11 a-clock at night. And in our mirth, I sang and sometimes fiddled (there being a noise* of fiddlers there) and at last we fell to dancing – the first time that ever I did in my life – which I did wonder to see myself to do. At last we made Mingo, Sir W. Battens black, and Jack, Sir W. Pens, dance; and it was strange how the first did dance with a great deal of seeming skill.

Home, where I find my wife all day in her chamber, and so to bed.

28. Up earely among my workmen. Then Mr. Creed coming to see me, I went along with him to Sir Robt. Slingsby[3] (he being newly maister*b* of that title by being made a Barronett) to discourse about Mr. Creeds accounts to be made up. And from thence by coach to my Cozen Tho. Pepys's to borrow 1000*l* for my Lord[4] – which I am to expect an answer to tomorrow. So to my Lord's and there stayed and dined; and after dinner did get my Lord to view Mr. Sheplys accounts as I had examined them – and also to sign me a bond for my*c* 500*l*.[5]

a MS. 'give'   *b* l.h. repl. s.h. 'maister'   *c* l.h. repl. '2'

---

1. A gratuity for Pepys's service at sea in 1660: cf. above, pp. 37, 51; below, p. 62.

2. John Harris, sailmaker.

3. Comptroller of the Navy.

4. See below, p. 63 & n. 1. Sandwich had also borrowed from the same Thomas Pepys (a Westminster business man) a few years before: Carte 73, f.325r.

5. This loan was increased to £700 on 24 August 1663: below, iv. 286. Pepys was in fact investing what were virtually his entire savings in this way: see his accounts below, at 8 September, 31 December 1661; 26 June, 31 December 1663. Of principal and interest just over £250 remained unpaid at 10 February 1665.

Then with Mr. Sheply to the Theatre and saw *Rollo*, ill acted.[1]
That done, to drink a cup of ale, and so by coach to London;
and having set him down in cheepeside, I went home – where I
find a great deal of work done today – and also 70*l* paid me by
the Treasurer upon the bill of exchange that I have had hopes of
so long.[2] So that, my heart in great content, I went to bed.

29. Up among my workmen with great pleasure.

Then to the office – where I find Sir W. Pen sent down
yesterday to Chatham to get two great ships in readiness, presently
to go to the East Indys upon some design against the Duch;
we think at Goa, but it is a great secret yet.[3]

Dined at home. Came Mr. Sheply and Moore, and did
business with both of them. After that to Sir W. Battens,
where great store of company at dinner. Among others, my
schoole fellow, Mr. Christmas. Where very merry. And hither
came letters from above for the fitting of two other ships for the
East Indys in all haste; and so we got orders presently for the
Hampshire and *Nonesuche*. Then home and there put some papers
in order; and not knowing what to do, the house being so dirty,
I went to bed.

30. At the office, we and Sir Wm. Rider, to advise what sort
of provisions to get ready for these ships going to the Indys.
Then the Controller and I by water to Mr. Coventry and there
discoursed upon the same thing.

So to my Cozen Tho. Pepys and got him to promise me a
1000*l* to lend my Lord upon his and my uncle Robt. and my
security. So to my Lord's and there got him to sign a bond to

---

1. *The bloody brother, or Rollo,
Duke of Normandy*, a tragedy by John
Fletcher and several others, written
c. 1617; published in 1639. Now at
the TR, Vere St. The cast listed by
Downes (pp. 5–6) includes Hart as
Rollo, Kynaston as Otto, Mrs Corey
as the Duchess and Mrs Marshall as
Edith. (A).

2. See above, p. 37 & n. 2.
3. These formed part of a fleet sent
to the Mediterranean under Sandwich:
below, pp. 79, 118. The suggestion
of action against the Dutch (three
years in advance of the outbreak of
hostilities) is interesting, though in-
accurate. Goa was Portuguese.

him, which I also signed too; and he did sign counter-security to us both.[1]

Then into London, up and down, and drank a pint of wine with Mr. Creed; and so home and sent a letter and the bonds to my uncle, to sign for my Lord.

This day I spoke with Dr Castle about making up the dividend for the last Quarter,[2] and agreed to meet about it on Monday.

31. *Sunday.*

At church, where a stranger preached like a fool.

From thence home and dined*a* with my*b* wife; [she] staying at home, she being unwilling to dress herself, the house being all dirty.

To church again. And after sermon I walked to my father's and to Mrs. Turner's – where I could not woo The to give me a lesson* upon the Harpsicon and was angry at it.

So home; and finding Will abroad at Sir W. Battens, talking with the people there (Sir W and my Lady being in the country) – I took occasion to be angry with him; and so to prayer and to bed.

a repl. 'with Sir W. Batten' (first word s.h.)   *b* repl. 'him'

---

1. The loan ran until 6 October next, at 6%, and was secured by Pepys and his uncle, Robert Pepys, in the sum of £2000, for which Sandwich gave counter-security on 6 April. The counter-security (in Latin, in Moore's hand), signed and sealed by Sandwich in the presence of Shipley and Howe, is in Rawl. A 174, f.434r. See below, iii. 17 & n. 1; vii. 32.

2. I.e. the fees of the Privy Seal Office; Castle was a colleague there.

APRILL.

1. This day my wayting at the Privy Seale comes in again.

Up earely among my workmen. So to the office and went home to dinner with Sir W. Batten. And after that to the Goate taverne by Charing-cross to meet Dr. Castle, where he and I drank a pint of wine and talked about Privy Seale business. Then to the Privy Seale Office and there find Mr. Moore, but no business yet. Then to White-fryers and there saw part of *Rule a Wife and Have a Wife*[1] – which I never saw before, but do not like it.

So to my father; and there finding a discontent between my father and mother about the mayde (which my father likes and my mother dislikes), I stayed till 10 at night, persuading my mother to understand* herself; and that in some high words – which I was sorry for, but she is grown, poor woman, very froward. So leaving them in the same discontent, I went away home – it being a brave mooneshine, and to bed.

2. Among my workmen earely. And then along with my wife and Pall to my father's by coach, there to have them lie a while till my house be done. I found my mother alone, weeping upon the last night's quarrel. And so left her and took my wife to Charing-cross and there left her to see her mother, who is not well. So I into St. James parke, where I saw the Duke of Yorke playing at *Peslemesle*[2] – the first time that I ever saw that sport.

Then to my Lord's, where I dined with my Lady; and after we had dined, in comes my Lord and Ned Pickering hungry, and there was not a bit of meat left in the house, the servants having eat up all – at which my Lord was very angry – and at last got something dressed. Then to Privy Seale and signed some things.

1. A comedy by John Fletcher, acted in 1624, and published in 1640; despite Pepys's verdict, one of Fletcher's most popular plays during the 17th century. For the usual cast, see Downes, p. 3. (A).

2. Pell-mell; forerunner of croquet; introduced under Charles I. 'A very princely play': Rugge, i. f.129v.

So to White-fryers and saw *The Little thiefe*, which is a very merry and pretty play – and the little boy doth very well.[1]

Then to my father's, where I find my mother and my wife in a very good moode; and so left them and went home.

Then to the Dolphin to Sir W. Batten and Pen and other company; among others, Mr. Delabar – where strange how these*a* men, who at other times are all wise men, do now in their drink betwitt and reproach one another with their former conditions and their actions as to public concernments, till I was shamed to see it.[2]

But parted all friends at 12 at night, after drinking a great deal of wine. So home and alone to bed.

3. Up among my workmen – my head akeing all day from last night's debauch. To the office all the morning; and at noon dined with Sir W. Batten and Pen, who would needs have me drink two good draughts of Sack today, to cure me of last night's disease – which I thought strange, but I think find it true.

Then home with my workmen all the afternoon. At night into the garden to play on my flagilette, it being Mooneshine – where I stayed a good while; and so home and to bed.

This day I hear that the Duch have sent the King a great present of money – which we think will stop the mach with Portugall; and judge this to be the reason that our so great haste in sending the two ships to the East Indys is also stayed.[3]

a MS. 'this'

---

1. *The night walker, or The little thief* was a comedy by John Fletcher written c. 1611, revised by James Shirley in 1633, and published in 1640. Now acted at the S. Ct, Whitefriars. The heroine, Alathe, carried out some comic deceptions disguised as a boy. A boy may in fact have played the part. (A).

2. All three had compromised themselves by service to the rebels – Batten and Penn in the navy, and Vincent Delabarr (a merchant) as collector of customs at Sandwich – an office from which he had just been dismissed for alleged disloyalty. *CSPD 1660-1*, pp. 134, 302-3.

3. For the marriage alliance between Charles II and Catherine of Braganza, see above, p. 52 & n. 1. Both Holland and Spain spent lavishly in unsuccessful attempts to stop it. For Charles's willingness to receive money himself, see *CSPVen. 1659-61*, p. 258. For the two ships, see above, p. 62, n. 3.

4. To my workmen. Then to my Lord's and there dined with Mr. Sheply. After dinner I went in to my Lord and there we had a great deal of Musique; and then came my Cozen Tom. Pepys, and there did accept of the Security which we give him for his 1000*l* that we borrow of him[1] – and so the money to be paid next week. Then to the Privy Seale; and so with Mr. Moore to my father's, where some friends did sup there and we with them, and late went home – leaving my wife still there. So to bed.

5. Up among my workmen. And so to the office and then to Sir Wm. Pen's with the other Sir Wm. and Sir John Lawson to dinner. And after that, with them to Mr. Lucy's a merchant, where much good company, and there drank a great deal of wine. And in discourse fell to talk of the waight of people, which did occasion some wagers; and where, among others, I won half a peece to be spent.

Then home; and at night to Sir W. Battens and there very merry with a good barrell of oysters; and this is the present life I lead.

Home and to bed.

6. Up among my workmen. Then to White-hall; and there at Privy Seale and elsewhere did business. And among other things, met with Mr. Townsend, who told of his mistake the other day to put both his legs through one of his Knees of his breeches, and went so all day.[2]

Then with Mr. Creed and Moore to the Legg in the Palace to dinner – which I gave them. And after dinner I saw the girl of the house, being very pretty, go into a chamber, and I went in after her and kissed her. Then by water, Creed and I, to Salsbury Court and there saw *Loves Quarrell*[3] acted the first time; but I do not like the designe nor words.

So calling at my father's, where they and my wife well; and so home and to bed.

---

1. See above, p. 62, p. 63 & n. 1.
2. This would be quite possible with the petticoat-breeches (sometimes called 'pantaloons') then fashionable:

Cunnington, pp. 149–50; figs. 71, 72.
3. There is no other reference, in the diary or elsewhere, to a play of this title. (A).

7. *Lords day.* /

All the morning at home making up my accounts (God forgive me) to give up to my Lord this afternoon. Then about 11 a-clock out a-doors toward Westminster, and put in at Pauls, where I saw our Minister, Mr. Mills, preaching before my Lord Major.[1] So to White-hall and there I met with Dr. Fuller of Twickenham, newly come from Ireland, and took him to my Lord's; where he and I dined and he did give my Lord and me a good account of the condition of Ireland and how it came to passe, through the joyning of the Fanatics and the Presbyterians, that the latter and the former are in their declaracion put together under the names of Phanatiques.[2]

After dinner my Lord and I and Mr. Sheply did look over our accounts and settle matter of money between us. And my Lord did tell me much of his mind about getting of money and other things, of his family, &c. Then to my father's, where I find Mr. Hunt and his wife at supper with my father and mother and my wife – where after supper I left them, and so home. And there I went to Sir W. Battens and resolved of a journey tomorrow to Chatham. And so home and to bed.

8. Up early, my Lady Batten knocking at her door that comes into one of my chambers – I did give directions to my people and workmen; and so about 8 a-clock we took barge at the Tower – Sir Wm. Batten and his Lady, Mrs. Turner, Mr. Fowler and I. A very pleasant passage. And so to Gravesend, where we dined; and from thence a coach took them and I and Fowler, with some others come from Rochester to meet us, on horseback – at

1. Weekly sermons had been given in the cathedral before the Lord Mayor and aldermen since 1644, when Paul's Cross and pulpit (scene of the traditional outdoor sermons) had been pulled down: cf. below, ix. 506 & n. 1. The Mayor was Sir Richard Browne.

2. A proclamation of 22 January had forbidden unlawful assemblies of 'Papists, Presbyterians, Independents, Anabaptists, Quakers and other fana-

tical persons': *CSP Ireland 1660–2,* p. 191. This news would strike most Englishmen as odd, for in England Presbyterians were not associated with the 'fanatics' and were at this very time engaged in parleys for church-union with Anglicans – the Savoy Conference began on 15 April. Dr William Fuller (formerly a schoolmaster at Twickenham) was now Dean of St Patrick's, Dublin.

Rochester, where light at Mr. Alcocks[1] and there drank and had good sport with his bringing out so many sorts of cheese. Then to the hill=house at Chatham,[2] where I never was before. And I find a pretty pleasant house – and am pleased with the armes that hang up there. Here we supped very merry, and late to bed; Sir Wm. telling me that old Edgeborow, his predecessor, did die and walk in my chamber – did make me somewhat afeared,

《9》 but not so much as for mirth sake I did seem.*[3] So to bed in the Treasurer's chamber and lay and sleep well – till 3 in the morning, and then waking; and by the light of the moon I saw my pillow (which overnight I flung from me) stand upright, but not bethinking myself what*[a] it might be, I was a little afeared. But sleep overcame all, and so lay till high morning – at which time I had a caudle brought me and a good fire made. And in generall, it was a great pleasure all*[b] the time I stayed here, to see how I am respected and honoured by all people; and I find that I begin to know now how to receive so much reverence, which at the beginning I could not tell how to do.

Sir Wm. and I by coach to the Dock and there viewd all the store-houses and the old goods that are this day to be sold, which was great pleasure to me; and so back again by coach home – where we had a good dinner. And among other strangers that came, there was Mr. Hempson[4] and his wife, a pretty woman and speaks Latin. Mr. Allen and two daughters of his, both very tall and the youngest very handsome,[5] so much as that I could not forbear to love her exceedingly – having, among other things, the best hand that ever I saw.

After dinner we went to fit books and things (Tom Hater

a l.h. repl. s.h. 'was'   *b* repl. 'it was'

---

1. Stephen Alcock, provision merchant and navy victualler; a relative by marriage of Batten; Mayor of Rochester in 1663.

2. An Elizabethan house near the dockyard, used as a pay-house and for the accommodation of official visitors.

3. Kenrick Edisbury, Surveyor of the Navy, 1632–8, had lived at Hill House, then the official residence of the surveyors. For Pepys's scepticism about ghosts, see below, iv. 186, n. 1.

4. William Hempson, Clerk of the Survey at Chatham.

5. John Allen was Clerk of the Ropeyard at Chatham. His younger daughter, Rebecca, who caught Pepys's roving eye both now and later, married Henry Jowles in 1662.

being this morning come to us) for the Sale by an inch of candle.[1]
And very good sport we and the ladies that stood by had to see
the people bid. Among other things sold, there was all the
State's armes;[2] which Sir W. Batten bought, entending to set up
some of the images in his gardens and the rest to burn on the
Coronacion night. The sale being done, the ladies and I and
Captain Pett and Mr. Castle[3] took barge; and down we went to
see the *Sovereigne*; which we did, taking great pleasure therein –
singing all the way; and among other pleasures, I put my Lady,
Mrs. Turner, Mrs. Hempson, and the two Mrs. Allen's into the
lantern[4] and I went in to them and kissed them, demanding it as a
fee due to a Principall officer. With all which we were exceeding
merry, and drank some bottles of wine and neat's tongue, &c.
Then back again home and so supped; and after much mirth,
to bed.

10. In the morning to see the Dock-houses. First, Mr. Pett's
the builder,[5] and there was very kindly received. And among
other things, he did offer my Lady Batten a parrot, the best ever I
saw – that knew Mingo[6] as soon as it saw him, having bred
formerly in the house with them. But for talking and singing,
I never heard the like. My Lady did accept of it.

Then to see Comissioner Petts house, he and his family being
absent. And here I wondered how my Lady Batten walked
up and down with envious looks to see how neat and rich everything is; and endeed, both the house and garden is most handsome – saying that she would get it, for it belonged formerly to
the Surveyor of the Navy.[7]

Then on board the *Prince*, now in the Dock; and endeed, it hath
one and no more rich cabbins for carved work, but no gold
in her.

1. Cf. above, i. 284, n. 2.
2. Carvings of the coats of arms of
the Commonwealth. The sale followed a council order of 13 February:
above, p. 50, n. 2.
3. Capt. Phineas Pett, late Clerk of
the Cheque, Chatham, whose father
(also named Phineas) had built the
Sovereign; and William Castle, shipbuilder, of Deptford.

4. Cf. above, p. 16.
5. Phineas Pett, Master-Shipwright,
Chatham, nephew of Capt. Phineas
Pett.
6. The Battens' black servant.
7. The Battens never used it. It
reminded Evelyn (iii. 359) of 'a villa
about *Rome*'.

After that back home and there eat a little dinner. Then to Rochester and there saw the Cathedrall, which is now fitting for use, and the Organ then a-tuning.[1] Then away thence, observing the great doors of the church, which they say was covered with the skins of the Danes.[2] And also had much mirth at a tombe on which was "Come sweet Jesu" and I read "Come sweet Mall," &c., at which Captain Pett and I had good laughter.[3]

So to the Salutacion tavern,[4] where Mr. Alcock and many of the towne came and entertained us with wine and oysters and other things; and hither came Sir John Mince to us, who is come today from London to see the *Henery*, in which he entends to ride as Vice-admirall in the Narrow-seas all this Sommer.[5] Here much mirth; but I was a little troubled to stay too long, because of going to Hempson's; which afterward we did – and find it in all things a most pretty house[a] and rarely furnished; only, it hath a most ill accesse on all sides to it, which is a greatest fault that I think can be in a house.

a   MS. 'hou'-

1. Cathedrals suffered serious spoliation in the revolution, if not used for worship. At Rochester the altar-rails had been removed, and parts of the buildings and precincts used as an inn and a saw-pit: *CSPD 1657–8*, pp. 121–2; R. Rawlinson, *Hist. Rochester* (1723), pp. 118–19; *Arch. Cant.*, 23/ 194–328. For a traveller's description of its ruinous condition (?1661), see HMC, *Rep.*, 13/2/277. It is there stated that the organ had been preserved during the Interregnum in a Greenwich tavern. It appears that this was one of the first organs to be made playable after the Restoration: A. Freeman, *Father Smith*, p. 14.

2. Similar traditions relating to Worcester Cathedral and Westminster Abbey were said to have been confirmed in the 1840s by a microscopic examination of the fabric alleged to be human skin: *Arch. Inst.*

Journ., 5 (1848)/185+ ; cf. J. Dart, *Westmonasterium* (1742), i. 64. There appears to be no record of the flaying of the Danes by the English.

3. The tomb has apparently disappeared, as many did when the level of the n. side of the graveyard was raised in the 18th century. The words Pepys mistakenly read may have been from a song.

4. On the Common, on the w. side of what is now Corporation St, between Northgate and the bridge; now no longer in existence.

5. A warrant from the Duke of York appointing Sir John Mennes Vice-Admiral in the Narrow Seas was issued on 18 May: *CSPD 1660–1*, p. 590. He was soon to become a close colleague of Pepys, succeeding Slingsby as Comptroller in November 1661.

Here we had, for my sake, two fiddles, the one a bass viall; on which he that played, played well some Lyra lessons,* but both together made the worst musique that ever I heard.

We had a fine collacion, but I took little pleasure in that, for the illnesse of the Musique and for the intentnesse of my mind upon Mrs. Rebecca Allen.

After we had done eating, the ladies went to dance; and among the men we had, I was forced to dance too – and did make an ugly shift. Mrs. R. Allen danced very well, and seems the best-humourd woman that ever I saw. About 9 a-clock Sir Wm. and my Lady went home, and we continued dancing an houre or two and so broke up very pleasant and merry; and so walked home, I leading Mrs. Rebecca – who seemed, I know not why, in that and other things to be desirous of my favours and would in all things show me respects.

Going home, she would needs have me sing; and did pretty well and was highly esteemed by them.

So to Captain Allens (where we was last night and heard him play of the Harpsicon; and I find him to be a perfect good Musician); and there, having no mind to leave Mrs. Rebecca, I did, what with talk and singing (her father and I), Mrs. Turner and I stayed there till 2 a-clock in the morning and was most exceeding merry; and I had the opportunity of kissing Mrs. Reb. very often.

Among other things, Captain Pett was saying that he thought that he had got his wife with Childe since I came thither.[1] Which I tooke hold of and was merrily asking him what he would take to have it said for my honour that it was of my getting?[a] He merrily answered that he would, if I would promise to be god-father to it if it did come within the time just; and I said that I would. So that I must remember to compute it when the time comes.

11. At 2 a-clock, with very great mirth, we went to our lodging and to bed. And lay till 7; and then called up by Sir W. Batten – so I rise. And we did some business; and then came Captain Allen and he and I withdrow and sung a song or

---

a followed by symbol (? 'which') crossed out

---

1. In January 1661.

two; and among others, took great pleasure in *Goe and bee hanged; that's twice god b'w'y*.[1]

The young ladies came too, and so I did again please myself with Mrs. Rebecca. And at about 9 a-clock, after we had breakfasted, we Sett*ª* forth for London; and endeed, I was a little troubled to part with Mrs. Rebecca – for which God forgive me. Thus we went away through Rochester, calling and taking leave of Mr. Alcocke at the door – Captain Cuttance going with us. We baited at Dartford, and thence to London.

But of all the journys that ever I made, this was the merriest, and I was in a strange moode for mirth. Among other things, I got my Lady to let her ⟨mayd⟩, Mrs. Ann, to ride all the way on horseback – and she rides exceeding well. And so I called [her] my clerk, that she went to wait upon me.

I met two little schoole-boys, going with pichers of ale to their schoolmaster to break up against Easter; and I did drink of some of one of them and give him two pence.

By and by we came to two little girls keeping cowes; and I saw one of them very pretty, so I had a minde to make her*ᵇ* aske my blessing. And telling that I was her godfather, she asked me innocently whether I was not Ned Wooding, and I said that I was; so she kneeled down and very simply cried, "Pray, godfather, pray to God to bless me" – which made us very merry and I gave her twopence.

In several places I asked women whether they would Sell*ᶜ* me their children; that they denied me all, but said they would give me one to keep for them if I would.

Mrs. Ann and I rode under the man that hangs upon Shooters

---

a   l.h. repl. s.h. 'went'   *b*   repl. ? 'all of'   *c*   l.h. repl. s.h. ? 'buy'

---

1. The last line of the fourth stanza of a bawdy song beginning 'I prithee sweet heart grant me my desire', printed in *Wit and drollery* (1656), pp. 123–4; ib. (1661), pp. 198–200; D'Urfey's *Wit and mirth* (1700), pp. 112–13. In broadside form (BM, Ballad Collection ?1660–?1710, C. 22. f. 6, f.211*r*), it begins 'Down in an Arbour devoted to *Venus*' and is 'To the Tune of, *Mars* and *Venus*'. Its point is that it strings together contemporary proverbs and catchphrases. Cf. J. Howell, *Lexicon Tetraglotton* (1660; 'Engl. Proverbs', p. 11). Pepys and Allen sang it again on 17 April. (E).

hill;[1] and a filthy sight it was to see how his flesh is shrunk to his bones.

So home. And I find all well, and a good deal of work done since I went.

I sent to see how my wife doth – who is well; and my brother John come from Cambrige.

To Sir W. Battens and there supped and very merry with the young ladies. So to bed, very sleepy for last night's work – concluding that it is the pleasantest journy, in all respects, that ever I had in my life.

12. Up among my workmen. And about 7 a-clock comes my wife to see me, and my brother John with her – who I am glad to see. But I sent them away because of going to the office, which I did, and then dined with Sir W. Batten; all fish-dinner, it being Goodfriday.

Then home and looked over my workmen; and then into the City and saw in what forwardness all things are for the Coronacion, which will be very magnificent. Then back again home, and to my chamber to set down in my Diary all my late journy, which I do with great pleasure; and while I am now writing, comes one with a tickett to invite me to Captain Robt. Blakes[2] buriall – for whose death I am very sorry; and do much wonder at it, he being a little while since a very likely man to live as any I knew.

Since my going out of towne, there is one Alexander Rosse taken and sent to the Counter by Sir Tho. Allen for counterfaiting my hand to a ticket – and we this day at the office have given order to Mr. Smith to prosecute him.[3] To bed.

1. A highwayman; it was common to erect gallows at the scene of the crime. The body of the malefactor would sometimes be soaked in tar to preserve it. Shooter's Hill, about eight miles out of London, was one of the most dangerous points on the Dover Road; the way was steep, narrow and fringed by woods. Many robberies were committed there until, under an act of 1739, a new road was built up the hill. E. Hasted, *Hist. Kent* (ed. Drake), i. 196.

2. Commander of the *Worcester*.

3. The offence dated from the previous November: *CSPD 1660–1*, p. 359. The Counter was one of the two city prisons of that name. Aleyn was an alderman. Robert Smith was the Navy Office messenger, whose duties included the conduct of such prosecutions. The city's court records are defective for this period, and nothing more has been discovered about the case.

13. To White-hall by water from towere=wharfe (where we could not pass the ordinary way, because they were mending of the great stone steps against the Coronacion) with Sir Wm. Pen. There to my Lords; and thence with Captain Cuttance and Captain Clerke to drink our morning draught together; and before we could get back again, my Lord was gone out. So to Whitehall again and met with my Lord above with the Duke. And after a little talk with him, I went to the Banquet-house and there saw the King heale, the first time that ever I saw him do it – which he did with great gravity; and it seemed to me to be an ugly office and a simple* one.¹ That done, to my Lord's and dined there; and so by water with parson Turner toward London; and upon my telling of him of Mr. Moore to be a fit man to do his business with Bishop Wren, about which he was going, he went back out of my boat into another to White-hall; and so I forwards home, and there by and by took coach with Sir W. Pen and Captain Terne and went to the buriall of Captain Robt. Blake at Wapping. And there had each of us a ring.² But it being dirty, we would not go to church with them, but with our coach we returned home. And there stayed a little; and then he and I alone to the Dolphin (Sir W. Batten being this day gone with his Lady to Walthamstowe to keep Easter) and there had a supper by ourselfs, we both being hungry. And staying late there drinking, I became very sleepy and so we went home, and I to bed.

14.*ᵃ* 《*Easter.*》 *Lords=day.* In the morning towards my father's. And by the way heard Mr. Jacomb at Ludgate, upon these words, "Christ loved you and therefore let us love one

a repl. '13'

---

1. Cf. above, i. 182, n. 1. The office is printed and the service described in Sir R. Crawfurd, *King's Evil*, pp. 114+; see also Evelyn, 6 July 1660; Magalotti, pp. 214–16. Pepys kept in his library an engraving by Robert White of Charles II performing the ceremony: PL 2973, 346 (b).

In February–April 1661, 1425 persons were touched: John Browne, *Charisma Basilicon* (1684), bk iii, App., n.p.

2. Rings were often provided for the principal mourners by the will of the deceased. Men's funerals were commonly attended by men only.

another."[1]   And made a lazy sermon, like a presbyterian.   Then to my father's and dined there, and Dr. Fairbrother (lately come to town) with us.   After dinner I went to the Temple and there heard Dr. Griffith;[2] a good sermon for the day.   So with Mr. Moore (whom I met there) to my Lord's – and there he showed me a Copy of my Lord Chancellor's patent for Earle, and I read the preamble, which is very short, modest, and good.[3]

Here my Lord saw us and spoke to me about getting Mr. Moore to come and governe his house while he goes to sea, which I promised him to do.   And did afterward speak to Mr. Moore and he is willing.

Then hearing that Mr. Barnwell[4] was come with some of my Lord's little children yesterday to town to see the Coronacion, I went and found them at the Goate at Charing-cross; and there I went and drank with them a good while – whom I find in very good health and very merry.   Then to my father's, and after supper seemed willing to go home; and my wife seeming to be so too,[5] I went away in a discontent; but she, poor wretch,[6] Fallowed me as far, in the rain and dark, as Fleete brige to fetch me back again; and so I did, and lay with her tonight – which I have not done these eight or ten days before.

15.[a]   From my father's (it being a very foule morning for the King and Lords to go to Windsor)[7] I went to the office; and there met Mr. Coventry and Sir Robt. Slingsby, but did no business but only appoint to go to Deptford together tomorrow.

a repl. '14'

1. A loose recollection of 1 John, iv. 11 (or possibly of Eph., v. 2). Thomas Jacombe, a leading Presbyterian, was Rector of St Martin-infra-Ludgate. This does not appear to be among his many published sermons.

2. Matthew Griffith, Rector of St Mary Magdalen, Old Fish St; a prominent royalist and episcopalian during the Interregnum.

3. See PRO, C 66/3000, no. 21, the passage beginning *Cum nihil magis ex Regia maiestate.* . . . For preambles to patents of title, see above, i. 188, n. 1.

Hyde's patent as Earl of Clarendon and Viscount Cornbury was not sealed until 21 April.

4. In Sandwich's service at Hinchingbrooke.

5. Sc. Pepys pretended to want to go home, and his wife pretended to be willing to let him go.

6. A term of endearment which Pepys often applies to his wife: modern equivalents would be 'poor thing', 'poor dear'.

7. They went to hold a chapter of the Order of the Garter on the 17th: *CSPD 1660-1*, p. 571.

Mr. Coventry being gone and I having at home laid up 200*l*, which I had brought this morning home from Alderman Backwells, I went home by coach with Sir R. Slingsby and dined with him – and had a very good dinner. His lady seems a good woman; and very desirous they were to hear this noon by the post how the eleccion*ᵃ* hath gone at New=castle – wherein he is concerned.[1] But the letters are not come yet.

To my Uncle Wights; and after a little stay with them, he and I to Mr. Rawlinsons and there stayed all the afternoon, it being very foule. And had a little talk with him what good I might make of these ships that go to Portugall, by venturing some money by them; and he will give me an answer to it shortly.[2] So home and sent for the Barber; and after that to bed.

16.*ᵇ* So soon as word was brought me that Mr. Coventry was come with the barge to the Tower, I went to him and find him reading of the psalmes in short-hand (which he is now busy about); and had good sport about the long marks that are made there for sentences in Divinity, which he is never like to make use of.[3] Here he and I sat till the Comptroller came; and then we put off for Deptford – where we went on board the Kings pleasure-boat that Comissioner Pett is making;[4] and endeed, it will be a most pretty thing.

a l.h. repl. s.h. 'ele'- (blotted)   b repl. '15'

---

1. The Duke of York had recommended Slingsby to the corporation of Newcastle-upon-Tyne in a letter of 5 March: PRO, Adm. 2/1745, f.29*v*. But two townsmen, Sir Francis Anderson and Sir John Marlay, were returned on 10 April, a third candidate, George Liddell, unsuccessfully petitioning. Cf. also J. Thurloe, *State Papers* (1742), vii. 346.

2. It was common and allowable at this time for the King's ships to carry private cargoes (usually plate or bullion), and for naval officers to receive payment for their services. Limits were imposed in 1686. For Pepys's views, see *Further Corr.*, i. 189; *Pepys' memoires of the royal navy* (ed. Tanner, 1906), p. 56. Cf. Ted-

der, p. 68; J. R. Tanner, *Pepys and navy*, pp. 66–7, 72.

3. Thomas Cross's edition of the Sternhold and Hopkins Psalms, engraved in the shorthand system of Jeremiah Rich (d. ?1660) had been published at an unknown date about this time. (This entry helps to fix the date.) Rich's use of special signs was lavish, and with their help he could write a sermon in a very small space. (Wavy lines represented 'the devills feare and tremble' etc.) Coventry did not write much shorthand: cf. Longleat, Coventry MSS 95, f.132*v*.

4. The *Catherine* yacht: see above, p. 12 & n. 2.

From thence to Comissioner Petts lodging and there had a good breakefast; and in came the two Sir Wms. from Walthamstow. And so we sat down and did a great deal of public business about the fitting of the fleet that is now going out.

That done, we went to the globe and there had a good dinner. And by and by took barge again and so home – and by the way they would have me sing, which I did to Mr. Coventry[1] – who went up*a* to Sir Wm. Battens; and there we stayed and talked a good while, and then broke up. And I home and then to my father's and there lay with my wife.

17.*b* By land and saw the Arches, which are now almost done and are very fine. And I saw the picture of the ships and other things this morning, set up before the East Indy-house – which are well done.[2] So to the office; and that being done, I went to dinner with Sir W. Batten. And then home to my workmen and saw them go on, with great content to me. Then comes Mr. Allen of Chatham and I took him to the Miter and there did drink with him; and did get of him the song that pleased me

a repl. 'str'-   *b* repl. '16'

---

1. Pepys would sing bass: cf. above, i. 19, n. 3. (E).

2. Four triumphal arches (90–100 ft high and costing over £10,000) were erected by the City, at each of which the royal procession from the Tower to Whitehall on 22 April 1661 (the day before the coronation) was due to halt for a ceremony of welcome. The first (in Leadenhall St) represented 'Monarchy and Rebellion'; the second (by the Royal Exchange) was a naval one; the third (on the site of Cheapside Cross) was a 'Temple of Concord'; the fourth (in Fleet St) a 'Garden of Plenty'. The pageantry was organised by John Ogilby and described in his official *Relation of his Majesty's entertainment passing thorough the city of London to his coronation* (1661), with plates by David Loggan, and in his more elaborate *Entertainment of his most excellent Majestie Charles II . . .* (1662), with plates by Hollar. The arches were designed by Peter Mills, Surveyor to the City, and by an anonymous architect; the paintings with which they were embellished were carried out by two City painters, Andrew Dacres and William Lightfoot. See E. Halfpenny in *Guildhall Misc.*, i, no. 10/19+; R. Strong in *Some portraits of Charles II*, National Portrait Gallery (1960), pp. 10–11. Pepys preserved in his library the Loggan prints: PL 2973, pp. 336–9. The 'picture' erected outside E. India House was put up by the company: Ogilby (1661), pp. 10–11. (OM).

so well there the other day – of *Shitten come Shits, the beginning of love.*[1]

His daughters are to come to town tomorrow, but I know not whether I shall see them or no. That done, I went to the Dolphin by appointment and there I met*a* Sir Wms. both and Mr. Castle and did eat a barrel of oysters and two lobsters which I did give them, and were very merry.

Here we had great talk of Mr. Warrens being Knighted by the King, and Sir W. Batten seemed to be very much incensed against him.[2]

So home.

18.*b* Up with my workmen. And then about 9 a-clock took horse with both the Sir Wms for Walthamstowe; and there we find my Lady and her daughters all.[3]

And a pleasant day it was and all things else, but that my Lady was in a bad moode, which we were troubled at; and had she been noble, she would not have been so with her servants when we came thither. And this Sir W. Penn took notice of as well as I. After dinner we all went to the Church stile – and there eate and drank.[4] And I was as merry as I could counterfeit myself to be. Then it raining hard, we left Sir W. Batten and we two returned – and called at Mr.   and drank some*c* brave wine there. And then homewards again. And in our way met with two country fellows upon one horse – which I did without much ado give the way to; but Sir W. Penn would not – but stroke them and they him – and so passed away; but they giving him some high words, he went back again and stroke them off of their horse in a simple fury, and without much honour in my mind. And so came away.

Home; and I sat with him a good while talking, and then home and to bed.

a MS. 'paid'   *b* repl. '17'   *c* MS. 'so'

---

1. The third line of the third stanza of the song sung by Pepys and Allen on 11 April: above, p. 72. (E).

2. Warren had been knighted on 12 April. Batten was usually critical of his work for the Navy Board.

3. Lady Batten's two daughters and her daughter-in-law.

4. The occasion would presumably be a church-ale (cf. the modern church-tea) held to collect funds for the church. Stalls would be erected at the church-stile at the entrance to the graveyard.

19.[a] Among my workmen. And then to the office. And after that dined with Sir W. Batten. And then home, where[b] Sir W. Warren came and I took him and Mr. Sheply and Moore with me to the Miter, and there I cleared with Warren for the deals I bought lately for my Lord of him.[1] And he went away and we stayed afterwards a good while and talked, and so parted – it being so foule that I could not go to White-hall to see the Knights of the Bath made today[2] – which doth trouble me mightily. So home; and having stayed awhile till Will came in (with whom I was vexed for staying abroad), he comes and then I went by water to my father's, and there after supper to bed with my wife.

20.[c] Here comes my boy to tell me that the Duke of Yorke hath sent for all the Principall officers &c to come to him today. So I went by water to Mr. Coventrys and there stayed and talked a good while with him till all the rest came. We went up and saw the Duke dress himself, and in his night habitt he is a very plain man. Then he sent us to his closet, where we saw, among other things, two very fine chests covered with gold and Indian varnish, given him by the East India Company of Holland. The Duke comes; and after he had told us that the fleet was designed for Algier (which was kept from us till now),[3] we did advise about many things as to the fitting of the fleet and so went away. And from thence to the Privy Seale, where little to do. And after that took Mr. Creed and Moore and gave them their morning draught. And after that to my Lord's, where Sir W. Penn came to me and dined with my Lord. After dinner he and others that dined there went away. And then my Lord looked upon his pages and footmens liverys, which are come home today and will be handsome, though not gawdy. Then with my Lady and my Lady Wright to White-hall; and in the banqueting-

---

a repl. '18'   *b* MS. 'Mr'.   *c* repl. '19'

---

1. Bought for the works at Hinch- ingbrooke: above, i. 324; above, p. 35.
2. For the names of the knights and a description of the ceremonies (in the Court of Requests and Chapel of Henry VII), see *Kingd. Intell.*, 29 April, pp. 242–7. Five royal commissioners acted on behalf of the King, the knights having spent their vigil (in bed) in the Painted Chamber.
3. Cf. above, p. 62 & n. 3.

house saw the King Create my Lord Chancellor and several other Earles; and Mr. Crew and several others Barons[1] – the first[a] being led up by Heralds and five old Earles to the King: and there the patent is read, and the King puts on his Vest and Sword and Coronett and gave him the patent. And then he kisseth the King's hand and rises and stands Coverd before the king. And the same for the Barons; only, he is led up but by three of the old Barons – and are girt with Swords before they go to the King.

That being done (which was very pleasant to see their habitts), I carried my Lady back. And there I find my Lord angry for that his page had let my Lord's new beaver be changed for an old hat.

Then I went away; and with Mr. Creed to the Exchange and bought some things, as gloves and band-strings, &c. So back to the Cockpitt; and there, by the favour of one Mr. Bowman,[2] he and I got in and there saw the King and Duke ⟨of Yorke⟩ and his Duchesse (which is a plain woman, and like her mother), my Lady Chanceller.

And so saw *The Humorsome Lieutenant*[3] acted before the King, but not very well done. But my pleasure was great to see the manner of it;[4] and so many great beauties, but above all Mrs. Palmer,[5] with whom the King[b] doth discover a great deal of Familiarity.

So Mr. Creed and I (the play being done) went to Mrs. Harpers

a repl. 'they'   b MS. 'here'

---

1. Description and lists in *Merc. Pub.*, 25 April, pp. 254–5, and other newsbooks. Six earls and six barons were invested.

2. Probably either Edward or Francis Bowman, both of whom were Gentlemen-Ushers to the King in 1663.

3. *The humorous lieutenant, or Demetrius and Enanthe*, a tragicomedy by John Fletcher, first acted c. 1619, and published in 1647. This performance was evidently given by the King's Company; according to Downes, it was one of its stock plays,

and the cast he lists (p. 3) includes Clun as the Lieutenant, Hart as Demetrius, Burt as Seleucus and Mrs Marshall as Celia. (A).

4. Pepys may be referring to a special method of presentation made necessary by the stage of the Cockpit at Whitehall, which probably had a semi-circular architectural façade with five doorways in it. (A).

5. Barbara Palmer (*née* Villiers); Countess of Castlemaine from December 1661; the King's mistress for about ten years from c. 1660.

and there sat and drank, it being about 12 at night. The ways being so dirty, and stopped up with the rayles which are this day set up in the streets, I could not go home, but went with him to his lodging at Mr. Wares and there lay all night.

21. In the morning we were troubled to hear it rain as it did, because of the great show tomorrow. After I was ready, I walked to my father's. And there find the late mayde to be gone and another come by my mother's choice, which my father doth not like; and so, great difference there will be between my father and mother about it. Here dined Dr. Tho. Pepys and Dr. Fayrebrother. And all our talk about tomorrow's Shewe – and our trouble that it is like to be a wet day.

After dinner comes in my Cozen Snow and his wife, and I think [to] stay there till the Shewe be*a* over. Then I went home; and all the way is so thronged with people to see the Triumphall Arches that I could hardly pass for them.

So home, people being at church; and I got home unseen. And so up to my chamber and set*b* down these last five or six days' Diarys.

My mind a little troubled about my workmen, which being foraigners[1] are like to be troubled by a couple of lazy rogues that worked with me the other day that are Citizens: and so my work will be hindered, but I must prevent it if I can.

22.*c*   *King's going from the Tower to White-hall*[2]

Up earely and made myself as fine as I could, and put on my velvet coat, the first day that I put it on though made half a year

a repl. ? 'being'   *b* MS. 'see'   *c* figure (blotted) repl. '21'

---

1. Men not enrolled as freemen of the city, though quite possibly living within its bounds. Freemen could properly object to their employment as skilled workmen within the city. (R).

2. The secular procession or royal entry held on the day before the coronation; omitted at the beginning of Charles I's reign because of the plague, and now of special magnificence because of the Restoration; never repeated after this occasion.

Pepys kept in his library Hollar's prints of the cavalcade: PL 2973, pp. 340–1. For accounts both of this and of the coronation itself, see Sir Edward Walker, *Circumstantial account of the . . . coronation of . . . Charles II* (1820); John Ogilby, *The relation of his Majesties entertainment . . .* (1661); Evelyn, s.d.; L. G. Wickham Legg (ed.), *Engl. coronation records*, pp. 276+; *Kingd. Intell.*, 29 April; W. Kennett, *Register* (1728), pp. 411+; Rugge, i, ff. 189+.

ago:[1] and being ready, Sir W. Batten, my Lady, and his two daughters and his son and wife, and Sir W. Penn and his son and I went to Mr. Young's the Flagg-maker in Cornhill;[2] and there we had a good room to ourselfs, with wine and good cake, and saw the Shew very well – in which it is impossible to relate the glory of that this day – expressed in the clothes of them that rid – and their horses and horse-cloths. Among others, my Lord Sandwich.

Imbroidery[3] and diamonds were ordinary among them.

The Knights of the Bath[4] was a brave sight of itself. And their Esquires, among which Mr. Armiger[5] was an Esquire to one of the Knights.   remarquable was the two men that represent*a* the two Dukes of Normandy and Aquitane.[6]

The Bishops came next after the Barons, which is the higher place; which makes me think that the next parliament they will be called to the House of Lords.[7] My Lord Monke rode bare after the King, and led in his hand a spare horse, as being Maister of the Horse.

The King, in a most rich imbrodered suit and cloak, looked most nobly.   Wadlow,[8] the vintner at the Devil in Fleetstreet, did lead a fine company of Souldiers, all young comely men, in white doublets.   There fallowed the Vice-Chamberlin, Sir G. Carteret, a company of men all like turkes; but I know not yet what they are for.[9]

The Streets all gravelled; and the houses, hung with Carpets

a repl. 'resemble'

---

1. Above, i. 227.
2. Near to John Young's house, by the Royal Exchange, was the principal arch dedicated to the navy: Ogilby, p. 12.
3. Probably gold- and silver-thread work, with jewels.
4. 'In Crimson robes exceeding rich, & the noblest shew of the whole *Cavalcade* (his Majestie Excepted)': Evelyn, 23 April.
5. Probably William Armiger, a distant relative of Pepys, lodging at the house of Tom Pepys, the tailor.
6. 'In fantastique habits of that

time' (Evelyn), personifying the royal claim to these duchies.
7. A bill restoring bishops to the Lords received royal assent in the following July. But they took no part in this secular cavalcade. Pepys may have been copying here from a broadsheet programme of the event (R. Williams, *A true copie . . .*, 1661) which makes the same error: E. Halfpenny in *Guildhall Misc.*, i. no. /1021 & n. 11.
8. A captain of militia.
9. They appear to have been a company of the royal footguard.

before them, made brave show, and the ladies out of the windows. One of which, over against us, I took much notice of and spoke of her, which made good sport among us.

So glorious was the show with gold and silver, that we were not able to look at*ᵃ* it – our eyes at last being so much overcome with it.

Both the King and the Duke of Yorke took notice of us as he saw us at the window.

The show being ended, Mr Young did give us dinner – at which we very merry, and pleased above imagination at what we have seen. ⟨Sir W. Batten going home, he and I called and drank some Mum and laid our wager about my Lady Faulconbrige's name, which he says not to be Mary;[1] and so I won above 20*s*.⟩*ᵇ*

So home – where Will and the boy stayed and saw the show upon tower hill – and Jane at T. Pepys the Turner and my wife at Charles Glascockes in Fleetstreete. In the evening, by water to White-hall to my Lord's. And there I spoke with my Lord. He talked with me about his suit, which was made in France and cost him 200*l*, and very rich it is with imbroidery.

23. I lay with Mr. Sheply, and about 4 in the morning I rose.

Coronacion day.

And got to the abby, where I fallowed Sir J. Denham the surveyour[2] with some company that he was leading in. And with much ado, by the favour of Mr. Cooper[3] his man, did get up into a great scaffold across the north end of the abby – where with a great deal of patience I sat from past 4 till 11 before the King came in. And a pleasure it was to see the Abbey raised in the middle, all covered with red and a throne (that is a chaire) and footstoole on the top of it. And all the officers of all kinds, so much as the very fidlers, in red vests.

---

a MS. 'up' *b* addition crowded into end of line

---

1. She was in fact Mary, daughter of Oliver Cromwell, who had married Thomas Belasyse, 2nd Viscount Fauconberg; Batten had probably confused one of her three sisters with her.

2. Sir John Denham (poet, courtier and dilettante architect) had been Surveyor-General of the King's Works since June 1660.

3. Henry Cooper, Clerk of the Works, Hampton Court.

At last comes in the Deane and prebends of Westminster with the Bishops (many of them in cloth-of-gold Copes); and after them the nobility all in their parliament-robes, which was a most magnificent sight.   Then the Duke and the King with a scepter (carried by my Lord of Sandwich) and Sword and mond before him, and the crowne too.[1]

The King in his robes, bare-headed, which was very fine. And after all had placed themselfs – there was a sermon and the service.   And then in the Quire at the high altar he passed all the ceremonies of the Coronacion – which, to my very great grief, I and most in the Abbey could not see.   The crowne being put upon his head, a great shout begun.   And he came forth to the Throne and there passed more ceremonies: as, taking the oath and having things read to him by the Bishopp,[2] and his lords (who put on their capps[3] as soon as the King put on his Crowne) and Bishopps came and kneeled before him.

And three times the King-at-armes[4] went to the three open places on the scaffold and proclaimed that if any one could show any reason why Ch. Steward should not be King of England, that now he should come and speak.

And a Generall pardon also was read by the Lord Chancellor;[5] and meddalls flung up and down by my Lord Cornwallis – of silver;[6] but I could not come by any.

But so great a noise, that I could make but little of the Musique; and endeed, it was lost to everybody.   But I had so great a list to pisse, that I went out a little while before the King had done all his ceremonies[a] and went round the abby to Westminster-hall,

a   repl. 'ceremonies' (blotted)

---

1. The regalia, sold or destroyed in 1649, had been replaced since the Restoration by Sandwich, as Master of the Great Wardrobe, and Sir Gilbert Talbot, Master of the Jewel House. Description in Sir E. Walker, *Circumstantial Account* (1820), pp. 30+.

2. Gilbert Sheldon, Bishop of London, conducted the greater part of the service, the Archbishop of Canterbury (Juxon) being old and ill.

3. For caps and coronets, see L. G. Wickham Legg (ed.), *Engl. coronation records*, pp. lxxxii+.

4. Sir Edward Walker, Garter King of Arms.

5. Steele, no. 3299.

6. For these coronation badges, see E. Hawkins *et al.*, *Medallic illust. hist. G.B.*, i. 472–7, nos 76–85; ib., portfolio, pl. 45. Cornwallis was Treasurer of the Household.

all the way within rayles, and 10000 people, with the ground coverd with blue cloth – and Scaffolds all the way. Into the hall I got – where it was very fine with hangings and scaffolds, one upon another, full of brave ladies. And my wife in one little one on the right hand.

Here I stayed walking up and down; and at last, upon one of the side-stalls, I stood and saw the King come in with all the persons (but the Souldiers) that were yesterday in the cavalcade;^a and a most pleasant sight it was to see them in their several robes. And the King came in with his Crowne on and his sceptre in his hand – under a Canopy borne up by six silver staves, carried by Barons of the Cinqueports – and little bells at every end.

And after a long time he got up to the farther end, and all set themselfs down at their several tables – and that was also a rare sight. And the King's first Course carried up by the Knights of the bath. And many fine ceremonies there was of the Heralds leading up people before him and bowing; and my Lord of Albimarles going to the Kitchin and eat a bit of the first dish that was to go to the King's table.[1]

But above all was these three Lords, Northumberland and Suffolke and the Duke of Ormond,[2] coming before the Courses on horseback and staying so all dinner-time; and at last, to bring up (Dymock) the King's Champion, all in armor on horseback, with his Speare and targett carried before him. And a herald[3] proclaim that if any dare deny Ch. Steward to be lawful King of England, here was a Champion that would fight with him; and with those words the Champion flings down his gantlet; and all this he doth three times in his going up toward the King's table. At last, when he is come, the King Drinkes to him and then sends him the Cup, which is of gold; and he drinks it off and then rides back again with the cup in his hand.

I went from table to table to see the Bishops and all others at their dinner, and was infinite pleased with it. And at the Lords'

a repl. 'progress'

---

1. For the custom of 'assaying' royal food, see S. Pegge, *Curialia* (1791), pt iii. 30–2; cf. below, viii. 428 & n. 1.

2. Lord High Constable, Earl Marshal and Lord High Steward respectively.

3. George Owen, York Herald. Pepys gives only a summary of the words used.

table I met with Wll. Howe and he spoke to my Lord for me
and he did give him four rabbits and a pullet; and so I got it,
and Mr. Creed and I got Mr. Michell to give us some bread and
so we at a Stall eat it, as everybody else did what they could get.

I took a great deal of pleasure to go up and down and look
upon the ladies – and to hear the Musique of all sorts; but above
all, the 24 viollins.[1]

About 6 at night they had dined; and I went up to my wife
and there met with a pretty lady (Mrs. Frankelyn, a Doctor's
wife, a friend of Mr. Bowyers) and kissed them both – and by
and by took them down to Mr. Bowyers. And strange it is, to
think that these two days have held up fair till now that all is
done and the King gone out of the hall; and then it fell a-raining
and thundering and lightening as I have not seen it do some
years – which people did take great notice of God's blessing of
the work of these two days – which is a foolery, to take too much
notice of such things.[2]

I observed little disorder in all this; but only the King's Footmen had got hold of the Canopy and would keep it from the
barons of the Cinqueports; which they endeavoured to force from
them again but could not do it till my Lord Duke of Albemarle
caused it to be put into Sir R. Pye's hand till tomorrow to be
decided.[3]

At Mr. Bowyers, a great deal of company; some I knew, others
I did not. Here we stayed upon the leads and below till it was
late, expecting to see the Fireworkes; but they were not performd

---

1. See above, i. 298, n. 1. (E).

2. Some were convinced it was
a good augury, others that it was evil:
Somers Tracts (ed. Scott), vii. 513–15.
Richard Baxter was reminded of the
earthquake that occurred during
Charles I's coronation, adding, 'I intend no Commentary . . . but only
to relate the Matter of Fact': M.
Sylvester, *Reliq. Baxt.* (1696), bk i,
pt ii. 303. Pepys himself was not
always proof against superstition: see
below, 21 January 1665.

3. The Barons had been dragged

along the hall, and had lost their
places at table. By a prompt command of the King, the footmen were
imprisoned and dismissed. Pepys
(himself a Baron of the Cinque Ports
at James II's coronation) has a note
about this squabble in *Naval Minutes*,
p. 157. Fuller accounts in J. Ogilby,
Entertainment (1662), p. 186; W.
Kennett, *Register* (1728), p. 421; Sir
E. Walker, *Circumstantial Account*
(1820), pp. 122–3. Pye was an
Exchequer official.

tonight.   Only, the City had a light like a glory round about it, with bonefyres.

At last I went to Kingstreete; and there sent Crockford to my father's and my house to tell them I could not come home tonight, because of the dirt and a coach could not be had.

And so after drinking a pot of ale alone at Mrs. Harpers, I returned to Mr. Bowyers; and after a little stay more, I took my wife and Mrs. Frankelyn (who I proferred the civility of lying with my wife at Mrs. Hunts tonight) to Axe yard. In which, at the further end, there was three great bonefyres and a great many great gallants, men and women; and they laid hold of us and would have us drink the King's health upon our knee, kneeling upon a fagott; which we all did, they drinking to us one after another – which we thought a strange Frolique.[1] But these gallants continued thus a great while, and I wondered to see how the ladies did tiple.

At last I sent my wife and her bedfellow to bed, and Mr. Hunt and I went in with Mr. Thornbury (who did give the company all their wines, he being yeoman of the wine-cellar to the King) to his house; and there, with his wife and two of his sisters and some gallant sparks that were there, we drank the King's health and nothing else, till one of the genlemen fell down stark drunk and there lay speweing. And I went to my Lord's pretty well. But no sooner a-bed with Mr. Sheply but my head begun to turne and I to vomitt, and if ever I was foxed it was now – which I cannot say yet, because I fell asleep and sleep till morning – only, when I waked I found myself wet with my spewing. Thus did the day end, with joy everywhere; and blessed be God, I have not heard of any mischance to anybody through it all, but only to Serjeant Glynne, whose Horse*^a* fell upon him yesterday and is like to kill him; which people do*^b* please themselfs with, to see how just God is to punish that rogue at such a time as this – he

a l.h. repl. s.h. 'horst'   *b* MS. 'to'

---

1. In 1681, in Anthony Wood's Oxford, the loyal toast was often   drunk kneeling: *L. & T.*, ii. 527 etc.

being now one of the King's Serjeants and rode in the Cavalcade with Maynard, to whom people wished the same fortune.[1]

There was also this night, in Kingstreet, [a woman] had her eye put out by a boy's flinging of a firebrand into the coach.

Now after all this, I can say that besides the pleasure of the sight of these glorious things, I may now shut my eyes against any other objects, or for the future trouble myself to see things of state and shewe, as being sure never to see the like again in this world.

24. Waked in the morning with my head in a sad taking through the last night's drink, which I am very sorry for. So rise and went out with Mr. Creed to drink our morning draught, which he did give me in Chocolate to settle my stomach. And after that to my wife, who lay with Mrs. Frankelyn at the next door to Mrs. Hunts.

And they were ready, and so I took them up in a coach and carried the lady to Pauls and there set her down; and so my wife and I home – and I to the office.

That being done, my wife and I went to dinner to Sir W. Batten; and all our talk about the happy conclusion of these last solemnitys.

After dinner home and advised with my wife about ordering things in my house; and then she went away to my father's to lie, and I stayed with my workmen, who do please me very well with their work.

At night set myself to write down these three days' diary; and while I am about it, I hear the noise of the chambers and other things of the Fireworkes, which are now playing upon the Thames before the King. And I wish myself with them, being sorry not to see them.

So to bed.

1. Sir John Glynne survived the accident by five years. He and Sir John Maynard were eminent lawyers who, after serving in high judicial office under Oliver Cromwell, made their peace with the King at the Restoration, and became knights and King's Serjeants. Their unpopularity is comprehensible but unde- served. Many horsemen were thrown during the procession – the Duke of York twice – their horses being apparently alarmed by the music. The King himself was said to have been in danger until he ordered the music to cease. M. H. Nicolson (ed.), *Conway Letters*, p. 187.

25. All the morning with my workmen, with great pleasure to see them near coming to an end. At noon Mr. Moore and I went to an ordinary at the Kings-head in Tower-street and there had a dirty dinner. Afterward home. And having done some business with him – in comes Mr. Sheply and Pierce the surgeon and they and I to the Miter and there stayed a while and drunk; and so home and after a little reading, to bed.

26. At the office all the morning; and at noon dined by myself at home on a piece of meat from the Cookes.
And so at home all the afternoon with my workmen. And at night to bed – having some thoughts to order my business so as to go to Portsmouth the next week with Sir Rt. Slingsby.

27. In the morning to my Lord's and there dined with my Lady; and after dinner, with Mr. Creede and Captain Ferrers to the Theatre to see *The Chances*[1] – and after that to the Cock ale-house, where we had a Harpe and Viallin played to us. And so home by Coach to Sir W. Battens – who seems to be so inquisitive when my house will be made an end of, that I am troubled to go thither. So home, with some trouble in my mind about it.

28. *Lords day.*
In the morning to my father's, where I dined. And in the afternoon to their church,[2] where come Mrs. Turner and Mrs. Edwd. Pepys[3] and several other ladies; and so I went out of that pewe into another. And after sermon home with them, and there stayed awhile and talked with them; and was sent for to my father's, where my Cosen Angier and his wife of Cambrige, to whom I went – and was glad to see them, and sent for wine for them. And they supped with my father. After supper my father told me of an odd passage the other night in bed between

1. A comedy by John Fletcher, written c. 1617, and published in 1647; now at the TR, Vere St. According to Downes (p. 16), Don John in this play was one of Charles Hart's best roles. Pepys probably saw the original version of the play on this occasion, but what he saw on 5 February 1667, was probably the Duke of Buckingham's revision of it. (A).

2. St Bride's, Fleet St.

3. Of Broomsthorpe, Norf.; sister-in-law of Mrs Turner.

my mother and him.   And she would not let him come to bed
to her, out of jealousy of him and a ugly wench that lived there
lately[1] – the most ill-favored slut that ever I saw in my life –
which I was ashamed to hear, that my mother should be become
such a fool.   And my father bid me to take notice of it to my
mother,[a] and to make peace between him and her – all which doth
trouble me very much.

So to bed to my wife.

29.   Up, and with my father toward my house; and by the
way met with Lieutenant Lambert, and with him to the Dolphin
in Tower-street – and drank our morning draught – he being
much troubled about his being offered a fourth-rate ship; to be
Lieutenant of her, now he hath been two years Lieutenant in a
first-rate.[2]

So to the office – where it is determined that I shall go tomorrow
to Portsmouth.

So I went out of the office to White-hall presently; and there
spoke with Sir W. Pen and Sir George Carteret and had their
advice as to my going.   And so back again home – where I
directed Mr. Hater what to do in order to our going tomorrow.
And so back again by Coach to White-hall and there eate something in the buttery at my Lord's, with John Goods and Ned
Osgood.

And so home again and give order to my work[men] what
to do in my absence.

At night to Sir W. Battens; and by his and Sir W. Pens per-
suasions, I sent for my wife from my father's – who came to us
to Mrs. Turners, where we were all at a collacion tonight till
12 a-clock – there being a gentlewoman there that did play well
and sing well to the Harpsicon.   And very merry we were.

So home and to bed – where my wife had not lien a great
while.

30.   This morning, after order given to my workmen, my

a   repl. 'aunt'

_____

1. Cf. above, p. 64.   Ehrman, p. 138. Cf. below, iii. 128,
2. His monthly pay would be   n. 1.
reduced from £4 4s. to £3 10s.:

wife and I and Mr. Creed took Coach, and in fish-street took up
Mr. Hater and his wife – who, through her maske,[1] seemed to me
at first an old woman – but afterward I find her to be a very pretty
modest black* woman.

We got a small bayte at Letherhead; and so to Godlyman,
where we lay all night and were very merry – having this day no
other extraordinary rancontre but my hat falling off of my head
at Newington into the water, by which it was spoiled and I
ashamed of it.

I am sorry that I was not at London, to be at Hide parke
tomorrow among the great gallants and ladies, which will be
very fine.[2]

1. A travelling mask used to protect her complexion.

2. For the May-day 'tour' in the
Park, see above, i. 121 & n. 1.

MAY[a]

1. Up earely and baited at Petersfield, in the room which the King lay in lately at his being there.[1]

Here very merry and played, us and our wifes, at bowles. Then we set forth again; and so to portsmouth, seeming to me a very pleasant and strong place.[2] And we lay at the Red lyon, where Haslerigg and Scott and Walton did hold their Councell when they were here, against[b] Lambert and the Committee of safety.[3]

Several officers of the Yard came to see us tonight; and merry we were, but troubled to have no better Lodgeings.

2. Up; and Mr. Creed and I to walk round the town upon the Walls. Then to our Inne; and there all the officers of the Yard to see me with great respect and I walked with them to the Dock and saw all the Stores, and much pleased with the sight of the place.

Back, and brought them all to dinner with me and treated

a l.h. repl. l.h. 'Ap'-   *b* repl. symbol rendered illegible

---

1. On 4–5 January 1661, when he travelled with his mother and sister Henrietta as far as Portsmouth on their way to France. The journey took two days from Guildford to Portsmouth: *Kingd. Intell.*, 7 January, p. 16; *CSPD 1660–1*, p. 466. There were three busy coaching inns at Petersfield – the Dolphin and the Red Lion on the Portsmouth Road, and the Castle in Market Place (now the Square).

2. The description (c. 1682) in HMC, *Rep.*, 13/2/286–7 makes it clear that the walls still served a useful purpose: visitors were closely examined on entering the town. Cf. also Celia Fiennes, *Journeys* (ed. Morris), p. 53. The old town was completely surrounded by earth-works and walls; bastions marked the angles; gates gave admittance. The fortifications, considerably strengthened under Elizabeth and later during the civil war, were also improved by both Charles II and James II: VCH, *Hants.*, iii. 189–90. The walls were mostly demolished in the 1870s.

3. In December 1659, when these republicans took action against the Army leaders, won over the garrison troops of Portsmouth and others sent against them, and prepared the way for Monck's march from Scotland. The old Red Lion inn was on the corner of High St and Church Lane: H. and J. Slight, *Chronicles of Portsmouth* (1828), p. 16.

them handsomely; and so after dinner by water to the Yard, and there we made the Sale of the old provisions.[1]   Then we and our wifes all to see the *Mountagu*, which is a fine ship.   And so to the towne again by water; and then to see the room where the Duke of Buckingham was killed by Felton.[2]

So to our lodgings and to supper and to bed.

Tonight came Mr. Stevens to town, to help us to pay off the *Fox*.[3]

3. earely to walk with Mr. Creed up and down the Towne; and it was in his and some others' thoughts to have got me made free of the towne; but the Mayor was it seems unwilling, and so they could not do it.[4]

Then to the pay=house and there paid off the ship.   And so to a short dinner and then took Coach, leaving Mrs. Hater there to stay with her husbands friends, and we to Petersfield – having nothing more of trouble in all my Journy but the exceeding unmannerly and most epicurelike* palate of Mr. Creed.

Here my wife and I lay in the room the Queene lately lay at her going into france.

4. Up in the morning and took Coach; and so to Gilford, where we lay at the Redlyon, the best Inne, and lay in the room the King lately lay in.   Where we had time to see the Hospitall,

---

1. The main object of this visit. Similar sales were held at the three other naval yards: cf. above, p. 50 & n. 2.   The Principal Officers were paid £66 10s. 1d. for their travelling expenses: PRO, Adm. 20/1, no. 1834.

2. Charles I's unpopular favourite, the 1st Duke of Buckingham, was murdered in August 1628 by John Felton at a house at the upper end of High St.

3. A frigate, now paid off for service since 24 June (£781): PRO, Adm. 20/1, no. 2051. Anthony

Stevens was a cashier in the Navy Treasury.

4. Pepys was made a burgess of Portsmouth a year later: below, iii. 74.   Creed was himself elected later this year.   It was a courtesy normally extended to naval officials and officers – Penn, Batten and Sandwich, for instance, were already burgesses. R. East, *Extracts from records of Portsmouth*, pp. 355, 356, 357. The Mayor was Richard Lardner: ib., p. 315.

built by Archbishop Abbott, and the free Schoole, and were civilly treated by the Mayster.[1]

So to supper and to bed – being very merry about our discourse with the Drawers concerning the Minister of the towne,[2] with a red face and a girdle. So to bed – where we lay and sleep well.

5. *Lords day.*

Mr. Creed and I went to the red-faced parsons church and heard a good sermon of him, better then I looked for. Then home and had a good dinner; and after dinner fell in some talk in Divinity with Mr. Stevens, that kept us till it was past church-time.

Anon we walked into the garden and there played the fools a great while, trying who of Mr. Creed or I could go best over the edge of ⟨an⟩ old fountaine-wall; and I won a Quart of sack of him.

Then to supper in the banquet-house;* and there my wife and I did talk high, she against and I for Mrs. Pierce (that she was a beauty), till we were both angry.

Then to walk in the fields; and so to our Quarters and to bed.

6. Up by 4 a-clock and took Coach. Mr. Creed rid and left us, that we knew not whither he went. We went on, thinking to be at home before the officers rose; but finding that we could not, we stayed by the way and eat some cakes, and so home.

Where I was much troubled to see no more work done in my absence then there was, but it could not be helped.

I sent my wife to my father's; and I went and sat till late with my Lady Batten, both the Sir Wms. being gone this day to pay off some ships at Deptford.

1. For a description (1673) of Guildford, see J. Aubrey, *Nat. hist. . . . Surrey* (1719), iii. 278+. The Red Lion (at the corner of Market St, now destroyed) had in Aubrey's time 50 bedrooms and was reckoned 'the best inn in England': James Yonge, *Journal* (ed. Poynter), p. 212; cf. also Evelyn, 22 August 1653. The King's visit had been in the previous January, when, on his way to Portsmouth, he had been feasted by the corporation: VCH, *Surrey*, iii. 561; *CSPD 1660–1*, p. 466. For Abbot's Hospital, see below, ix. 273 & n. 3. The Free School (in High St) dated from c. 1520; the buildings Pepys saw were erected c. 1557. O. Manning and W. Bray, *Hist. Surrey* (1804–14), i. 75–94. John Graile was Master from 1645 to 1698: VCH, *Surrey*, ii. 170.

2. John Holland (d. 1671), Rector of Holy Trinity.

So home*ᵃ* and to bed without seeing of them.

I hear tonight that the Duke of Yorkes son is this day dead, which I believe will please everybody;[1] and I hear that the Duke and his Lady themselfs are not much troubled at it.

7. In the morning to Mr. Coventry, Sir G. Carteret, and my Lord's, to give them an account of my return. My Lady, I find, is since my going gone to the Wardrobe.[2] Then with Mr. Creed into London to Severall places about his and my businesses – being much stopped in our way by the City trayne bands, who go in much Solemnity and pomp this day to muster before the King and the Duke, and the*ᵇ* shops in the City are shut up everywhere all this day.[3]

He carried me to an Ordinary by the old Exchange, where we came a little too late; but we had very good cheer for our 18*d* a-piece,[4] and an excellent Droll too, my hoste; and his wife so fine a woman, and sung and play[ed] so well, that I stayed a great while and drank a great deal of wine.

Then home and stayed among my workmen all day, and took order for things for the finishing of their work.

And so at night to Sir W. Battens and there supped; and so home and to bed – having sent my Lord a letter tonight to excuse myself for not going with him tomorrow to the Hope, whither he is to go to see in what condition the fleete is in.

8. This morning came my Brother John to take his leave of me, he being to return to Cambrige tomorrow; and after I had chidd him for his*ᶜ* going with my Will the other day to Deptford with the Principall Officers, I did give him some good counsel and 20*s* in money; and so he went away.

     a l.h. repl. s.h. 'to'   *b* MS. 'I'   *c* MS. 'is'

---

1. The baby Charles Stuart, designated Duke of Cambridge, born on 22 October 1660, the first of eight children of the marriage, was buried this day in Westminster Abbey. Both the Duke of York and his secret marriage were unpopular. Cf. above, p. 38.

2. Sandwich, as Master, had the right of residence at the King's Wardrobe, near Puddle Dock.

3. The muster, involving elaborate military exercises, was held in Hyde Park. Description in *Merc. Pub.*, 9 May, p. 284.

4. For prices at ordinaries, see J. Parkes, *Travel in Engl. in 17th cent.*, pp. 325–6.

All this day I stayed at home with my workmen, without eating anything.   And took much pleasure to see my work go forward. At night comes my wife, not well, from my father's, having had a foretooth drawn out today[1] – which doth trouble me, and the more because I am now in the greatest of all my dirt.

My Will also returned tonight pretty well, he being gone yesterday, not very well, to his father's.

Today I received a letter from my Uncle to beg an old fiddle of me for my Cosen Perkin the Miller,[2] whose mill the wind hath lately broke down and now he hath nothing to live but by fiddling – and he must needs have it against Whitsuntide to play to the country girles.   But it vexed me to see how my Uncle writes to me, as if he were not able to buy him one.   But I entend tomorrow to send him one.   At night I set down my Journall of my late Journy to this time, and so to bed – my wife not being well and I very angry with her for her coming hither in that condition.

9.   With my workmen all the morning – my wife being ill and in great pain with her*a* old payne;[3] which troubled me much, because that my house is in this condition of dirt.

In the afternoon, I went to White-hall and there spoke with my Lord at his Lodgeings; and there being with him my Lord Chamberlin, I spoke for my old waterman Payne to get into White's place, who was waterman to my Lord Chamberlain and is now to go Master-of-the-Barge to my Lord to sea.   And my Lord Chamberlain*b* did promise that Payne should be entertained in Whites place with him.   From thence to Sir G. Carteret, and there did get his promise for the payment of the remainder of the bill of Mr. Creeds wherein of late I have been so much concerned;[4] which did so much rejoice me, that I meeting with

---

a   word blotted   *b*   l.h. repl. s.h. 'doth'

---

1. ? by Leeson (below ix. 557) or by de la Roche, the dentist who lived not far from Pepys's father. Methods of extraction are described in J. Woodall, *The surgeons mate* (1639), pp. 10–11; Charles Allen, *The operator for the teeth* (Dublin, 1686).

2. Frank Perkin, of Parson Drove, Cambs. The uncle was Robert Pepys of Brampton.

3. See above, i. 213 & n. 2.

4. Order for the payment of Creed's bill for £1035, for expenses incurred as Deputy-Treasurer of the fleet, was made on 15 May: PRO, Adm. 20/1, p. 143.   See below, p. 97.

Mr. Childe, took him to the Swan taverne in King-street and there did give him a tankard of white wine and sugar. And so I went by water home. And set myself to get my Lord's accounts made up, which was till 9 at night before I could finish; and then I walked to the Wardrobe – being the first that I was there*ᵃ* since my Lady came thither – who I find all alone; and so she showed*ᵇ* me all the lodgings as they are now fitted and they seem pretty pleasant. By and by comes in my Lord; and so after looking over my accounts, I returned home – being a dirty and dark walk. So to bed.

10. At the office all the morning, and the afternoon at home among my workmen with great pleasure, because being near an end of their work. This afternoon came Mr. Blackburne and Creed to see me, and I took them to the Dolphin and there drank a great deal of Rhenish wine with them. And so home, having some talk with Mr. Blackburne about his kinsman, my Will;[1] and he did give me good satisfaccion, in that it is his desire that his kinsman should do me all service, and that he would give*ᶜ* him the best counsel he could to make him good – which I begin of late to fear that he will not, because of the bad company that I find that he doth begin to take. This afternoon Mr. Hater received for me the 225*l.* due up[on] Mr. Creeds bill, in which I am concerned so much; which doth make me very glad.

At night to Sir W. Battens and sat a while; and so to bed.

11. This morning I went by water with Payne (Mr. Moore being with me) to my Lord Chamberlain at Whitehall and there spoke with my Lord, and he did accept of Payne for his waterman, as I had lately endeavoured to get him to be. After that, Mr. Cooling[2] did give Payne an order to be entertained; and so I left him. And Mr. Moore and I went to Grayes Inne and there to a barbers, where I was trimmed and had my haire cutt – in which I am lately become a little curious,* finding that the length of it doth become me very much.

So calling at my father's, I went home; and there stayed and

a repl. 'at'   *b* MS. s.h. 'should'   *c* repl. 'do'

1. Will Hewer, Blackborne's ne-   2. Secretary to the Lord Chamber-
phew and Pepys's clerk.   lain.

saw my workmen fallow their work, which this night is brought to a very good condition.

This afternoon Mr. Sheply, Moore, and Creed came to me all about their several accounts with me; and we did something with them all – and so they went away. This evening Mr. Hater brought my last Quarter's salary,[1] of which I was very glad – because I have lost my first bill for it, and so this morning was forced to get another signed by three of my fellow-officers for it.

All this evening, till late, setting my accounts and papers in order; and so to bed.

12. My wife had a very troublesome night this night, and in great pain; but about the morning her swelling broke, and so she was at great ease presently – as she useth to be. So I put in a tent (which Dr Williams sent me yesterday) into the hole, to keep it open till all the matter be come out – and so I question not but she will soon be well again.

I stayed at home all this morning, being the Lords day – making up my private accounts and setting papers in order. At noon went out, thinking to have dined with my Lady Mountagu[2] at the Wardrobe. But I found it so late that I came back again, and so dined with my wife in her chamber.

After dinner I went awhile to my chamber to set my papers right.

Then I walked forth toward Westminster; and at the Savoy heard Dr. Fuller preach upon Davids words ("I will wait with patience all the days of my appointed time until my change comes"); but methought it was a poor dry sermon. And I am afeared my former high esteem of his preaching was more out of opinion then judgement.[3]

From thence homeward; but met with Mr. Creed, with whom I went and walked in Grayes Inn walks; and from thence to Islington and there eate and drank at the house[4] my father and we

1. PRO, Adm. 20/1, p. 217 (25 March; £87 10s. for Pepys, £15 for his two clerks).

2. Probably Lady (Ann) Mountagu, Sandwich's step-mother.

3. The text, as cited, was a loose recollection of Job, xiv. 14. The preacher was the author Thomas Fuller, lecturer at the Savoy, whose Anglican sermons in the city in the 1650's had been popular.

4. The King's Head: below, 27 March 1664.

were wont of old to go to. And after that walked homeward, and parted in Smithfield; and so I home – much wondering to see how things are altered with Mr. Creed, who twelve months ago might have been got to hang himself almost, as soon as to go to a drinking-house on a Sunday.

13. All the morning at home among my workmen. At noon Mr. Creed and I went to the ordinary behind the Exchange, where we lately was; but I do not like it so well as I did. So home with him and to the office, where we sat late and he did deliver his accounts to us.

The office being done, I went home and took pleasure to see my work draw to an end.

14. Up earely, and by water to White-hall to my Lord and there had much talk with him about getting some money for him. He told me of his intention to get the Muster Maisters place for Mr. Pierce the purser, who he hath a mind to carry to sea with him. And spoke very slightingly of Mr. Creed, as that he hath no opinion at all of him; but only, he was forced to make use of him because of his present accounts.[1] Thence to drink with Mr. Sheply and Mr. Pinkny; and so home and among my workmen all day. In the evening Mr. Sheply came to me for some money; and so he and I to the Mitre and there we had good wine and a gammon of bacon. My Uncle Wight, Mr. Talbott, and others were with us, and we were pretty merry. So at night home and to bed – finding my head grow weak nowadays if I come to drink wine; and therefore hope that I shall leave it off of myself, which I pray God I could do.

15. With my workmen all day till the afternoon; and then to the office, where Mr. Creeds accounts were passed.

Home; and found all my Joyners work[2] now done but only a small jobb or two, which please me very well.

1. John Creed was, however, appointed Deputy-Treasurer and Muster-Master to Sandwich's fleet in 1661 – the same office he had held in 1660. Pierce had been purser of the *Naseby* (later *Royal Charles*) in 1660.

2. The making of the new staircase, begun on 25 March.

This evening there came two men with an order from a Comittee of Lords to demand some books of me out of the office, in order to the examining of Mr. Huchinson's accounts; but I gave them a surly* answer, and they went away to complain; which put me into some trouble with myself – but I resolve to go tomorrow myself to those Lords and answer them.¹

To bed – being in great fear because of the shavings which lay all up and down the house and Seller, for fear of fire.

16.   Up earely to see whether the work of my house be quite done, and I find it to my mind.   Stayed at home all the morning; and about 2 a-clock went in my velvet coat by water to the Savoy; and there having stayed a good while, I was called into the Lords;² and there, quite contrary to my expectations, they did treat me very civilly, telling me that what they had done was out of zeal to the King's service, and that they would joyne with the governors of the Chest³ with all their hearts, since they knew that there was any, which they did not before.   I gave them very respectful answer; and so went away to the Theatre and there saw the latter end of *The Mayds tragedy*,⁴ which I never saw before, and methinks it is too sad and melancholy.

Thence homewards; and meeting Mr. Creed, I took him by water to the Wardrobe with me and there we find my Lord newly gone away with the Duke of Ormond and some others, whom he had had to the collation.   And so we, with the rest of the servants in the Hall, sat down and eat of the best cold meats that ever I eat on in all my life.

1. John Price had petitioned for arrears of money due to him, and asked that Richard Hutchinson (Treasurer of the Navy, 1651–60) should be examined, and his books scrutinised: HMC, *Rep.*, 7/141. The power of the Lords' Committee for Petitions to call witnesses was confirmed by order of the House on the 18th: *LJ*, xi. 258.

2. Parliamentary and government committees often met in the Savoy Hospital, Strand, or in one of the houses in its precinct.   Pepys's velvet coat had been bought in August 1660 and worn only once before, at the coronation.

3. The Chatham Chest, a benevolent fund for disabled seamen.

4. A tragedy by Beaumont and Fletcher, written c. 1611; published in 1619;   now at the TR, Vere St. The cast in Downes (p. 5) includes Hart as Amintor, Mohun as Melantius, Wintersel as the King and Mrs [Rebecca] Marshall as Evadne.   (A).

From thence I went home (Mr. Moore with me to the water-side, telling me how kindly he is used by my Lord and my Lady since his coming thither as a servant),[1] and to bed.

17. All the morning at home: at noon Lieutenant Lambert came to me, and he and I to the Exchange and thence to an ordinary over against it – where to our dinner we had a fellow play well upon the bagpipes and whistle like a bird exceeding well. And I had a fancy to learn to whistle as he doth, and did promise to come some other day and give him an Angell to teach me. To the office and sat there all the afternoon till 9 at night. So home to my musique; and my wife and I sat singing in my chamber a good while together. And then to bed.

18. Toward Westminster from the towre by water; and was fain to stand upon one of the peeres about the bridge before the men could drag their boat through the lock,* and which they could not do till another was called to help them.

Being through bridge, I find the Thames full of boats and gallys; and upon enquiry find that there was a wager to be run this morning.[2] So spying of Payne in a galley, I went into him and there stayed, thinking to have gone to Chelsy with them; but upon the start, the wager-boats fell foul one of another, till at last one of them goes over, pretending foule play; and so the other rew away alone – and all our sport lost. So I went ashore at Westminster; and to the hall I went, where it was very pleasant to see the hall in the condition it is now, with the judges in the benches at the further end of it – which I had not seen all this tearme till now.[3]

Thence with Mr. Spicer, Creed and some others to drink; and so away homewards by water with Mr. Creed, whom I left in London going about business; and I home – where I stayed

---

1. Above, p. 75. Moore, originally in the service of John Crew, was now Sandwich's man of business.

2. Boat races on the Thames were rare, partly because of the amount of river-traffic.

3. After the Restoration, Westminster Hall was renovated and the Courts of Chancery and King's Bench moved from the sides to the upper (southern) end of the hall. In 1663–4 it was repaired. (R).

all the afternoon. ⟨And in the garden reading *Faber fortunae* [1] with great pleasure. So home to bed.⟩[a]

19. *Lords day.* I walked in the morning toward Westminster; and seeing many people at Yorke-house, I went down and find them at Masse, it being the Spanish Embassadors; and so I got into one of the gallerys and there heard two masses – done, I think, in not so much state as I have seen them heretofore.[2] After that into the garden and walked a turn or two; but find it not so fine a place as I alway took it for by the outside. Thence to my Lord's and there spoke with him about business; and then he went to White-hall to dinner – and Captain Ferrers and Mr. Howe and myself to Mr. Wilkinsons at the Crowne. And though he had no meat of his owne, yet we happened to find our Cooke Mr. Robinson[3] there, who had a dinner for himself and some friends; and so he did give us a very fine dinner.

Then to my Lord's, where we went and sat talking and laughing in the drawing-room a great while. All our talk about their going to sea this voyage, which Captain Ferrers is in some doubt whether he shall go or no. But swears that he would go if he were sure never to come back again. And I giving him some hopes, he grew so mad with joy that he fell a-dancing and leaping like a madman.

Now it fell out so that the balcone windows were open; and he went to the rayle and made an offer to leap over and asked what if he should leap over there. I told him I would give him

a addition crowded in between entries

---

1. Francis Bacon's *Faber Fortunae sive Doctrina de ambitu vitae*; one of the pieces collected in his *Sermones Fideles*, of which duodecimo editions had been published at Leyden in 1641, 1644 and 1659. (Pepys retained the Amsterdam duodecimo of 1662: PL 48.) He often slipped the book into his pocket to read in the open air, and always it was *Faber Fortunae* which he read. He set his brother to translate it on 29 October 1666. Pepys's fondness for this essay on self-help ('every man the architect of his own fortune') is perhaps significant. It is to be distinguished from Bacon's essay 'Of Fortune'.

2. The Catholic envoys' chapels (with those of the Queen Mother and later the Queen) were the only places where Catholic services could legally be held, and the presence of unprivileged persons was forbidden. Pepys's attendance was in defiance of the law, but enforcement was often lax: cf. W. R. Trimble in *Journ. Mod. Hist.*, 18/97+.

3. 'Our Cooke' in that Pepys bought cooked meats from his shop.

40*l* if he did not go to sea. With that, though I shut the door and W. Howe hindered him all we could, yet he opened them again and with a vault leaps down into the garden – the greatest and most desperate frolic that ever I saw in my life. I run to see what was become of him, and we find him crawled upon his knees – but could not rise. So we went down into the garden and dragged him to the bench, where he looked like a dead man – but could not stir. And though he had broke nothing, yet his pain in his back was such as he could not endure. With this, my Lord (who was in the little new room) came to us in an amaze and bid us carry him up; which by our strength we did and so laid him in Easts bed by the doore – where he lay in great pain. We sent for Doctor and Chyrurgeon, but none to be found; till by and by, by chance comes in Dr Clerke – who is afeared of him. So we sent to get a lodgeing for him; and I went up to my Lord, where Captain Cooke, Mr. Gibbons, and others of the King's Musique were come to present my Lord with some songs and Symphonys,* which were performed very finely; which being done, I took leave and supped at my father's – where was my Cozen Beck, come lately out of the country.

I am troubled to see my father so much decay of a suddaine as he doth, both in his seeing and hearing – and as much, to hear of him how my Brother Tom doth grow disrespectfull to him and my mother.

I took leave and went home. Where to prayers (which I have not had in my house a good while), and so to bed.

20. At home all the morning. Paid 50*l* to one Mr. Grant for Mr. Barlow for the last half year.[1] And was visited by Mr. Anderson, my former Chamber fellow at Cambrige, with whom I parted at The Hague. But I did not go forth with him; only gave him a morning draught at home.

At noon Mr. Creed came to me; and he and I to the Exchange, and so to an ordinary to dinner; and after dinner to the Miter and there sat drinking while it rained very much. Then to the office, where I find Sir Wms. both, choosing of Maisters for the new fleet of ships that is ordered to be set forth. And Pen

1. See above, i. 202 & n. 1. John Grant, the pioneer social statistician, had received power of attorney from William Petty, Barlow's agent: Rawl. A 174, f. 319*r*.

seeming to be in an ugly humour, not willing to gratify one that I mentioned to be put in, did vex me.[1]

We sat late, and so home. Mr. Moore came to me when I was going to bed, and sat with me a good while, talking about my Lord's business and our own. And so good-night.

21. Up earely and with Sir R. Slingsby (and Major Waters, the deafe gentleman, his friend, for company's sake) to the Victualling-office (the first time that ever I knew where it was); and there stayed while he read a commission for enquiry into some of the King's lands and houses thereabouts, that are given his Brother.[2] And then we took boat to Woolwich, where we stayed and gave order for the fitting out of some more Shipps presently. And then to Deptford,[a] where we stayed and did the same. And so took barge again, and was overtaken by the King in his barge – he having been down the River with his Yacht this day for pleasure, to try it. And as I hear, Comissioner Petts doth prove better then the Duch one and that that his Brother[3] built.

While we were upon the water, one of the greatest showers of rain fell that ever I saw.

The Comptroller and I landed with our barge at the Temple; and from thence I went to my father's, and there did give order about some clothes to be made – and did buy a new hatt, cost between 20 and 30s, at Mr. Holdens. So home.

22. To Westminster and there missed of my Lord; and so about noone I and W. Howe by water to the Wardrobe, where my Lord and all the officers of the Wardrobe dined, and several other friends of my Lord, at a venison pasty. Before dinner my Lady Wright and my Lady Jem. sang songs to the Harpsicon.

a word blotted

---

1. For this dispute, see below, pp. 108, 111.

2. Henry Slingsby, Deputy-Master of the Mint. The Victualling Office was on Tower Hill, and the Royal Mint in the Tower. The Crown owned much leasehold property in the neighbourhood, and this grant may have been for the benefit of Slingsby personally or for that of some of his workmen. Cf. *CSPD 1661-2*, p. 548.

3. Christopher Pett of Woolwich, who had built a yacht for the Duke of York. For these yachts, see *Comp.*: 'Mary', 'Catherine', 'Anne'; and cf. above, p. 12, n. 2.

Very pleasant and merry at dinner. And then I went away by water to the office; and there stayed till it was late. At night, before I went to bed, the barber came to trim me and wash me, and so to bed, in order to my being clean tomorrow.

23. This day I went to my Lord, and about many other things at White-hall – and there made even my accounts with Mr. Sheply at my Lord's. And then with him and Mr. Moore and John Bowles to the Renish wine-house, and there came Jonas ⟨Moore⟩ the Mathematician to us. And there he did by discourse make us fully believe that England and France were once the same continent,[1] by very good arguments. And spoke very many things, not so much to prove the Scripture false, as that the time therein is not well*a* computed nor understood.[2] From thence home by water and there shifted myself into my black*b* silke sute (the first day I have put it on this year); and so to my Lord Mayors by coach, where a great deal of Honourable company – and great entertainment.[3]

At table I had very good discourse with Mr. Ashmole, wherein he did assure me that froggs and many other insects do often fall from the Sky ready-formed.[4]

Dr. Bates's singularity, in not rising up nor drink the King's nor other healths at the table, was very much observed.[5]

From thence we all took coach and to our office. And there sat till it was late.

a repl. 'com'-   *b* l.h. repl. l.h. 's'-

---

1. A common view: cf. W. Camden, *Britannia* (1637 ed.), p. 1; H. Peacham, *Compleat Gentleman* (1634 ed.), p. 69.

2. The difficulty which had troubled most commentators was the longevity of the patriarchs – e.g. Adam's 930 and Methuselah's 969 years. The theory that 'years' in these cases were equivalent to the modern months was not supported by 17th-century authorities: cf. James Ussher, *Annals of the world* (1658); Matthew Poole, *Synopsis* (1669–76), i. 69, 70; Thomas Burnet, *Telluris theoria sacra* (1681). Cf. Augustine, *City of God*, bk xv, chs ix–xiv.

3. An Ascension Day dinner: cf. below, viii. 218; ix. 179 & n. 1.

4. The 'generation of insects' had been discussed at the Royal Society (of which Ashmole was a member) on the day before: Birch, i. 24. For contemporary theories of spontaneous generation, see above, i. 318 & n. 1: P. H. Maty, *Gen. index to Philos. Trans.* (1787), pp. 246–8.

5. William Bates (Presbyterian Vicar of St Dunstan-in-the-West) objected, like many Puritans, to the drinking of toasts. He was not a republican.

And so I home and to bed by day light.　This day was kept*a* a Holyday through the towne.　And it pleased me to see the little boys go*b* up and down in procession with their broomestaffes in their hands, as I have myself long ago gone.[1]

24.　At home all the morning making up my private accounts; and this is the first time that I do find myself to be clearly worth 500*l* in money, besides all my goods in my house, &c.

In the afternoon at the office late.　And then I went to the Wardrobe, where I find my Lord at supper and therefore I walked a good while till he had done; and then I went in to him, and there looked over my accounts and they were committed to Mr. Moore to see me paid what remained due to me. Then down to the Kitchin to eat a bit of bread and butter, which I did.　And there I took one of the maids by the chin, thinking her to be Susan; but it proved to be her sister, which is very like her.

From thence home.

25.　All the morning at home about business.　At noon to the Temple; where I stayed and looked over a book or two at Playfords[2] and then to the Theatre, where I saw a piece of *The Silent woman*,[3] which pleased me.　So homewards, and in my way bought *The Bondman*[4] in Pauls church-yard.　And so home – where I find all clean and the harth and range, as it is now enlarged, set up; which pleases me very much.

a MS. 'keep'　　　*b* MS. 'good'

---

1. The customary processions of boys perambulating the parish bounds on Ascension Day.　They used their broomstaves to strike the stones etc., marking the limits – hence 'beating the bounds'.　Sometimes the boys themselves were beaten: below, ix. 179 & n. 1; W. E. Tate, *Parish Chest*, p. 74.　Perambulations held every four years continued in full force into the 19th century, when the decline of the parish as a unit of civil government, combined with the widespread use of maps, caused them to disappear or to decline into a quaint survival.

See A. R. Wright, *Brit. cal. customs: Engl.* (ed. Lones), i. 130+; J. Hastings (ed.), *Encycl. religion and ethics*, vii. 794.

2. The music shop near the Inner Temple. (E).

3. A comedy by Ben Jonson (see above, i. 171, n. 2); now at the TR, Vere St. (A).

4. One of Pepys's favourite plays, a tragicomedy by Philip Massinger: see above, p. 47, n. 2.　The copy he bought (1638 ed.) is now PL 1075(3). (A).

26. *Lords day.*

Lay long in bed. To church and heard a good sermon at our own church, where I have not been a great many weeks. Dined with my wife alone at home, pleasing myself in that my house doth begin to look as if at last it would be in good order.

This day the Parliament received the Communion of Dr. Gunning at St. Margaret, Westminster.[1]

In the afternoon both the Sir Wms. came to church; where we had a dull stranger. After church, home; and so to the Miter, where I find Dr Burnett[2] (the first time that ever I met him to drink with him) and my Uncle Wight, and there we sat and drank a great deal. And so I to Sir Wm. Battens, where I have on purpose made myself a great stranger only to get a high opinion, a little more of myself, in them.[3] Here I heard how Mrs. Browne, Sir W. Batten's sister, is brought to bed; and I to be one of the godfathers – which I could not nor did deny – which, however, did trouble me very much, to be at charge to no purpose. So that I could not sleep hardly all night. But in the morning I bethought myself and I think it is very well I should do it.

Sir Wm. Batten told me how Mr. Prin (among the two or three that did refuse today to receive the Sacrament upon their knees) was offered by a mistake the drinke afterwards; which he did receive, being denied the drink by Dr. Guning unless he would take it on his knees. And after that, by another the bread was brought him; and he did take it sitting – which is thought very preposterous.[4] Home and to bed.

27. To the Wardrobe; and from thence with my Lords Sandwich and Hinchingbrooke to the Lord's House by boat at Westminster; and there I left them. Then to the Lobby; and

1. The House of Commons, not parliament, is here referred to. An order was made on 13 May that all members should receive Anglican communion on pain of exclusion: *CJ*, viii. 247. For the history of this test of membership (applied 1614–72), see E. and A. G. Porritt, *Unreformed H. of Commons*, i. 130+ ; C. H. Smyth, *Church and parish*, pp. 7–19.

2. Alexander Burnet; Pepys's regular physician.

3. Cf. above, p. 89.

4. Puritans objected to kneeling at the receipt of communion. On the following day, in the House, Prynne opposed the vote of thanks to Dr Gunning. For another, slightly different, version of the incident, see HMC, *Rep.*, 5/160.

after waiting for Sir G. Downings coming out (to speak with him about the giving me up of my bond for my honesty when I was his clerk) but to no purpose, I went to Clerkes at the legg; and there I find both Mr. Pierces, Mr. Rolt (formerly too great a man to meet upon such even termes)[1] and there we dined very merry – there coming to us Captain Ferrers, this being his first day of his going abroad since his leape a week ago[2] – which I was greatly glad to see.   Then by water to the office and there sat late – Sir George Carteret coming in – who, among other things, did inquire into the nameing of the maisters for this fleete and was very angry that they were named as they are.   And above all, to see the master of the *Adventure* (for whom there is some kind of difference between Sir W. Penn and I) turned out, who had been in her last.[3]

The office done, I went with the Comptroller to the Coffeehouse and there we discoursed of this, and I seem to be fond of him; and endeed, I find I must carry fair with all, as far as I see it safe.   But I have got of him leave to have a little room from his lodgings to my house, of which I am very glad.   Besides, I do open him a way to get lodgings himself in the office, of which I should be very glad.

Home and to bed.

28.   This morning to the Wardrobe; and thence to a little alehouse hard by to drink with John Bowles, who is now going to Hinchingbrooke this day.

Thence with Mr. Sheply to the Exchange about business; and there, by Mr. Rawlinson's favour, got into a balcone over against the Exchange and there saw the hangman burn, by vote of Parliament, two old acts; the one for constituting us a Comonwealth and the other I have forgot.[4]

1. Edward Rolt was a relative by marriage of Oliver Cromwell, a gentleman of the Protector's chamber, and envoy to Sweden, 1655–6.

2. Above, pp. 102–3.

3. Cf. above, pp. 103–4.

4. They were the two acts of 1649 and 1650 establishing the Commonwealth and requiring the subscription of an engagement to it; others were burnt on this and the following day. The Commons made an order to this effect on the 27th, and, with a nice regard for language, refused to call them 'acts' and referred to them as 'treasonable parchment writings': *CJ*, viii. 259.

Which still doth make me think of the greatness of this late turne and what people will do tomorrow against what they all, through profit or fear, did promise and practise this day.

Then to the Mitre with Mr. Sheply and there dined with D. Rawlinson and some friends of his, very well. So home, and then to Cheapeside about buying a piece*a* of plate to give away tomorrow to Mrs. Brownes Childe. So to the Starre in Chepeside, where I left Mr. Moore telling 5*l.* out for me – who I find in a great strait for my coming back again and so he went his way at my coming.

Then home, where Mr. Cooke[1] I met and he paid me 30*s.*, an old debt of his to me. So to Sir W. Pens, and there sat alone with him till 10 at night in talk – with great content; he telling me things and persons that I did not understand in the late times; and so I home to bed. My Cozen John Holcroft (whom I have not seen many years) this morning came to see me.

29. *Kings birth day.*

Rose earely; and having made myself fine and put six spoons and a porringer of Silver in my pocket to give away today, Sir W. Pen and I took Coach and (the weather and ways being foule) went to Waltamstowe. And being come thither, heard Mr.*b* Ratcliffe (my former schoolefellow at Pauls, who is yet a mere boy) preach upon "Nay, lett him take all, since my Lord the King is returned," &c:[2] he reads all, and his sermon very simple – but I looked for no better. Back to dinner to Sir Wms; and then after a walk in the fine gardens, we went to Mrs. Brown's, where Sir W. Pen and I were godfathers and Mrs. Jordan and Shipman godmothers to her*c* boy. And there, before and after the Christening, we were with the women above in her chamber; but whether we carried ourselfs well or ill, I know not – but I was directed by young Mrs. Batten.[3] One passage, of a lady

a repl. 'p'-   *b* 'Mr.' repeated in l.h.   *c* l.h. repl. s.h. 'his'

---

1. A servant of Sandwich.

2. A loose recollection of 2 Sam., xix. 30. For the service, established by an act of 1660 to commemorate both the King's birthday and his

restoration, see *A form of prayer with thanksgiving* ... (1661). The preacher was about 27 – one year younger than Pepys.

3. See above, p. 30, n. 3.

that eate wafers with her dog, did a little displease me. I did give the midwife 10s and the nurse 5s and the maid of the house 2: but for as much as I expected to give the name to the Childe, but did not, it being called John, I forbore then to give my plate – till another time, after a little more advice.

All being done, we went to Mrs. Shipmans, who is a great butterwoman; and I did see there the most of milke and cream, and the cleanest, that*ᵃ* ever I saw in my life.   After we had filled our bellies with cream, we took our leaves and away.   In our way we had great sport to try who should drive fastest, Sir W. Batten's coach or Sir W. Pen's charriot, they having four and we two horses, and we beat them.   But it cost me the spoiling of my clothes and velvet coate with dirt.

Being come home, I to bed; and gave my breeches to be dried by the fire against tomorrow.

30. To the Wardrobe and there with my Lord went into his new barge to try her; and find her a good boat and like my Lord's contrivance of the door to come out round and not square, as they use to do.   Back to the Wardrobe with my Lord and then with Mr. Moore to the temple; and thence I to Greatrex, who took me to Arundell-house and there showed me some fine flowers in his garden and all the fine Statues in the galery; which I formerly had seen and is a brave sight.[1]   And then to a blind dark sellar, where we had two bottles of good ale; and so after giving*ᵇ* him direccion for my silver side table, I took boat at Arundel-stayres and put in at Milford and there behind the doore of the stairs shit, there being a house of office there.

So home – and find Sir Wms both and my Lady going to Deptford to christen Captain Rooths child; and would have had me with them, but I would not go.

To the office, where Sir R. Slingsby was; and he and I went

---

a   MS. 'time'   b   MS. 'given'

---

1. The collection of antique sculpture, built up by the 2nd Earl of Arundel (d. 1646) before the Civil War, had perhaps already been partly dispersed, but was still impressive. A section of it, the Arundel Marbles, passed ultimately to the Ashmolean Museum. Aubrey, *Nat. hist. . . . Surrey* (1719), v. 282; J. Hess in *Engl. Misc.*, 1/197–220. (OM).

into his and my lodgings to take a view of them, out of a design he hath to have mine of me, to join to his and give me Mrs. Turners.

To the office again; where Sir G. Carteret came and sat a while, he being angry for Sir Wms. making of the maisters of this fleet upon their own heads, without a full table.[1] Then the Comptroller and I to the Coffee-house and there sat a great while, talking of many things.

So home and to bed.

This day I hear the parliament hath ordered a bill to be brought in for the restoring the Bishops to the House of Lords – which they had not done so soon but to spite Mr. Prynne, who is every day so bitter against them in his discourse in the House.[2]

31. I went to my father's, thinking to have met with my Cozen John Holecroft; but he came not. But to my great grief, I find my father and mother in a great deal of discontent one with another;[3] and endeed, my mother is grown now so pettish that I know not how my father is able to bear with it. I did talk to her so as did not endeed become me; but I could not help it, she being so unsufferably foolish and simple – so that my father, poor man, is become a very unhappy man.

There I dined; and so home and to the office all the afternoon, till 9 at night; and then home and to supper and to bed.

Great talk now how the parliament entends to make a Collection of free gifts to the King through the Kingdom. But I think it will not come to much.[4]

1. Cf. above, pp. 103–4, 108. For much business two was a quorum (see below, iv. 314–15), but the issue of warrants of appointment to ships' masters could be lucrative: below, iv. 74.

2. Cf. the resolution adopted *nem. con.* in the Commons: *CJ*, viii. 261. An act to this effect (13 Car. II, stat. I, c. 2) was passed at the end of the session. The bill was hurried along for more important reasons than this.

3. Cf. above, pp. 89–90.

4. The Commons had on the 30th resolved that a bill for this purpose should be brought in: *CJ*, viii. 262. Passed in July (13 Car. II, stat. I, c. 4), it declared that it constituted no precedent, and that the commissioners appointed to collect the gifts should cease to act in June 1662. For the slow rate at which gifts came in, see below, p. 168, n. 1.

JUNE

1. Saturday.

Having taken our leaves of Sir W. Batten and my Lady, who
are gone this morning to Chatham to keep their Whitsuntide,
Sir W. Penn and I and Mr. Gauden by water to Woolwich;
and there went from ship to ship to give order for and take notice
of their forwardness to go forth.   And then to Deptford and did
the like – having*a* dined at Woolwich with Captain Poole at the
taverne there.[1]

From Deptford we walked to Redriffe, calling at the Half-way
house; and there came into a room where there was infinite of
new cakes placed, that are made against Whitsuntide; and there
we were very merry.

By water home and there did businesses of the office.   Among
others, got my Lord's imprest of 1000*l* and Mr. Creeds of 10000*l*
against this voyage, their bills signed.   Having writ letters into the
country and read something, I went to bed.

2. Sunday. Whitsunday.

The barber*b* having done with me, I went to church and there
heard a good sermon of Mr. Mills, fit for the day.   Then home
to dinner.   And then to church again.   And going home, I find
Gratorex[2] (whom I expected today at dinner) come to see me.
And so he and I in my chamber, drinking of wine and eating of
anchoves an hour or two – discoursing of many things in Mathe-
matiques; and among other, he showed me how it comes to pass
the strength that Levers have; and he showed me that what is
got as to matter of strength is lost by them as to matter of time.

It rained very hard (as it hath done of late, so much that we

a s.h. repl. 'and then on the towne' (all s.h. exc. 'towne')   *b* l.h. repl. s.h. 'ber'-

---

1. The ships were about to sail
under Sandwich to the Mediterranean: they set off on 13 June and
returned on 14 May 1662. Jonas

Poole had married a sister of Penn.
2. Ralph Greatorex, mathematical
instrument maker.

begin to doubt a famine);[1] and so he was forced to stay longer then I desired.

At night, after prayers, to bed.

3. To the Wardrobe – where, discoursing with my Lord, he did instruct me as to the business of the wardrobe, in case in his absence Mr. Townsend should die; and told me that he doth intend to joyne me and Mr. Moore with him as to that business, now he is going to sea.[2] And spoke to me many other things, as to one that he doth put the greatest confidence in – of which I am proud. Here I have a good occasion to tell him (what I have had long in my mind) that since it hath pleased God to bless me with something, I am desirous to lay out something for my father, and so have pitched upon Mr. Yong's place in the wardrobe – which I desired he would give order in his absence if the place should fall, that I might have the refusal of – which my Lord did freely promise me.[3] At which I was very glad – he saying that he would do that at the least. So I saw my Lord in the barge going to White-hall; and I and Mr. Creed home to my house, whither my father and my Cosen Scott came to dine with me. And so we dined together very well, and before we had done, in comes my father Bowyer and my mother and four daughters,[4] and a young gentleman and his sister, their friends, and there stayed all the afternoon – which cost me great store of wine and were very merry.

By and by I am called to the office, and there stayed a little. So home again and took Mr. Creed and left them; and so he and

1. The sharp rise in prices of grain from 1660 to 1661 is shown in J. E. Thorold Rogers, *Hist. Agric.* etc., vi. 68–9.

2. Thomas Townshend, sen., was Sandwich's deputy at the Wardrobe. Pepys and Moore now supervised the Wardrobe finances, rendering an account to Sandwich on his return in May 1662: below, iii. 92–3. Moore (already in charge of Sandwich's household) did most of the work; Pepys's functions (to judge by the

diary) were mainly fulfilled by frequent dinners taken at the Wardrobe. In June 1662 Pepys recommended Sandwich to appoint Moore as Townshend's assistant: below, iii. 102 & n. 3.

3. Cf. above, p. 42 & n. 1.

4. Robert and Elizabeth Bowyer had a large family (13 children in all), of which Pepys and his wife enjoyed a sort of honorary membership: above, i. 84, n. 3.

I to the Tower to speak for some ammunicion for ships for my Lord. And so he and I with much pleasure walked quite round the tower, which I never did before. So home; and after a walk with my wife upon the leads, I and she went to bed.

This morning I and Dr. Pierce went over to the beare at the bridge-foot – thinking to have met my Lord Hinchingbrooke and his brother, setting forth for France. But they being not come, we went over to the Wardrobe and there find that my Lord Abbot Mountagu being not at Paris, my Lord hath a mind to have them stay a little longer before they go.[1]

4. The Comptroller came this morning to get me to go see a house or two near our office, which he would take for himself or Mr. Turner and then he would have me have Mr. Turners lodgings and himself mine and Mrs. Davis. But the houses did not like us, and so that design at present is stopped.

Then he and I by water to the bridge; and then walked over the Bank-side till we came to the Temple; and so I went over and to my father's, where I met with my Cosen J. Holecroft and took him and my father and my brother Tom to the beare tavern and gave them wine – my Cosen being to go into the country again tomorrow. From thence to my Lord Crew's to dinner with him. And had very good discourse about having of young noblemen and gentlemen to think of going to sea, as being as honourable service as the land war.[2] And among other things, told us how in Queen Elisabeth's times,[a] young noblemen would wait with a trencher at the back of another till he is come to age himself. And witnessed in my Lord, young Lord of Kent that then was, who waited upon my Lord Bedford at table, when a letter came to my Lord Bedford that the Earldome of

a symbol blotted in red ink

1. Hinchingbrooke and his brother Sidney were about to go to school in Paris, where they were in the charge of their cousin the Abbé Walter Mountagu. Sidney returned in May 1664; his brother toured Italy and came home in August 1665. Harris, i. 218+, 234–9; J. W. Stoye, *Engl. traveller abroad, 1604–1667*, pp. 434–6.

2. It was necessary to attract men of honour into the service, but also to maintain standards of technical skill and to keep the navy as free as possible from political graft. Pepys, in common with most naval administrators of his time, came to see that the admission of gentlemen captains led to intolerable inefficiency.

Kent was fallen to his servant, the young Lord; and so rose from table and made him sit down in his place, and took a lower for himself – for so he was by place to sit.[1]

From thence to the theatre and saw *Harry the Fourth*,[2] a good play. That done, I went over the water and walked over the fields to Southworke; and so home and to my lute. At night to bed.

5. This morning, did give my wife 4*l* to lay out upon lace and other things for herself. I to Wardrobe and so to White-hall and Westminster; where I dined with my Lord and Ned Pickering – alone at his lodgings. After dinner to the office, where we sat and did business; and then Sir W. Penn and I went home with Sir R. Slingsby to bowles in his ally and there had good sport; and afterward went in and drank and talked. So home, Sir William and I; and it being very hot weather, I took my flagilette and played upon the leads in the garden, where Sir W. Penn came out in his shirt into his leads and there we stayed talking and singing and drinking of great draughts of Clarret and eating botargo and bread and butter till 12 at night, it being moonshine. And so to bed – very near fuddled.

6. My head hath aked all night and all this morning with my last night's debauch.

Called up this morning by Lieutenant Lambert, who is now made Captain of the *Norwich*; and he and I went down by water to Greenwich, in our way observing and discoursing upon the things of a ship; he telling me all I asked him – which was of good use to me.

There we went and eat and drank and hear musique at the Globe; and saw the simple motion that is there, of a woman with a

1. The earldom of Bedford dated from 1550; that of Kent from 1465. Both families lived in Bedfordshire. Lord Bedford was probably Francis, 2nd Earl (d. 1585); the Earl of Kent was either Reynold, 5th Earl (succ. 1572, d. 1573), or more probably Henry, 6th Earl (succ. 1573, d. 1615).

That either of the Kents should have been waiting at table seems a little unlikely, since the 5th Earl must have been at least 27, and the 6th Earl, 32. Neither was a ward of Bedford.

2. Shakespeare's Henry IV, Part I, at the TR, Vere St; see above, i. 325 & n. 1. (A).

rod in her hand, keeping time to the music while it plays – which is simple methinks.[1]

Back again[a] by water, calling at Captain Lamberts house, which is very handsome and neat, and a fine prospect at top. So to the office, where we sat a little. And then the Captain and I again to Bridewell, to Mr.[b] Holland; where his wife also (a plain dowdy) and his mother was. Here I paid Mrs. Holland the money due from me to her husband.[2] Here came two young gentlewomen to see Mrs. Holland and one of them could play pretty well upon the viallin; but good God, how these ignorant people did cry her up for it. We were very merry.

I stayed and supped here; and so home and to bed. The weather very hot; this night I left off my wastecoate.*

7. To my Lord's at White-hall; but not finding him, I went to the Wardrobe and there dined with my Lady and was very kindly treated by her. After dinner to the office and there till late at night. So home and to Sir Wm. Battens, who is come this day from Chatham with my Lady, who is and hath been much troubled with the toothach. Here I stayed till late; and so home and to bed.

8. To White-hall to my Lord, who did tell me that he would have me go to Mr. Townsend, whom he hath ordered to discover to me the whole mystery of the Wardrobe, and none else but me; and that he will make me deputy with him, for fear that he should die in my Lord's absence – of which I was glad.[3]

Then to the Cookes with Mr. Sheply and Creed and dined together; and then I went to the Theatre and there saw *Bartlemew*

a followed by blot   *b* MS. 'Mrs.'

---

1. The music was provided by an organ: below, iv. 283. The 'motion' was that of an automaton, not a human conductor. Cf. Donne, Satyre II, ll. 15–16: 'As in some Organ, Puppits dance above/And bellows pant below, which them do move.' The removal of organs from churches to taverns during the revolution possibly gave an impetus to concert life in England: P. A. Scholes, *Puritans and music*, pp. 244+. (E).

2. Probably Capt. Philip Holland.

3. See above, p. 113, n. 2.

faire, the first time it was acted nowadays.[1] It is [a] most admirable play and well acted; but too much profane and abusive.

From thence, meeting Mr. Creed at the door, he and I went to the tobacco-shop under Temple-bar gate and there went up to the top of the house and there sat drinking Lambeth ale a good while. Then away home; and in my way called upon Mr. Rawlinson (my uncle Wight being out of town) for his advice to answer a letter of my uncle Rob., wherein he doth offer me a purchase to lay some money upon, that joynes upon some of his owne lands. And plainly telling me that the reason of his advice is the convenience that it will give me as[a] to his estate – of which I am exceeding glad and am advised to give up wholly the disposal of my money to him.[2] Let him do what he will with it – which I shall do. So home and to bed.

9. *Lords day.*

This day my wife put on her black silk gown, which is now laced all over with black gimp lace, as the fashion is – in which she is very pretty.

She and I walked to my Lady's at the Wardrobe and there dined and was exceeding much made of. After dinner I left my wife there and I walked to White-hall and there went to Mr. Pierces and sat with his wife a good while (who continues very pretty) till he came in; and then he and I and Mr. Symons (dancing-master that goes to sea with my Lord) to the Swan tavern and there drank; and so I again to White-hall and there met with Deane Fuller and walked a great while with him; among other things, discoursed of the liberty the Bishops (by name, he of Galloway) takes to admit into orders anybody that

a repl. symbol rendered illegible

---

1. A comedy by Ben Jonson, first acted in 1614, and published in 1631; now performed at the TR, Vere St. This is the first record of a post-Restoration performance; according to Downes (p. 17), the role of Cokes was one of Wintersel's best interpretations. On this occasion the puppet-show in Act V was omitted. Much of the satire in the play is directed against Puritans; hence its popularity now. (A).

2. Pepys was the residuary legatee of the estate of Robert Pepys of Brampton. The proposal here mentioned appears to have come to nothing: below, p. 124. Daniel Rawlinson (landlord of the Mitre, Fenchurch St) was a friend or relative of Uncle Wight.

will; among others, Roundtree, a simple mechanique that was a parson formerly in the Fleete.[1]   He told me he would complain of it.   By and by we went and got a Sculler; and landing him at Worcester-house, I and W. Howe (who came to us at White-hall) went to the Wardrobe.

Where I met with Mr. Townsend, who is very willing, he says, to communicate anything for my Lord's advantage to me as to his business.   I went up to Jane Shores towre[2] and there W. Howe and I sang; and so took my wife and walked home and so to bed.   ⟨After I came home, a messenger came from my Lord to bid me come to him tomorrow morning.⟩[a]

10.   earely to my Lord – who privately told me how the King hath made him embassador in the bringing over the Queen. That he is to go to Algier &c. to settle that business and to put the fleet in order there; and so to come back to Lisbone with three ships, and there to meet the fleet that is to fallow him.[3]

He sent for me to tell me that he doth intrust me with the seeing of all things done in his absence as to this great preparation, as I shall receive orders from my Lord Chancellor and Mr. Edw. Mountagu.   At all which, my heart is above measure glad – for my Lord's honour, and some profit to myself I hope.

a addition crowded into bottom of page

---

1. I.e. in the Fleet (debtors') prison; or in the surrounding area where prisoners were allowed to reside. Ralph Roundtree on 6 June had been appointed chaplain of the *Breda*: PRO, Adm. 2/1745, f.45r. Sydserff of Galloway, the only Scottish bishop to survive the Interregnum, was now in London, angling (in vain) for advancement to the primacy of Scot-land.   Burnet (i. 236) tells how his reputation suffered from these indis-criminate ordinations. (Many clergy-men were now anxious for episcopal orders so that they should not lose their livings.) Burnet places the incidents in the following year.

2. Little appears to be known about this Tower and its association with Jane Shore, Edward IV's mistress: see

R. Allen Brown *et al.*, *King's Works*, ii. 980–1. The Wardrobe build-ing had been used by Edward as a royal residence: Stow, *Survey* (ed. Strype, 1720), vol. i, bk iii. 224.

3. Sandwich had been given com-mand of the fleet on 10 May, and was later made ambassador-extraordinary-The treaty arranging the marriage between Charles II and Catherine of Braganza was signed on 23 June, and Sandwich's instructions in that matter (based on art. iv of the treaty) are in Carte 74, f.449r. His instructions with regard to Algiers were to con-clude a treaty for free passage of ships, and failing that to attack the town; ib., ff. 388–9 (printed in Sandwich, pp. 288–90). In the event, he made an abortive attack in August.

By and by out with Mr. Sheply, Walden, parliament-man for Huntingdon, Rolt, Mackworth, and Alderman Backwell to a house hard by to drink Lambeth ale. So I back to the Wardrobe and there find my Lord going to Trinity-house, this being the solemn day of choosing Master; and my Lord is chosen[1] – so he dines there today.

I stayed and dined with my Lady; but after we were sat, comes in some persons of condition; and so the children and I rise and dined by ourselfs, all the children and I, and were very merry – and they mighty fond of me. Then I to the office, and there sat a while. So home; and at night to bed – where we lay in Sir R. Slingsby's lodgings – in the dining-room there, in our green bed – my house being now in its last work of painting and whiting.

11. At the office this morning, Sir G. Carteret with us. And we agreed upon a letter to the Duke of Yorke,[2] to tell him the sad condition of this office for want of money. How men are not able to serve us more without some money. And that now, the credit of the office is brought so low, that none will sell us anything without our personal security given for the same.[3]

All the afternoon abroad about several businesses; and at night home and to bed.

12. *Wednesday*, a day kept*a* between a fast and a feast, the Bishops not being ready enough to keep the fast for foule weather before fair weather come; and so they were forced to keep it between both.[4]

a MS. 'keep'

---

1. He succeeded Albemarle and served for the usual term of one year.
2. Dated 14 June; copy in PL 2265, no. 7.
3. Carteret, as Treasurer, used his personal credit extensively: cf. below, viii. 290 & n. 2.
4. A fast had been ordered to avert 'those sicknesses and diseases' which might follow 'the late immoderate rain'. But by the time that arrangements for the fast had been made, the weather had changed; the fast was accordingly kept, but, in addition, thanksgiving was ordered to be given for the fair weather. The proclamation (7 June) is in Steele, no. 3307. For the service, see E. Cardwell (ed.), *Synodalia* (1842), ii. 643–4.

I to White-hall; and there with Captain Rolt and Ferrers we
went to Lambeth to drink our morning draught. Where at the
Three Marriners, a place noted for their ale, we went and stayed
awhile, very merry. And so away; and wanting a boat, we find
Captain Bun going down the River; and so we went into his
boat, having a lady with him, and he landed them at Westminster and me at the Bridge.

At home all day with my workmen and doing several things.
Among others, writing the letter resolved of yesterday to the
Duke.

Then to White-hall, where I met my Lord, who told me that
he must have 300 laid out in Cloth to give in Barbary as presents
among the Turkes.

At which occasion of getting something by it I was very glad.

Home to supper. And then to Sir R. Slingsby; who with his
Brother and I went to my Lord's at the Wardrobe and there stayed
a great while; but he being now taking his leave of his friends,
stayed out late; and so they went away.

Anon came my Lord in and I stayed with him a good while.
And then to bed with Mr. Moore in his chamber.

13. I went up and down to Alderman Backwells, but his
servants not being up, I went home and put on my gray cloth
suit and faced white coate, made of one of my wife's pettycoates –
the first time that I have had it on. And so, in a riding garbe,
back again and spoke with Mr. Shaw at the Aldermans; who
offers me 300*l*, if my Lord pleases, to buy this cloth with – which
pleased me well. So to the Wardrobe and got my Lord to
order Mr. Creed to imprest so much upon me, to be paid by
Alderman Backwell.

So with my Lord to White-hall by water. And he having
taken leave of the King, comes to us at his lodgeings and from
thence goes to the garden Staires and there takes barge. And at
the stairs was met by Sir R. Slingsby, who there took his leave
of my Lord; and I heard my Lord thank him for his kindness to
me, which Sir Robert answered much to my advantage.

I went down with my Lord in the barge to Deptford; and there
went on board the Duch yacht and stayed there a good while,
W. Howe not being come with my Lord's things, which made
my Lord angry. By and by he comes and so we set sayle;

and anon went to dinner. My Lord and we very merry. And after dinner I went down below and there sang and took leave of W. Howe, Captain Rolt, and the rest of my friends; then went up and took leave of my Lord, who gave me his hand and parted with great respect.

So went, and Captain Ferrers with me, into our wherry. And my Lord did give five guns, all they had charged, which was the greatest respect my Lord could do me and of which I was not a little proud.[1] So with a sad and merry heart I left them, sailing pleasantly from Erith, hoping to be in the Downes tomorrow earely.

We toward London in our boat. Pulled off our Stockings and bathed our legs a great while in the River – which I had not done some years before.

By and by we came to Greenwich; and thinking to have gone on the King's Yacht,[2] the King was in her, so we passed by; and at Woolwich went on shore in the company of Captain Poole of Jamaica[3] and young Mr. Kenersly and many others. And so to the Taverne, where we drank a great deal, both wine and beere. So we parted thence and went home with Mr. Falconer, who did give us cherrys and good wine.[4] So to boat and young Poole took us on board the *Charity* and gave us wine there, with which I had full enough; and so to our wherry again. And there fell asleep till I came almost to the tower; and there the Captain and I parted. And I home – and with wine enough in my head went to bed.

14. To White-hall to my Lord's. Where I find Mr. Edwd. Mountagu and his family come to lie during my Lord's absence. I sent to*ᵃ* my house, by my Lord's order, his shipp[5] and Triangle

a l.h. repl. s.h. 'my'

---

1. Pepys, as a 'gentleman of quality', was entitled to a salute of seven guns: cf. above, p. 16 & n. 2.
2. The *Catherine*.
3. Jonas Poole had commanded the *Swiftsure* in which Penn had sailed in 1654 to the conquest of Jamaica.
4. John Falconer was Clerk of the Ropeyard, Woolwich. The Navy Board had recently secured for him a salary of £60 p.a.: Duke of York, *Mem. (naval)*, p. 21.
5. A model of the *Royal James* which Pepys hung in his room: below, p. 192.

virginall.¹ So to my father's and did give him order about the
buying of this cloth to send to my Lord.   But I could not stay
with him myself; for having got a great cold by my playing the
foole in the water yesterday, I was in great pain and so went home
by coach to bed, and went not to the office at all.   And by keeping
myself warme, I broke wind and so came to some ease.   Rise and
eat some supper and so to bed again.

15.   My father came and drank his morning draught with me,
and sat with me till I was ready; and so he and I about the
business of the cloth.   By and by I left him and went and dined
with my Lady; who now my Lord is gone, is come to her poor
housekeeping again.   Then to my father's, who tells me what he
hath done; and we resolved upon two pieces of scarlet, two of
purple, and two of blackes – and 50*l* in Linnen.

I home, taking 300*l* with me home from Alderman Backwells.
After writing to my Lord to let him know what I had done,
I was going to bed.   But there coming the purser of the King's
Yacht for victuals presently, for the Duke of Yorke is to go down
tomorrow, I got him to promise*ᵃ* stowage for these things there.
And so I went to bed, bidding Will go and fetch the things from
the Carriers hither – which about 12 a-clock were brought to my
house and laid there all night.

16.   But no purser coming in the morning for them, I hear
that the Duke went last night, and so I am at a great losse what
to do.   And so this day (though the Lords day) stayed at home,
sending Will up and downe to know what to do.   Sometimes
thinking to continue my resolution of sending by the Carrier,
to be at Deale on Wednesday next.   Sometimes to send them by
sea by a vessell on purpose.   But am not yet come to a resolucion,
but am at a very great loss and trouble in mind what in the
world to do herein.   The afternoon, while Will is abroad, I

a   MS. 'present' (similar symbol)

---

1. Virginals   and   harpsichords
could be made with other than rectangular cases: some were pentagonal,
shaped like a triangle with two corners
cut off.   (E).

spent in reading *The Spanish Gypsy*,[1] a play not very good, though commended much. At night resolved to hire a Marget Hoy,[2] who would go away tomorrow morning – which I did, and sent the things all by him. And put them on board about 12 this night – hoping to have them, as the wind now serves, in the Downes tomorrow night.

To bed with some quiet of mind, having sent the things away.

17. visited this morning by my old friend Mr. Ch. Carter[3] – who stayed and went to Westminster with me. And there we parted and I to the Wardrobe and dined with my Lady. So home to my paynters, who are now about painting my stayres.[4] So to the office. And at night we all went to Sir W. Pens and there sat and drank till 11 at night. And so home and to bed.

18. All this morning at home, vexing about the delay of my painters. And about 4 in the afternoon, my wife and I by water to Captain Lamberts. Where we took great pleasure in their turret-garden and seeing the fine needleworkes of his wife, the best I ever saw in my life. And afterwards had a very handsome treate, and good musique that she made upon the Harpsicon. And with a great [deal] of pleasure stayed till 8 at night; and so home again – there being a little pretty witty child that they keep in their house that would not let us go without her and so fell a-crying by the water-side. So home – where I met Jack Cole, who stayed with me a good while, and is still of the old good humour that we were of at schoole together and I am very glad to see him. He gone, we went to bed.

19. All the morning almost at home, seeing my stairs finished

1. A tragicomedy by Thomas Middleton and William Rowley, acted in 1623, and published in 1653; not in the PL. (A).

2. See Pepys to Sandwich, 16 June (two letters, one headed '9 at night', the other referring to a previous letter of 15 June on the same subject): Carte 73, ff. 523r, 525r. The hoy was the *Martha and Mary*; the hire-charge (from Tower Wharf to the Downs) was £6: PRO, Adm. 20/1/261, no. 1623.

3. A parson; at Magdalene with Pepys.

4. The new stairs out of the parlour: above, p. 59 & n. 2. A painter's bill (8 January 1662) for £15 7s. for work done in Pepys's lodgings is registered in PRO, Adm. 20/4, p. 358.

by the painter, which please me well. So with Mr. Moore to Westminster-hall, it being terme, and then by water to the Wardrobe – where very merry with him.*ᵃ* So home to the office all the afternoon. And at night to the Exchange to my uncle Wight about my intentions of purchasing at Brampton.¹ So back again home and at night to bed.

Thanks be to God, I am very well again of my late payne.² And tomorrow hope to be out of my pain of dirt and trouble in my house, of which I am now become very weary.

One thing I must observe here, while I think of it; that I am now become the most negligent man in the world as to matter of newes.*ᵇ* Insomuch, that nowadays I neither can tell any nor aske any of others.

20. At home the greatest part of the day, to see my workmen make an end; which this night they did, to my great content.³

21. This morning, going to my father's, I met him and so he and I went and drank our morning draught at the Samson in Pauls churchyard, and eat some gammon of Bacon &c; and then parted, having bought some green Say for curtains in my parlour. Home; and so to the Exchange, where I met with my uncle Wight and home with him to dinner. Where among others (my aunt being out of towne), Mr. Norbury,⁴ and he and I did discourse of his wife's house and land at Brampton, which I find too much for me to buy.

Home and in the afternoon to the office; and much pleased at night to see my house begin to be cleane, after all this dirty time.

22. Abroad all the morning about several businesses. At noon went and dined with my Lord Crew – where very much

a   MS. 'her'   *b*   repl. word rendered illegible

---

1. See above, p. 117.
2. See above, p. 122.
3. Cf. above, p. 59 & n. 2.
4. George Norbury ('Uncle

Norbury'), a Londoner had married the sister of Aunt Wight. Both he and his wife had property in Brampton.

made of by him and his Lady. Then to the Theatre, *The Alchymist*,[1] which is a most incomparable play. And that being done, I met with little Luellin and Blirton, who took me to a friend's of theirs in Lincoln's Inn fields, one Mr. Hodges; where we drank great store of Rhenish wine and were very merry. So I went home, where I find my house now very clean, which was great content to me.

23. *Lords day.* In the morning to church; and my wife not being well, I went with Sir W. Batten home to dinner (my Lady being out of towne), where there was Sir W. Pen, Captain Allen and his daughter Rebecca, and Mr. Hempson and his wife. After dinner to church, all of us, and had a very good sermon of a stranger. And so I and the young company to walk first to Grayes Inn walks – where great store of gallants; but above all, the ladies that I then saw, or ever did see, Mrs. Frances Butler (Monsieur L'impertinent's sister) is the greatest beauty. Then we went to Islington, where at the great house[2] I entertained them as well as I could; and so home with them and so to my own home and to bed. Pall (who went this day to a child's christening of Kate Joyces) stayed out all night at my father's, she not being well.

24. *Midsummer day.* We kept*a* this a holiday, and so went not to the office at all. All the morning at home. At noon my father came to see my house now it is done; which is now very neat. He and I and Dr Williams (who is come to see my wife, whose soare belly is now grown dangerous as she thinks) to the ordinary over against the Exchange, where we dined. And had great wrangling with the master of the house when the Reckoning was brought to us, he setting down exceeding high everything.

a symbol written incorrectly

---

1. A comedy by Ben Jonson, first acted in 1610, and published in 1612. Now at the TR, Vere St. It was the third of Jonson's comedies to be revived after the Restoration and Pepys's is the first specific record of a post-Restoration performance, though a broadside entitled *Prologue to the reviv'd alchemist* appeared in 1660.

Subtle, the alchemist, was one of Walter Clun's best roles, as Pepys notes at 4 August 1664. The cast listed by Downes (pp. 4–5) is probably the one for the 1669 revival, not for this performance; see below, ix. 523 & n. 1. (A).

2. The King's Head, famous for its cheesecakes: cf. below, iii. 57 etc.

I home again and to Sir W. Batten, and there sat a good while. So home.

25. Up this morning to put my papers in order that are come from my Lord's, so that now I have nothing there remaining that is mine, which I have had till now.[1]

This morning came Mr. Goodgroome to me, recommended by Mr. Mage.[2] With whom I agreed presently to give him 20s entrance; which I then did, and 20s a month more to teach me to sing. And so we begun and I hope I shall come to something in it. His first song is *La cruda la bella*.[3] He gone, my Brother Tom comes; with whom I made even with my father and the two drapers for the cloths I sent to sea lately.[4]

At home all day. In the afternoon came Captain Allen and his daughter Rebecca and Mr. Hempson; and by and by both Sir Wms., who sat with me till it was late. And I had a very gallant collacion for them.

At night to bed.

26. To Westminster about several businesses. Then to dine with my Lady at the Wardrobe – taking*a* Deane Fuller along with me. Then home, where I heard that my father had been to find me out about special business; so I took coach and went to him; and find by a letter to him from my aunt that my uncle Robert is taken with a dizzinesse in his head.[5] So that they desire my father to come downe to look after his business – by which we guess that he is very ill; and so my father doth think to go tomorrow. And so God's will be done.

Back by water to the office. There till night; and so home to my musique and then to bed.

a l.h. repl. s.h. 'So'

---

1. Cf. Pepys to Sandwich, 25 June: Carte 73, f.538*r*.

2. Theodore Goodgroome was probably brother of the John Goodgroome who (like Humphrey Madge) was a royal musician. (E).

3. *La cruda la bella mia pastorella.* Probably a MS. copy; not published

in England until 1667, in Playford's *Catch that catch can, or The musical companion*, pp. 192–3. (E).

4. The cloth (which included £50-worth of fine linens) was to be used as gifts: Carte 73, f.538*r*.

5. Robert Pepys of Brampton died on 5 July.

27. To my father's and with him to Mr. Standings to drink our morning draught. And there I told him how I would have [him] speak to my Uncle Robt. when he comes thither, concerning my buying of land; that I would pay ready money, 600*l*, and the rest by 150*l* per annum, to make up as much as will buy 50 per annum. Which I do, though I am not worth above 500*l* ready money, that he may think me to be a greater saver then I am. Here I took my leave of my father, who is going this morning to my uncle, upon my aunts letter this week that he is not well and so needs my father's helpe.

At noon home; and then with my Lady Batten, Mrs. Rebecca*ᵃ* Allen, Mrs. Hempson &c., two coaches of us, we went and saw *Bartholmew fayre*,[1] acted very well. And so home again and stayed at Sir Wm. Batten's late; and so home and to bed. This day Mr. Holden sent me a bever, which costs me 4*l*-5*s*-0*d*.

28. At home all the morning, practising to sing, which is now my great trade. And at noon to my Lady and dined with her. So back and to the office. And there sat till 7 at night; and then Sir W. Penn in his coach and I, we went to Moore-fields and there walked; and stood and saw the wrestling, which I never saw so much of before – between the North and West countrymen.[2]

So home; and this night had our bed set up in our room that we called the Nursery, where we lay; and I am very much pleased with the room.

29. By a letter from the Duke, complaining of the delay of the ships that are to be got ready, Sir Wms. both and I went to Deptford and there examined into the delays and were satisfyed. So back again home and stayed till the afternoon and then I walked to the Bells at the maypoole in the Strand; and thither came to me by appointment Mr. Chetwin, Gregory and Hartlibb, so many of our old clubb,[3] and Mr. Kipps; where we stayed and drank and talked with much pleasure till it was late; and so I walked home and to bed.

a blot above word

---

1. See above, p. 117 & n. 1. (A).
2. Exponents of the Cornish–Devon and Cumberland–Westmorland styles of wrestling often competed in this way in London parks etc.

3. See above, i. 208 & n. 4.

Mr. Chetwind, by chawing of tobacco, is become very fat and lusty, whereas he was consumptive.*1   And in our discourse he fell commending of Hooker's *Ecclesiastical policy* as the best book, and the only one that made him a Christian, which puts me upon the buying of it, which I will do shortly.2

30. *Lords day.*

To church; where we observe the trade of briefes is come now up to so constant a course every Sunday, that we resolve to give no more to them.3   A good sermon; and then home to dinner, my wife and I all alone.

After dinner, Sir Wms. both and I by water to White-hall; where having walked up and down, at last we met with the Duke of Yorke according to an order sent us yesterday from him, to give him an account where the fault lay in the not sending out of the ships.   Which we find to be only the wind hath been against them, and so they could not get out of the River.   Hence I to Grayes Inn walk all alone; and with great pleasure seeing the fine ladies walk there – myself humming to myself (which now-adays is my constant practice since I begun to learn to sing) the *trillo*;4 and find by use that it doth come upon me.   Home, very weary, and to bed – finding my wife not sick but yet out of order, that I fear she will come to be sick.   This day the Portu-guese Embassador came to White-hall to take leave of the King,

1. In the 16th and 17th centuries tobacco was frequently used as a medicine.

2. Richard Hooker's *Of the lawes of ecclesiastical politie*, the classic state-ment of the claims of the Anglican church, was first published in 1593 or 1594.   For Pepys's copy, see below, p. 157 & n. 2.

3. Briefs were collections author-ised by the Lord Chancellor for charit-able objects (commonly for losses by fire); at this time particularly nu-merous because of the civil war.   In GL, MS. 863 (printed incompletely in *Gent. Mag.*, 24 (1845)/353) are details

of the sums collected at St Olave's. On this day £1 2s. 7d. was collected for losses from a fire in the parish of St Dunstan-in-the-West, and this was the fifteenth successive Sunday on which appeals of this sort had been made in the church.   The practice was abolished in 1828.   See W. A. Bewes, *Church Briefs*; W. E. Tate, *Parish Chest*, pp. 121–2.

4. Not the modern trill but the accelerated reiteration of the same note.   He was still hoping that Good-groome could teach him the *trillo* on 7 September 1667.   (E).

he being now going to end all with the Queene and to send her over.[1]

The weather now very fair and pleasant, but very hot. My father gone to Brampton to see my Uncle Robt., not knowing whether to find him dead or alive. Myself, lately under a great expense of money upon myself in clothes and other things; but I hope to make it up this summer, by my having to do in getting things ready to send with the next fleet for the Queene.

Myself in good health; but mighty apt to take cold, so that this hot weather I am fain to wear a cloth before my belly.[a]

[a] Here end the entries in the first volume of the MS. Eight blank pages follow.

---

1. The ambassador (Francesco de Mello, Marquez de Sande) was now about to go to Portugal to complete the arrangements for the Infanta Catherine's journey to England. He had dinner with the King and was treated with unusual ceremony: *CSPVen. 1661–4*, p. 6.

1. *Monday.* This morning I went up and down into the City to ⟨buy⟩ several things (as I have lately done for my house): among other things, a fair chest of drawers for my own chamber and an Indian gown for myself. The first cost me 33s, the other 34s. Home and dined there, and Mr. Goodgroome my singing master with me; and then to our singing. After that to the office. And then home.

2. To Westminster-hall and there walked up and down, it being term-time. Spoke with several; among others, my Cosen Rogr. Pepys, who was going up to the parliament-house and enquired whether I had heard from my father since he went to Brampton – which I had done yesterday, who writes that my uncle is by fits stupid and like a man that is drunk, and sometimes speechless.

Home; and after my singing master had done and took Coach and went to Sir Wm. Davenant's opera – this being the fourth day that it hath begun, and the first that I have seen it.[1] Today was acted the second part of *The Siege of Rhodes*.[2] We stayed a

1. Pepys here refers to the new theatre in Portugal Row, Lincoln's Inn Fields, to which Davenant had transferred the Duke of York's Company from the Salisbury Court Theatre, Whitefriars. Like Thomas Killigrew's Theatre Royal in nearby Vere St, the Lincoln's Inn Fields Theatre was a converted tennis-court building. Though the stage was small, Davenant equipped it with a proscenium arch and proscenium doors and used movable scenery on it. These facts partly explain Pepys's application of the term 'opera' to this theatre, for opera at this time was closely associated with the use of painted scenery and stage machines. Pepys's reference is now generally accepted as fixing the date of the opening of this theatre at 28 June 1661. Downes states (p. 20) that the opening was 'in Spring, 1662', but his dating is evidently incorrect, for Pepys mentions another performance at this theatre on 11 September 1661. (A).

2. The first part of Davenant's *The siege of Rhodes*, the first English opera, was produced and published in 1656. He subsequently revised it and published it with the second part in 1663. This reference by Pepys is the first record of a performance of the second part. The cast that he saw, as listed by Downes (p. 20), includes Betterton as Solyman, Harris as Alphonso, Mrs Davenport as Roxalana and Mrs Sanderson (later Betterton's wife) as Ianthe. (A).

very great while for the King, and the Queene of Bohemia.[1]
And by the breaking of a board over our heads, we had a great
deal of dust fell into the ladies' necks and the men's haire, which
made good sport. The King being come, the Scene opened;[2]
which endeed is very fine and magnificent, and well acted, all but
the Eunuches, who was so much out that he was hissed off the
stage.[3]

Home and wrote letters to my Lord to Sea; and so to bed.

3. To Westminster to Mr. Edwd. Mountagu about business
of my Lord's; and so to the Wardrobe and there dined with my
Lady, who is in some mourning for her brother, Mr. Sam. Crew,
who died yesterday of the spotted feavor.[4] So home through
Duck lane[5] to enquire for some Spanish books, but found none
that pleased me. So to the office; and that being done, to Sir
W. Battens with the Controller; where we sat late, talking and
disputing with Mr. Mills the parson of our parish. This day my
Lady Batten and my wife were at the burial of a daughter of Sir

---

1. I.e. Charles, King of England,
and Elizabeth his aunt, widow of
Frederick, Elector Palatine, elected
King of Bohemia in 1619.

2. Throughout the Restoration
period, and indeed, until the later
19th century, the main scenic system
of the English theatre consisted of
wings fronting pairs of large flats, all
of which were moved in grooves
arranged at intervals on the floor and
flies of the stage. During the Restoration period the stage curtain was
rarely used to conceal a change of
scene; as Pepys indicates here, one
pair of large flats was usually drawn
aside to reveal another scene arranged
behind them on wings backed by
another pair of flats. The scenery
for *The siege of Rhodes* was designed by
John Webb. According to Downes
(p. 20), the 'Scenes and Decorations'
at Lincoln's Inn Fields were 'the first
that e're were Introduc'd in *England*'.
It is more accurate to say, however,
that the Lincoln's Inn Fields Theatre
was the first public theatre in England
in which painted settings were con-
tinuously used. (A).

3. This part was taken by John
Downes, who became prompter at
this theatre in 1662, and in 1708
published his invaluable *Roscius Angli-
canus*, in which he admits (p. 34) his
failure in this performance and attri-
butes it to the 'August *presence*' of
Charles II. (A).

4. Samuel Crew was a parson who
had taken his B.A. at Oxford in 1658.
The fever was an intermittent type
(? typhus or cerebrospinal), common
in London 1661–4; evidence and
analysis in C. Creighton, *Hist.
epidemics in Brit.*, ii. 4+. See below,
pp. 155, 168; cf. Evelyn, 22 September 1661; M. H. Nicolson (ed.),
Conway Letters, pp. 189–90, 194, 195.

5. Largely inhabited by book-
sellers.

Joh. Lawson's and had rings for themselfs and their husbands.[1]
Home and to bed.

4.   At home all the morning.   In the afternoon I went to the
Theatre and there I saw *Claracilla*[2] (the first time I ever saw it),
well acted.   But strange to see this house, that use to be so
thronged, now empty since the opera begun – and so will continue for a while I believe.[3]   Called at my father's, and there I
hear that my Uncle Robt. continues to have his fits of stupe-
faccion[a] every day, for 10 or 12 houres together.

From thence to the Exchange at night; and there went with
my Uncle Wight to the Mitre.   And were merry; but he takes
it very ill that my father would go out of town to Brampton on
this occasion and would not tell him of it – which I endeavoured to
remove, but could not.

Here Mr. Batersby the apothecary was, who told me that if my
uncle had formerly had the Emerods (which I think he had)
and that now they are stopped, he will lay his life that bleeding
behind by leeches will cure him. But I am resolved not to meddle
in it.

Home and to bed.

5.   At home; and in the afternoon to the office; and that being
done, we all went to Sir W. Battens and there had a venison
pasty and were very merry.   At night home and to bed.

6.   Waked this morning with news, brought me by a messenger on purpose, that my Uncle Robert is dead – and died
yesterday.   So I rose, sorry in some respect; glad in my expectations in another respect.   So I made myself ready.   Went and
told my Uncle Wight – my Lady – and some others thereof.
And bought me a pair of boots in St. Martins and got myself

a   MS. l.h. 'supefaccion'

---

1. Abigail Lawson was this day
buried at St Dunstan-in-the-East. For
funeral rings, see above, p. 74, n. 2.
2. A tragicomedy by Thomas
Killigrew, first acted in 1636, and
published in 1641: now at the TR,
Vere St.   (A).

3. Killigrew did not use painted
scenery at the TR, and the novelty of
it at the 'Opera' (q.v. above, p. 130,
n. 1) was evidently a strong counter-
attraction.   (A).

ready; and then to the post-house and set out about 11 or[a] 12 a-clock, taking the messenger with me that came to me; and so we rode and got well by 9 a-clock to Brampton, where I find my father well. My Uncles corps in a coffin, standing upon joynt-stooles in the chimny in the hall; but it begun to smell, and so I caused it to be set forth in the yard all night and wached by two men. My aunt I find in bedd in a most nasty ugly pickle, made me sick to see it. My father and I lay together tonight, I greedy to see the Will but did not aske to see it till tomorrow.

7. *Lords day.* In the morning my father and I walked in the garden and read the Will; where though he gives me nothing at present till my father's death, or at least very little, yet I am glad to see that he hath done so well for us all – and well to the rest of his kindred.[1] After that done, we went about getting things, as ribbands and gloves, ready for the burial. Which in the after-noon was done; where it being Sonday, all people far and near came in and in the greatest disorder that ever I saw; we made shift to serve them what we had of wine and other things;[2] and then to carry him to the church, where Mr. Taylor buried him and Mr. Turner preached a funerall Sermon[b][3] – where he spoke not perticularly of him anything, but that he was one so well-known for his honesty, that it spoke for itself above all that he could say for it. And so made a very good sermon.

a MS. 'and'   *b* l.h. repl. s.h. 'sm'-

---

1. The will of Robert Pepys of Brampton (dated 12–15 August 1657, and proved 23 August 1661) is in PCC, May, 128 and is summarised in Whitear, pp. 145–8. The house at Brampton, together with the greater part of the estate, was left to Pepys's father, and was after his death to pass to Pepys, who was also to have an annuity of £30 (after debts and legacies were paid) during the life-time of his uncle Thomas Pepys. This was to be increased, after Thomas Pepys's death, to a half-interest in the estate. There were legacies to most of the deceased's relatives, except his widow. Pepys and his father were appointed executors. Pepys gained his half-interest on his uncle Thomas's death in 1676, and full possession on his father's death in 1680. He then made over the house and profits to his sister Paulina who enjoyed them until her death in 1689.

2. The funeral costs, together with the apothecary's bills, came to £80 (or, according to another account, £95): PL (unoff.), Freshfield MSS, nos 8 and 9.

3. Thomas Taylor was master of the grammar school at Huntingdon, and John Turner Rector of Eynesbury (Hunts.) and chaplain to Sandwich.

Home with some of the company who supped there; and things being quiet, at night to bed.

《 8》 I fell to work, and my father, to look over his papers and
《 9》 clothes.   And continued all this week upon that business—
《10》 much troubled with my aunts base ugly humours.¹   We
《11》 had news of Tom Trices putting in a caveat against us in
《12》 behalfe of his mother, to whom my Uncle hath not given
《13》 anything, and for good reason therein expressed; which
            troubled us also.²   But above all, our trouble is to find
that his estate appears nothing as we expected and all the world

1. Was she always – illness and the present crisis apart – a difficult person? Her son Jasper Trice had occasion in 1641 to consult an astrologer-physician about her health. He was Sir Richard Napier, of Great Linford, Bucks., and the horoscope, notes and prescription which he then made survive in Bodl., Ashmole 412, f.290r. Trice had reported that his mother was 'distracted.   Sometymes she will be quiett and of a sudden she will be in a passion, feares every body will betray her, and if any body give her anything she will refuse it, and thereafter of her selfe she will take it. Cannot sleep . . . Discontent and greife.'   She was then 45.
2. When in 1630 Robert Pepys married Anne, widow of Richard Trice of Brampton, she had induced him to enter a bond for £200 on her behalf so that she could leave this money to her children.   Otherwise, her first husband's property would have passed to her second husband. But her first husband left much less than she made out, and Robert Pepys felt cheated.   He bequeathed nothing to his widow, and simply required his executors to be civil to her.   Whereupon her sons of the first marriage

(Jasper and Thomas Trice, both lawyers) entered a caveat against the will.   Though the caveat was later withdrawn, this affair caused Pepys much worry and litigation.   The relevant passage in the will runs: 'And whereas much will be said for my not giveing of my wife a large legacie the reason I doe vow to God is this that she gott me to enter into Bond to leave her at libertie to bestowe Two hundred pounds of Goods as Cloathes and monyes at the time of her death pretending that shee was to have the benefitt of her former husbands Estate dureing her sonnes Minoritie without being accomptable to her said sonne And that she was to have a Joynture as large againe as it was in both which [. . .?] I lost halfe and then paid 281 pounds^li [*sic*] in leiue of accompting for the revenues of the Estate for which cause as she suggested she was not to be answerable was the Bond given yet after she did see how unworthily I was dealt with still shee would hold what advantage she hath gott And so let her hold what she can Soe I doe require my Executors to be very Civell unto her in all respects although shee knowes she hath done me much wrong.'

believes.[1] Nor his papers so well sorted as I would have had them, but all in confusion, that break my brains to understand them. We missed also the Surrenders of his Coppyhold land, without which the land could not come to us but to the heire-at-law.[2] So that what with this and the badness of the drink and the ill opinion I have of the meat, and the biting of the gnatts by night[3] – and my disappointment in getting home this week – and the trouble of sorting all the papers, I am almost out of my wits with trouble. Only, I appear the more contented, because I would not have my father troubled.

The latter end of the weeke, Mr. Philips[4] comes home from London; and so we advised with him and had the best counsel he could give us. But for all that, we were not quiet in our minds.

14. *Lords day.* At home, and Rob. Barnwell with us and dined. And in the evening my father and I walked round porthome[5] and viewed all the fields, which was very pleasant. Then to Hinchingbrooke, which is now all in dirt because of my Lord's building, which will make it very magnificent.[6] Back to Brampton and to supper and to bed.

15. Up by 3 a-clock this morning and rode to Cambridge, and was there by 7 a-clock. Where after I was trimmed, I went to Christ College and find my brother John at 8 a-clock in bed, which vexed me. Then to Kings College chappell, where I find the schollers in their surplices at the service with the organs –

1. There was real estate worth £128 p.a., and £372 in personalty (excluding household goods), out of which had to be paid legacies of £324 in cash, annuities of £55, and debts of £869 10s. 0d. The executors' legacy amounted to £23 p.a. in land (less lord's rents, taxes and parish duties). See the valuations in PL (unoff.), Freshfield MSS, nos 8 and 9. Cf. below, iv. 119, n. 1, ib. 141, n. 3. On 24 July Pepys 'to put an esteem' on himself let it be known at the Navy Board that he had inherited £200 p.a. in land alone.

2. For the consequent dispute (not settled until early 1663), see *Comp.*: 'Pepys, Robert'. The heir-at-law was Thomas Pepys, elder of the two surviving brothers of the deceased.

3. For Fenland gnats, see below, iv. 311, n. 1.

4. Lewis Phillips of Brampton, the executors' attorney in this affair.

5. Portholme; reputedly the largest meadow in England; c. 300 acres.

6. See above, p. 49, n. 1.

which is a strange sight to what it used in my time to be here.[1]
Then with Dr. Fairebrother (whom I met there) to the Rose
taverne and called for some wine; and there met fortunately with
Mr. Turner of our office and sent for his wife and were very merry
(they being come to settle their son here);[2] and sent also for Mr.
Sanchy of Magdalen, with whom and other gentlemen, friends of
his, we were very merry and I treated them as well as I could;
and so at noon took horse again, having taken leave of my Cosen
Angier, and rode to Impington – where I find my old Uncle[3]
setting all alone, like a man out of the world. He can hardly see;
but all things else he doth pretty livelyly. Then with Dr. John
Pepys[4] and him, I read over the Will and had their advice therein;
who, as to the sufficiency thereof, confirmed me, and advised me
as to the other parts thereof.

Having done there, I rode to Gravely with much ado, to
enquire for a Surrender of my uncles in some of the Coppy-
holders hands there; but I can hear of none, which puts me into
very great trouble of mind; and so with a sad heart rode home
to Brampton, but made myself as cheerful as I could to my father.
And so to bed.

《16》 These four days we spent in putting things in order –
《17》 letting of the cropp upon the ground – agreeing with
《18》 Stankes to have a care of our business in our absence, and
《19》 we think ourselfs in nothing happy but in lighting*a* upon
　　　him to be our bayly – in riding to Offord and Sturtlow,
and up and down all our lands; and in the evening walking, my

a l.h. repl. s.h. ? 'this'

---

1. The organ at King's had been
removed in 1643, and by the time
Pepys came into residence at Magdalene in 1651 the choristers had
dwindled to one. There are signs
that an organ was used after 1654.
In 1660 a small organ belonging to
Henry Loosemore the organist was
used. Lancelot Pease was paid £200
for a 'chaireorgan' in 1661. See T.
Fuller, *Hist. univ. Cambridge* (1655),
p. 167; R. Willis and J. W. Clark,
Archit. hist. Cambridge, i. 519–21; ii.

141–4, 205–14, 572–81; P. A. Scholes,
Puritans and music, p. 237; W. L.
Sumner, *The Organ* (1962 ed.), pp.
125, 132; VCH, *Cambs.*, iii. 391.
(E).

2. Thomas Turner of Westminster
School; admitted to Trinity College
on 22 May.

3. Talbot Pepys, Pepys's great-
uncle; lawyer and landowner, now
aged 78.

4. Second son of Talbot Pepys;
lawyer and Fellow of Trinity Hall.

father and I, about the fields talking. And had advice from Mr. Moore from London by my desire, that the three Witnesses[1] of the Will being all Legattées will not do the Will any wrong. Tonight Serjeant Bernard,[2] I hear, is come home into the country. To supper and to bed – my aunt continuing in her base hypocriticall tricks, which both Jane Perkin[3] (of whom we make great use) and the mayd do tell us every day of.

20. Up to Huntington this morning to Sir Robt. Bernard, with whom I met Jespar Trice. So Sir Robt. caused us to sit down together and begun discourse very fairly between us, so I drow out the Will and shew it him and spoke between us as well as I could desire, but could come to no issue till Tom. Trice comes. Then Sir Robt. and I fell to talk about the money due to us upon Surrender from Piggott, 164*l*, which he tells me will go, he doubts, to the heire-at-law,[4] which breaks my heart on the other side.

Here I stayed and dined with Sir Robt. and his Lady, my Lady Digby,[5] a very good woman.

After dinner I went into the Towne and spent the afternoon sometimes with Mr. Philips, sometimes with Dr. Symcottes,[6] Mr. Vinter, Rob. Ethell, and many more friends; and at last Mr. Davenport, Phillips, Jespr Trice, myself and others at Mother   over against the Crowne,[7] we sat and drank ale

1. John Holcroft, Thomas Holcroft, and John Pepys. But the second of these does not appear to have been a legatee.

2. Robert Bernard, cr. bt 1662, Sergeant-at-law; Recorder of Huntingdon, and lord of the manor of Brampton.

3. The late Robert Pepys's niece, brought up by him and his wife.

4. This was a mortgage owed by Richard Pigott of Brampton to the late Robert Pepys, on the security of his lands and houses in Brampton. Despite the challenge from the heir-at-law (Thomas Pepys), it passed to the executors in the settlement of 14 February 1663: below, iv. 42. But

Pigott could not repay it without selling the land, and for this Thomas Pepys's consent was not obtained until July 1663: below, iv. 133.

5. Sir Robert Bernard's second wife, Elizabeth, widow of George, 1st Baron Digby; still called Lady Digby because her remarriage to a man of lower rank than her first husband did not deprive her of her superior title. Cf. 'Lady Mountagu': below, p. 171.

6. John Symcottes (Simcotes), a Huntingdon physician; he had attended Oliver Cromwell.

7. In High St; no longer in existence. See VCH, *Hunts.*, ii. 127. The name after 'Mother' is missing.

and were very merry till 9 at night and so broke up. I walked home, and there find Tom Trice come and he and my father gone to Goody Gorrum's;[1] where I find them and Jespar Trice got before me, and Mr. Greene, and there had some calme discourse, but came to no issue and so parted. So home and to bed – being now pretty well again of my left hand, which lately was stung and very much swelled.

21. *Lords*[a] *day*. At home all the morning, putting my papers in order against my going tomorrow and doing many things else to that end. Had a good dinner, and Stankes and his wife with us. To my business again in the afternoon; and in the evening came the two Trices, Mr. Greene, and Mr. Philips, and so we begun to argue; at last it came to some agreement, that for our giving of my aunt 10*l*, she is to quit the house; and for other matters, they are to be left to the law, which doth please us all; and so we broke up pretty well satisfyed.

Then came Mr. Barnwell and J. Bowles and supped with us, and after supper away; and so I having taken leave of them and put things in the best order I could against tomorrow, I went to bed.

Old Wm. Luffe having been here this afternoon and paid us his bond of 20*l*; and I did give him into his hand my Uncles surrender of Sturtlow to me before Mr. Philips, R. Barnwell, and Mr. Pigott – which he did acknowledge to them my Uncle did in his lifetime deliver to him.

22. Up by 3 and going by 4 on my way to London. But the day proves very cold; so that having put on noe stockings but thread ones under my boots, I was fain at Bigglesworth to buy a pair of coarse woollen ones and put them on. So by degrees, till I came to Hatfield before 12 a-clock – where I had a very good dinner with my hostesse at my Lord of Salsburys Inn;[2] and after dinner, though weary, I walked all alone to the Vine-

a repl. '21'

---

1. Widow Gorham's alehouse, owned by Robert Pepys, was to pass first to Pepys's father and then to

Pepys himself after the death of the tenant.

2. The Salisbury Arms, Fore St.

yard,[1] which is now a very beautiful place again; and coming back, I met with Mr. Looker my Lord's gardener (a friend of Mr. Eglins), who showed me the house,[2] the chappell with rare pictures,[3] and above all the gardens, such as I never saw in all my life; nor so good flowers nor so great goosburys, as big as nutmegs.

Back to the Inne and drank with him; and so to horse again, and with much ado got to London and set him up in Smithfield; so called at my uncle Fenners, my mother's, my Lady's; and so home, in all which I find all things as well as I could expect. So, weary and to bed.

23. Put on my mourning. Made visits to Sir W. Pen and Batten. Then to Westminster and at the hall stayed talking with Mrs. Michell a good while; and in the afternoon, finding myself unfit for business, I went to the Theatre and saw *Breneralt*;[4] I never saw before. It seemed a good play, but ill acted; only, I sat before Mrs. Palmer, the King's mistress, and filled my eyes with her, which much pleased me. Then to my father's, where by my desire I met my Uncle Thomas and discourse of my Uncles Will to him, and did satisfye as well as I could. So to my Uncle Wights, but find him out of doors; but my aunt I saw and stayed a while; and so home – and to bed. Troubled to hear how proud and Idle Pall is grown, that I am resolved not to keep her.

1. Planted on either side of the river Lea, about a mile from the inn. Description in T. Fuller, *Worthies* (1811 ed.), i. 426.

2. Description of house and park in VCH, *Herts.*, iii. 94+. Hatfield House, originally a palace of the bishops of Ely, and after 1538 a royal residence, had passed to the Cecils in 1607, and Robert Cecil, 1st Earl of Salisbury was responsible for most of the building (c. 1607–11) which Pepys saw, and for the vineyard. The second Earl (William, d. 1668) was the owner at this time. Cf. Evelyn, 11 March 1643, and his letter describing the gardens in Sir Thomas Browne, *Works* (ed. Keynes), vi. 305; S. Sorbière, *Relation d'un voyage en*

Angleterre (Cologne, 1667), pp. 110+.

3. Rowland Buckett (d. 1639) and Richard Butler (fl. 1609–?50) are the only artists recorded by name as having worked for the first Earl in the chapel. Buckett was at work there in 1609–12, and of the early 17th-century religious pictures still there (all except one are in the chapel), two are apparently by Buckett, in addition to decorative painting throughout the house: E. Croft-Murray, *Decorative painting in Engl.*, i. 32, 194–5. (OM).

4. *Brennoralt, or The discontented colonel*, a tragicomedy by Sir John Suckling, first acted between 1639 and 1641, and published in 1646. Now at the TR, Vere St. (A).

24. This morning in bed my wife tells me of our being robbed of our silver tankard; which vexed me all day for the negligence of my people to leave the door open.

My wife and I by water to White-hall, where I left her to her business; and I to my Cosen Tho. Pepys and discoursed with him at large about our business of my uncles Will. He can give us no light at all into his estate. But upon the whole, tells me that he doth believe that he hath left but little money, though something more then we have found, which is about 500*l*.

Here came Sir G. Lane by chance, seeing a bill upon the doore to hire the house, with whom my Cosen and I walked all up and down; and endeed it is a very pretty place. And he doth entend to leave the agreement*a* for the house, which is 400*l* fine and 46*l* rent a year to me between them.[1] Then to the Wardrobe; but came too late and so dined with the servants. And then to my Lady, who doth show my wife and me the greatest favour in the world – in which I take great content.

Home by water, and to the office all the afternoon; which is a great pleasure to me again – to talk with persons of Quality and to be in command; and I gave it out among them that the estate left me is 200*l* a year in land, besides money – because I would put an esteem upon myself.

At night home and to bed, after I had set down my Journall ever since my going from London this journy, to this houre.

This afternoon I hear that my man Will hath lost his cloak with my tankard, at which I am very glad.

25. This morning came my box of papers from Brampton, of all my uncles papers, which will now set me at work enough. At noon I went to the Exchange, where I met my uncle Wight and find him so discontented about my father (whether that he takes it ill that he hath not been acquainted with things, or

a repl. 'house'

---

1. Sc. Pepys was to draw up the terms of the lease agreed between Lane and Thomas Pepys. Sir George Lane was a clerk to the Privy Council, and secretary to Ormond, Lord Steward of the Royal Household. The house was in the fields near St Martin's Lane. Thomas Pepys now moved to Newport St, Covent Garden, where he stayed until 1663, when he went to live at Hatcham, Surrey.

whether he takes it ill that he had nothing left him, I cannot tell); for which I am much troubled, and so stayed not long to talk with him.

Thence to my mother's, where I find my wife and my aunt Bell and Mrs. Ramsey; and great store of tattle there was between the old women; and above [all], my mother, who thinks that there is God knows what fallen to her – which makes me mad, but it was not a proper time to speak to her of it; and so I went away with Mr. Moore and he and I to the Theatre and saw *The Joviall Crew*,[1] (the first time I saw it); and endeed, it is as merry, and the most innocent play that ever I saw, and well performed. From thence home and wrote to my father, and so to bed – full of thoughts to think of the trouble that we shall go through before we come to see what will remain to us of all our expectations.

26. At home all the morning; and walking, met with Mr. Hill of Cambrige in Popes-head ally with some women with him; whom he took and me into the taverne there and did give us wine. And would fain seem to be very knowing in the affairs of state, and tells me that yesterday put a change to the whole state of England as to the Church; for the King now would be forced to favour Presbytery,*a* or the City would leave him;[2] but I heed not what he says, though upon enquiry I do find that things in the Parliament are at a great disorder.[3]

Home at noon, and there find Mr. Moore and with him to an ordinary alone and dined; and there he and I read my Uncles Will and I had his opinion on it, and still find more and more trouble like to attend it.

a l.h. repl. l.h. 'Episcopacy'

1. *The jovial crew, or The merry beggars*, a comedy by Richard Brome, first acted in 1641, and published in 1652. Now at the TR, Vere St. (A).

2. Joseph Hill was a Fellow of Magdalene. On 25 July the Savoy Conference between Presbyterians and Anglicans had ended without agreement. Hill's forecast was wide of the mark; he was himself a Presby-terian and his prophecy was perhaps illegitimately fathered by his wishes. Even the loss of his fellowship in the next year on account of his noncon-formity did not subdue his optimism: see below, iv. 243.

3. A great volume of legislation had still to be passed, and attendance, particularly among government sup-porters, had fallen off.

Back to the office all the afternoon. And that done, home for all night.

Having the beginning of this week made a vowe to myself to drink no wine this week (finding it to unfit me to look after business), and this day breaking of it against my will, I am much troubled for it – but I hope God will forgive me.

27. To Westminster; where at Mr. Mountagu's chamber I heard a Frenchman play (a friend of Monsieur Eschar's)[1] upon the Gittar most extreme well; though, at the best, methinks it is but a bawble.[2] From thence to Westminster-hall, where it was expected that the Parliament was to be*a* adjourned for two or three months; but something hinders it for a day or two. In the Lobby I spoke with Mr. George Mountagu and advised about a ship to carry my Lord Hinchingbrooke and the rest of the young gentlemen to France; and have resolved of going in a hired vessell from Rye, and not in a man-of-Warr.[3] He told me in discourse that my Lord Chancellor is much envyed and that many great men, such as the Duke of Buckingham and my Lord of Bristol, do endeavour to undermine him. And that he believes it will not be done, for that the King (though he loves him not in the way of a companion, as he doth these young gallants that can answer him in his pleasures), yet cannot be without him for his policy and service.

From thence to the Wardrobe, where my wife met me, it being my Lord of Sandwiches Birth=day. And so we had many friends here, Mr. Townsend and his wife and Captain Ferrers' lady and Captain Isham, and were very merry and had a good venison pasty. Mr. Pargiter the Merchant was with us also.

After dinner Mr. Townsend was called upon by Captain Cooke;[4] so we three went to a taverne hard by and there he did give us a song or two; and without doubt, he hath the best manner of singing in the world. Back to my wife and with my Lady

a MS. 'be been'

---

1. Edward Mountagu's servant.
2. For the growing popularity of the guitar, see above, i. 172, n. 2. (E).
3. For their journey and stay abroad, see above, p. 114, n. 1. They sailed in late August: below,

p. 163. George, son of George Mountagu and grandson of the 1st Earl of Manchester, went with them: below, iii. 15.
4. Henry Cooke, Master of the Children of the Chapel Royal. (E).

Jem. and Pall[1] by water through bridge, and showed them the ships with great pleasure; and then took them to my house to show it them (my Lady their mother having been lately all alone to see it and my wife, in my absence in the country) and we treated them well and were very merry. Then back again through bridge and set them safe at home; and so my wife and I by coach home again. And after writing a letter to my father at Brampton, who, poor man, is there all alone and I have not heard from him since my coming from him, which troubles me – to bed.

28. *Lords day*. This morning, as my wife and I were going to church, comes Mrs. Ramsy to see us; so we sent her to church and we went too, and came back to dinner and she dined with us and was welcome.

To church again in the afternoon. And then came home with us Sir W. Pen and drank with us and then went away; and my wife after him to see his daughter that is lately come out of Ireland.[2] I stayed at home at my book. She came back again, and tells me that whereas I expected she should have been a great beauty, she is a very plain girl.

This evening my wife gives me all my linen, which I have put up and entend to keep it now in my own custody.

To supper and to bed.

29. This morning we begin again to sit in the mornings at the office.[3] But before we sat down, Sir R. Slingsby and I went to Sir R. Fords to see his house; and we find it will be very convenient for us to have it added to the office, if he can be got to part with it.[4]

1. Jemima and Paulina, daughters of Sandwich.

2. Penn had estates in co. Cork, and was Governor of Kinsale. This was his only daughter, Margaret (Peg).

3. The parliamentary recess (beginning on the 30th) would enable members of the Board who were M.P.'s to attend in the mornings.

4. This was a large house (of 18 hearths in the hearth-tax assessment of 1666) on the e. side of Seething Lane, next to and south of the Navy Office. Sir Richard Ford (a great merchant) had been a tenant there since 1653, and had taken out a 21-year lease in 1655. He let out parts of it both now and later, but the proposal here mentioned came to nothing. The house was destroyed in the Navy Office fire of 1673, and its site included in the rebuilt Navy Office. (R).

Then we sat down and did business in the office. So home to dinner – and my brother Tom dined with me; and after dinner he and I alone in my chamber had a great deal of talk, and I find that unless my father can forbear to make profit of his house in London and leave it to Tom, he hath no mind to set up the trade anywhere else. And so I know not what to do with him.

After this I went with*ᵃ* him to my mother and there told her how things do fall out short of our expectacions; which I did (though it be true) to make her leave off her spending, which I find she is nowadays very free in, building upon what is left us by my uncle to bear her out in it – which troubles me much.

While I was here, word is brought that my aunt Fenner is exceeding ill and that my mother is sent for presently to come to her. Also, that my Cozen Charles Glascoke (though very ill himself) is this day gone to the country to his brother John Glascock,¹ who is a-dying there.

Home.

30. After my singing-master² had done with me this morning, I went to White-hall and Westminster-hall, where I find the King expected to come and adjourne the parliament.

I find the two Houses at a great difference about the Lords challenging their priviledges not to have their houses searched; which makes them deny to pass the House of Commons' bill for searching for pamphlets and seditious books.³

Thence by water to the Wardrobe (meeting the King upon the

a   repl. 'home'

---

1. Rector of Little Canfield, Essex. He had made his will on the 28th, and died shortly afterwards.

2. Theodore Goodgroome. (E).

3. The Commons objected to a proviso inserted by the Lords which would have protected peers' houses from search. At a conference with the Lords on the 29th, the Commons had asserted that the exemption would be too dangerous a loophole, and that, in any case, 'all Houses, as well of Commons as of Peers, are equally the Castles and Proprieties of the owners': *CJ*, viii. 315. The bill was now abandoned, and passed in May 1662 in a form which allowed search of peers' houses only under special licence from the King: Licensing Act, 14 Car. II c. 33, sect. xviii.

water, going in his barge to adjourne the House); where I dined
with my Lady and there met Dr. Tom. Pepys,[1] who I find to be a
silly talking fellow, but very good-natured.

So home to the office, where we met about the business of
Tanger this afternoon.[2] That done, at home I find Mr. Moore
and he and I walked into the City and there parted; and I to
Fleetstreete to find when the Assizes begin at Cambrige and
Huntington, in order to my going to meet with Roger Pepys for
counsel.

So in*a* Fleetstreete I met with Mr. Salsbury,[3] who is now
grown, in less then two years' time, so great a limner that he is
become excellent, and gets a great deal of money at it. I took
him to Hercules pillars to drink and there came Mr. Whore
(whom I formerly have known) a friend of his to him, who is a
very ingenious fellow and there I sat with them a good while;
and so home and wrote letters late to my Lord and to my father
and then to bed.

31. Singing-master came to me this morning. Then to the
office all the morning. In the afternoon I went to the Theatre
and there I saw *The Tamer tamed*,[4] well done. And then home
and prepared to go to Walthamstowe tomorrow.

This night I was forced to borrow 40*l* of Sir Wm. Batten.[5]

a l.h. repl. s.h. 'on'

---

1. Physician; son of Pepys's great-uncle, Talbot Pepys of Impington.

2. Tangier had just been acquired, as part of the dowry of Catherine of Braganza, by the marriage treaty signed on 23 June. It was formally surrendered to Sandwich in January 1662. From October 1662 Pepys was a member of the committee of Council which controlled its government; in March 1665 he became Treasurer.

3. See above, p. 23, n. 2.

4. A comedy by John Fletcher (see above, i. 278 & n. 1); now at the TR, Vere St. (A).

5. It was repaid on 1 March 1662: below, iii. 39.

AUGUST. *1661.*

1. This morning, Sir Wms. both and my wife and I and Mrs. Margt. Penn (this, first time that I have seen her since she came from Ireland) went by coach to Walthamstowe, a-gossiping* to Mrs. Browne – where I did give her six silver spoons for her boy. Here we had a venison pasty brought hot from London, and were very merry. Only, I hear how nurses husband hath spoke strangely of my Lady Batten, how she was such a man's whore; who endeed is known to leave her her estate – which we would fain have reconciled* today, but could not. And endeed, I do believe that the story is too true.

Back again at night home.

2. At the office all the morning. At noon Dr. Tho. Pepys dined with me; and after dinner my Brother Tom came to me. And then I made myself ready to get a-horseback for Cambridge. So I set out and rode to Ware this night, in my way having much discourse with a fellmonger, a Quaker, who told me what a wicked man he had been all his life-time till within this two years.

[3.] Here I lay, and got up earely the next morning and got to Barkeway, where I stayed and drank; and there met with a letter-Carrier of Cambrige, with whom I rode all the way to Cambrige, my horse being tired and myself very wet with rayne.

I went to the Castle hill, where the Judges were at the Assizes, and I stayed till Roger Pepys rose.[1] And went with him and dined with his Brother Doctor and Claxton at Trinity hall.[2] Then parted, and I went to the Rose and there, with Mr. Pechell and Sanchy and others, sat and drank till night and were very merry. Only they tell me how high the old Doctors are in the

---

1. The assizes were held in Shire House, Castle Hill, until 1747: VCH, *Cambs.*, iii. 118. Roger Pepys attended as Recorder of the borough.

2. I.e. his brother John Pepys, lawyer, and his brother-in-law Hammond Claxton, of Booton, Norf.

University over those they find there,[1] though a great deal better
Schollers then themselfs – which I am very sorry – and above all,
Dr. Gunning.[2] At night I took horse and rode with Rogr
Pepys and his two brothers to Impington; and there with great
respect was led up by them to the best chamber in the house, and
there slept.

4. *Lords day.* Got up, and by and by walked into the orchard
with my Cosen Roger and there plucked some fruit; and then
discoursed at large about the business I came for; that is, about
my Uncles Will; in which he did give me good satisfaccion, but
tells me I shall meet with a great deal of trouble in it. However,
in all things he told me what I am to expect and what to do.

To church and had a good plain sermon – and my Uncle
Talbott[3] went with us. And at our coming in, the country-
people all rise, with so much reverence. And when the parson
begins, he begins "Right Worshipfull and dearly beloved" to us.

Home to dinner – which was very good – and then to church
again; and so home and to walk up and down, and so to supper –
and after supper to talk about public matters, wherein Roger
(who I find a very sober man, and one whom I do now honour
more then ever before, for this discourse sake only) told me how
basely things have been carried in parliament by the young men,
that did labour to oppose all things that were moved by serious
men.[4] That they are the most profane swearing fellows that ever

1. John Peachell and Clement
Sankey had been elected to their
fellowships at Magdalene during the
Protectorate. They probably feared
the power of the dispossessed heads of
houses and fellows who were now
restored to the places from which
they had been extruded during the
revolution.

2. Peter Gunning, elected Master
of St John's in June 1661, was quick
to 'rout out the old leaven', according
to Thomas Baker (d. 1740): *Hist.
St John's,* i. 233. But he is said to
have allowed 'a very considerable
annuity' to Anthony Tuckney, whom
he replaced both in the mastership and

as professor: Wood, *Ath. Oxon.* (ed.
Bliss), iv. 142.

3. Talbot Pepys, lord of the manor,
Pepys's great-uncle. The church (St
Andrew's) lay a short distance to the
north of the house. The parson was
probably T- Bradshaw, who served
the cure for the non-resident Vicar,
Thomas Wilborough.

4. The first session of the new
parliament, ending on 30 July, had
seen many victories for the cavalier
(or 'young men's') interest over that
of the Presbyterians, or 'serious men'.
Roger, son of Talbot Pepys, was M.P.
for Cambridge borough.

he heard in his life – which makes him think that they will spoil all, and bring things into a warr again if they can.

So to bed.

5. earely to Huntington.   But was fain to stay a great while at Stanton because of the rayne; and there borrowed a coat of a man for 6*d*, and so he rode all the way, poor man, without any. Stayed at Huntington a little, but the Judges are not yet come hither.   So I went to Brampton and there find my father very well – and my aunt gone from the house; which I am glad of, though it costs us a great deal of money, *viz.*, 10*l*.

Here I dined, and after dinner took horse and rode to Yelling to my Cosen Nightingales, who hath a pretty house here.   And did learn of her all she could tell me concerning my business, and hath given me some light by her discourse how I may get a Surrender made for Graveley lands.

Hence to Graveley; and there at an alehouse met with Chandler and Jackson (one of my tenants for Cotton=closes) and another, with whom I had a great deal of discourse, much to my satisfaccion.

Thence back again to Brampton; and after supper to bed – being now very quiett in the house, which is a content to us.

6.   Up earely and went to Mr. Phillips's; but lost my labour, he lying at Huntington last night.   So I went back again and took horse and rode thither, where I stayed with Tho. Trice and Mr. Philips drinking till noone; and then Tho. Trice and I to Brampton, where he to Goody Gorums and I home to my father (who could decerne that I had been drinking, which he did never see or hear of before), so I eat a bit of dinner and went with him to Gorums and there talked with Tom. Trice.   And then I went and took horse for London; and with much ado, the ways being very bad, got to Baldwick and there lay and had a good supper by myself – the landlady being a pretty woman, but I darst not take notice of her, her husband being there.

Before supper I went to see the church, which is a very handsome church;[1] but I find that both here and everywhere else

---

1. St Mary the Virgin, with an interior mostly of the 14th century; 'a wealthy town church': N. Pevsner, *Buildings of Engl., Herts.*, p. 47.

that I come, the Quakers do still continue, and rather grow then lessen.[1]

To bed.

7. Called up at 3 a-clock and was a-horseback by 4. And as I was eating my breakfast, I saw a man riding by that rode a little way with me upon the road last night; so I called to him, and he being going with a venison in his panyards to London, I called him in and did give him his breakfast with me. And so we went together all the way. At Hatfield we bayted and walked into the great House through all the Courts; and I would fain have stolen a pretty dog that fallowed me, but I could not, which troubled me.

To horse again; and by degrees, with much ado got to London; where I find all well at home and at my father's and my Lady's. But no news yet from my Lord where he is.

At my Lady's (whither I went with Deane Fuller, who came to my house to see me just as I was come home) I met with Mr. Moore, who told me at what a loss he was for me, for tomorrow is a Seale day[2] at the Privy Seale; and it being my month, I am to wait upon my Lord Roberts, Lord privy=Seale, at the Seale. Home and to bed.

8. earely in the morning to White-hall; but my Lord Privy Seale came not all the morning. At noon Mr. Moore and I to the Wardrobe to dinner – where my Lady and all merry and well. Back again to the Privy Seale; but my Lord comes not all the afternoon – which made me mad and gives all the world reason to talk of his delaying of businesse[3] – as well as of his Severity and ill using the Clerkes of the Privy Seale. In the evening I took Monsieur Eschar and Mr. Moore and Dr. Pierce's brother (the Souldier) to the taverne next the Savoy and there

1. Joseph Besse records a meeting at Baldock in 1661 and others elsewhere in the county: *Collections of sufferings* (1753), vol. i, ch. xvii. 'Many hundreds' gathered at Baldock in 1668 to hear George Fox: Fox, *Journal* (ed. Penney), ii. 119.

2. A public sealing day: see below, p. 150. In the 18th century they were

held weekly: Sir H. Maxwell Lyte, *Hist. notes on Great Seal*, p. 39. Cf. the 'public seal' held by the Chancellor: above, i. 226.

3. Cf. Clarendon (*Life*, ii. 23): 'To shew his extraordinary talent, [Robartes] found a way more to obstruct and puzzle business . . . than any man in that office had ever done before.'

stayed and drank with them. Here I met with Mr. Mage; and discoursing of Musique, Monsieur Eschar spoke so much against the English and in praise of the French[1] that made him mad, and so he went away. After a stay with them a little longer, we parted and I home.

9. To the office, where word is brought me by a Son-in-law of Mr. Pierce the Purser that his father is a-dying and that he desires that I would come to him before he dies. So I rise from the table and went, where I found him not so ill as I thought, but he hath been ill. So I did promise to be a friend to his wife and family if he should die, which was all he desired of me. But I do believe he will recover.

Back again to the office, where I find Sir G. Carteret had a day or two ago invited some of the officers to dinner today at Dept-ford.[2] So at noon, when I heard that he was a-coming, I went out, because I would see whether he would send to me or no to go with them. But he did not, which doth a little trouble*a* me till I see how it comes to pass. Although in other things, I am glad of it, because of my going again today to the Privy Seale.

I dined at home; and having dined, news is brought by Mr. Hater[3] that his wife is now falling into labour; so he is come for my wife, who presently went with him.

I to White-hall; where after 4 a-clock comes my Lord Privy Seale and so we went up to his chamber over the Gate[4] at White-hall, where he asked me what deputacion I had from my Lord; I told him none, but that I am sworne my Lord's deputy by both the Secretarys,[5] which did Satisfye him. So he caused Mr. Moore to read over all the bills,[6] as is the manner, and all ended very well – so that I still see the Lyon is not so fierce as he is painted.

That being done, Monsieur Eschar (who all this afternoon hath been waiting at the Privy Seale for the warrant for 5000*l* for

a l.h. repl. s.h. 'till'

---

1. Cf. above, i. 298, n. 1. (E).

2. Carteret, as Treasurer of the Navy, had an official residence there: *Cat.*, 1. 22.

3. Tom Hayter, one of Pepys's two clerks.

4. The main entry gate into the palace. (R).

5. See above, i. 206.

6. The privy seal bills authorising the issue of instruments under the Great Seal.

my Lord of Sandwich's preparacion for Portugall)[1] and I took some wine with us and went to visitt *la belle* Pierce.[2] Who we find very big with child, and a pretty lady, one Mrs. Clifford, with her; where we stayed and were extraordinary merry. From thence I took Coach to my father's, where I find him come home this day from Brampton (as I expected) very well. And after some discourse about business and it being very late, I took Coach again home – where I hear by my wife that Mrs. Hater is not yet delivered, but continues in her pains.

So to bed.

10. This morning came the mayde that my wife hath lately hired for a Chamber=mayd. She is very ugly, so that I cannot care for her; but otherwise she seems very good.[3] But however, she doth come about three weeks hence, when my wife comes back from Brampton, if she do go with my mother.

By and by came my father to my house; and so he and I went and find out my Uncle Wight at the Coffee-house and there did agree with him to meet the next week with my Uncle Thomas and read over the Captains Will[4] before them both, for their satisfaccion.

Having done with him, I went to my Lady's and dined with her; and after dinner took the two young Gentlemen and the two ladies[5] and carried them and Captain Ferrer to the Theatre and showed them *The Merry divell of Edmunton*,[6] which is a very merry play, the first time I ever saw it, which pleased me well: and that being done, I took them all home by Coach to my house

---

1. The warrant is listed in PRO, Index 6751, n.p., *sub* August. Cf. also *CSPD 1661-2*, p. 59; *CTB*, i. 267.

2. Elizabeth, wife of James Pearse, naval surgeon. Her good looks always impressed Pepys, though he was later horrified to discover that she used paint: below, 16 September 1667. To James Yonge, another naval surgeon, who saw her in 1678, she was 'a miracle of her sex', looking not a day over 20 despite having had 19 children. He wrote of her com-

plexion as 'florid and pure red without paint, so smooth and plump . . .': *Journal* (ed. Poynter), p. 156.

3. This was Doll: but see below, p. 174 & n. 3.

4. Robert Pepys of Brampton had been a captain in the Huntingdonshire militia until 1659.

5. Lady Sandwich's children.

6. A comedy of unknown authorship, popular at the Globe in 1604, and published in 1608; now at the TR, Vere St. (A).

and there gave them fruit to eat and wine. So by water home with them; and so home myself.

11. ⟨*Lords day*⟩
To our own church in the forenoon; and in the afternoon to Clerkenwell church,¹ only to see the two fayre Botelers; and I happened to be placed in the pew where they afterwards came to sit. But the pew by their coming being too full, I went out into the next and there sat and had my full view of them; but I am out of conceit now with them, Collonell Dillon being come back from Ireland again and doth still court them and comes to church with them, which makes me think they are not honest.* Thence to Grayes Inn walks and there stayed a good while – where I met with Ned Pickering, who told me what a great match of hunting of a Stagg the King had yesterday; and how the King tired all their horses and came home with not above two or three able to keep pace with him.² So to my father's and there supped, and so home.

12. At the office this morning. At home in the afternoon, and had notice that my Lord Hinchingbrooke is fallen ill – which I fear is with the fruits that I did give them on Saturday last at my house.³ So in the evening I went thither and there find him very ill, and in great fear of the small-pox. I supped with my Lady and did consult about him, but we find it best to let him lie where he doth; and so I went home with my heart full of trouble for my Lord Hinchingbrooke's sickness, and more for my Lord Sandwich's himself; whom we are now confirmed is sick

---

1. St James-the-Less. (R).
2. For Charles II's interest in hunting and his prowess at riding (he had been well taught by the Marquess of Newcastle), see 'Sabretache' (A. S. Barrow), *Monarchy and the chase*, pp. 87–96. He won several horse-races at Newmarket.
3. Some fevers, as well as colic, were attributed to the eating of fruit. 'In Summer time crude Humors

breed . . . by eating of fruits, and over-much drinking [which] being mixed with Choller, do breed bastard Tertians': L. Riverius, *The practice of physick* . . . (1672), p. 580. The sale of certain fruits was forbidden in London during plague-time: C. Hole, *Engl. home-life, 1500–1800*, p. 13. See also *Priv. Corr.*, ii. 63, 85; Burton's *Anat. of melancholy* (ed. Shilleto), i. 253–4; ii. 29.

ashore at Alicante[1] – who if he should miscarry, God knows in what a condition would his family be.

I dined today with my Lord Crew, who is now at Sir H. Wrights while his new house[2] is making fit for him. And he is much troubled also at these things.

13. To the privy Seale in the morning. Then to the Wardrobe to dinner, where I met my wife and find my young Lord very ill. So my Lady intends to send her other three Sons, Sidney, Oliver, and John, to my house, for fear of the small-pox. After dinner I went to my father's, where I find him within and went up to him; and there find him settling his papers against his removall, and I took some old papers of difference between me and my wife and took them away.[3] After that, Pall being there, I spoke to my father about my intention not to keep her longer for such and such reasons; which troubled him and me also, and had like to have come to some high words between my mother and me, who is become a very simple woman.

By and by comes in Mrs. Cordery to take her leave of my father, thinking that he was to go presently into the country – and will have us to come and see her before he doth go.

Then my father and I went forth to Mr. Rawlinsons; where afterward comes my uncle Tho. and his two sons and then my uncle Wight, by appointment of us all; and there we read the Will and told them how things[a] are and what our thoughts are of kindness to my Uncle Tho if he doth carry himself peaceably; but otherwise if he persist to keep his Caveat up against us. So he promised to withdraw it, and seemed to be very well contented with things as they are.

After a while drinking, wc paid all and parted; and so I home and there find my Lady's three sons come, of which I am glad that I am in condition to do her and my Lord any service in this kind.

a repl. ? 'accounts'

---

1. Sandwich had been ashore at Alicante (on the s.-e. coast of Spain) from 12 to 19 July, suffering from a high fever: Sandwich, p. 90.
2. In Lincoln's Inn Fields: he was moving to the house next door. (R).
3. The papers have not survived, and nothing is known of any such 'difference' except the fact that Pepys and his wife separated temporarily sometime during the early years of their marriage, she going to live with 'friends' (?relatives) at Charing Cross: below, iv. 277.

but my mind is yet very much troubled about my Lord of Sandwichs health, which I am afeared of.

14. This morning Sir W. Batten and Sir W. Penn and I waited upon the Duke of Yorke in his Chamber, to give him an account of the condition of the Navy for lack of money and how our own very bills are offered upon the Exchange to be sold at 20 in the 100 loss.[1] He is much troubled at it, and will speak to the King and Council of it this morning.[2]

And*a* so I went to my Lady's and dined with her, and find my Lord Hinchingbrooke somewhat better.

After dinner Captain Ferrer and I to the Theatre and there saw *The Alchymist*;[3] and there I saw Sir W. Penn, who took us when the play was done and carried the Captain to Pauls and set him down, and me home with him; and he and I to the Dolphin but not finding Sir W. Batten there, we went and carried a bottle of wine to his house and there sat a while and talked; and so home to bed.

At home I find a letter from Mr. Creed of the 15 of July last, that tells me that my Lord is rid of his pain (which was Wind got into the Muscles of his right side) and his feaver, and is now in hopes to go aboard in a day or two; which doth give me mighty great comfort.

15. To the Privy Seale and White-hall, up and down; and at noon Sir W. Penn carried me to Pauls; and so I walked to the Wardrobe and dined with my Lady, and there told her of my Lord's sicknesse (of which, though it hath been the towne-talk this fortnight, she hath heard nothing)[4] and recovery, of which she was glad – though hardly persuaded of the latter. I find my Lord Hinchingbrooke better and better, and the worst past.

a At the beginning of this paragraph, half a line is so effectively crossed out that only a few l.h. words ('Sir W.P.', 'P'.) are now legible.

---

1. At the end of the month they stood at 10% discount: below, p. 168.
2. Presumably a committee meeting; the Council itself did not meet this day. A statement of the navy debts at the end of the year revealed a deficit of £374,000: below, p. 241.
3. See above, p. 125 & n. 1. (A).
4. She was about to give birth to a child: below, p. 159.

Thence to the Opera, which begins again today with *The Witts*,[1] never acted yet with Scenes; and the King and Duke and Duchesse was there (who dined today with Sir H. Finch, Reader at the Temple, in great state);[2] and endeed, it is a most excellent play – and admirable Scenes.

So home; and was overtaken by Sir W. Penn in his Coach, who hath been this afternoon with my Lady Batten &c at the Theatre.

So I fallowed them to the Dolphin, where Sir W. Batten was, and there we sat awhile; and so home – after we had made shift to fudle Mr. Falconer of Woolwich.

So home.

16. At the office all the morning, though little to be done because all our Clerkes are gone to the buriall of Tom. Whitton, one of the Controllers Clerkes, a very ingenious and a likely young man to live as any in the office. But it is such a sickly time, both in City and country everywhere (of a sort of fever) that never was heard of almost, unless it was in a plague-time.[3]

Among others, the famous Tom. Fuller[4] is dead of it – and Dr. Nichols,[5] Deane of Pauls; and my Lord Generall Monke is very dangerous ill.

Dined at home with the Children and were merry, and my father with me – who after dinner, he and I went forth about

1. A comedy by Davenant, first acted in 1634 and published in 1636. The cast listed by Downes (p. 21) includes Betterton as 'the elder *Pallatine*', Harris as 'the younger Pallatine', Underhill as Sir Morglay Thwack, and Mrs Davenport as Lady Ample. The 'Opera' was the new theatre in Lincoln's Inn Fields which made use of moveable painted scenery: cf. above, p. 131, n. 2. (A).

2. Sir Heneage Finch, Solicitor-General, was Treasurer and autumn Reader of the Inner Temple (4–17 August). The dinner is described in Sir W. Dugdale, *Origines Juridiciales* (1680), pp. 157–8. The King had sent venison for it: M. H. Nicolson

(ed.), *Conway Letters*, p. 189. The costliness of these feasts was one of the reasons for the abandonment c. 1680 of public readings: R. North, *Life of . . . Guilford* (1742), pp. 74–6; Sir W. Holdsworth, *Hist. Engl. law*, vi. (1924), pp. 491–2.

3. According to the bills of mortality, 3490 deaths from fever occurred this year in London: C. Creighton, *Hist. epidemics in Brit.*, i. 576. Cf. above, p. 131 & n. 4; below, iii. 10.

4. Author of the *Worthies*: he died this day at his lodgings in Covent Garden.

5. Matthew, brother of Sir Edward Nicholas, Secretary of State; he had died on the 15th.

business.   Among other things, we found out Dr. John Williams at an alehouse, where we stayed till past 9 at night, in Shooe-lane, talking about our country business; and I find him so well acquainted with the matters of Gravely that I expect he will be of great use to me.   So by link home.   I understand my aunt Fenner is upon the poynt of death.

17.   At the Privy Seale, where we had a Seale this morning.[1] Then met with Ned Pickering and walked with him into St. James parke (where I have not been a great while); and there find great and very noble alteracions.[2]   And in our discourse he was very forward to complain and to speak loud of the lewdnesse and beggary of the Court;[3] which I am sorry to hear and which I am afeared will bring all to ruine again.   So he and I to the Wardrobe to dinner.   And after dinner Captain Ferrers and I to the Opera and saw *The Witts* again, which I like exceedingly. The Queen of Bohemia was here, brought by my Lord Craven.[4]

So the Captain and I and another to the Divell tavern and drank; and so by coach home – troubled in mind that I cannot bring myself to mind my business, but to be so much in love with plays.

We have been at a great loss a great while for a vessell that I sent about a month ago with things of my Lord's to Lynne and cannot[a] till now hear of them; but now we are told that they are put into Soale bay, but to what purpose I know not.

18.   *Lords day*.   To our owne church in the morning; and so

---

a repl. 'cart'

---

1. Probably a private seal-day, at which beneficiaries were charged more than at the public seal mentioned above, at 7 and 9 August.

2. Cf. above, i. 246 & n. 2. Short descriptions in Monconys, ii. 14; Mundy, v. 155–6.

3. Pickering's brother, Sir Gilbert, had been Lord Chamberlain to both Oliver and Richard Cromwell. His testimony here, though tainted, is true.

4. William, 1st Earl of Craven, was the lifelong champion and benefactor of Elizabeth, 'Winter-Queen' of Bohemia. From the time of her arrival in England in May 1661 until shortly before her death in the follow-ing February, she lived as his guest at his house in Drury Lane. The story that they were secretly married is unfounded.

home to dinner, where my father and Dr. Tom. Pepys came to me to dine – and were very merry. After dinner I took my wife and Mr. Sidny to my Lady to see my Lord Hinchingbrooke, who is now pretty well again – and sits up and walks about his chamber.

So I went to White-hall and there hear that my Lord Generall Monke continues very ill. So I went to *la belle* Pearse and sat with her; and then to walk in St. James parke and saw great variety of fowle which I never saw before.[1] And so home.

At night fell to read in Hookers *Ecclesiastical policy*, which Mr. Moore did give me last Wednesday, very handsomely bound; and which I shall read with great pains and love for his sake.[2]

So to supper and to bed.

19. At the office all the morning. At noon the children are sent for by their mother, my Lady Sandwich, to dinner, and my wife goes along with them by coach; and she to my father's and dines there and from thence with them to see Mrs. Cordery, who doth invite them before my father goes into the country; and thither I should have gone too, but that I am sent for to the Privy Seale: and there I find a thing of my Lord Chancellors[3] to be sealed this afternoon and so I am forced to go to Worcester-house, where several Lords are met in council this afternoon. And while I am waiting there, in comes the King in a plain common riding-suit and velvet capp, in which he seemed a very

1. The modern Birdcage Walk preserves the memory of this aviary, which was greatly extended, if not founded, by Charles II. Most of the birds were water-birds living on the ponds or in a decoy; others – e.g. the exotic varieties presented by the E. India Company – were kept in a 'poultry-house'. In 1661 there were parrots and cassowaries; in 1663 pelicans, Indian ducks, Muscovy ducks and white crows. Descriptions in Mundy, v. 156–8 [1663]; Monconys, ii. 22–3, 58 [1663]; Evelyn, 9 February 1665; Magalotti, p. 168 [1669]. For its history, see Sir William Foster, *John Company*,

pp. 89–90. Cf. Marvell, *The Kings vowes*, ll. 52–4 (q.v. above, i. 126, n. 1); *CTB*, i. 262; *CSPVen. 1661–4*, p. 250.

2. Cf. above, p. 128 & n. 2. Pepys retained the 1666 edition: PL 2499. This also is 'very handsomely bound', possibly in the style of Moore's, in black morocco, with gilt-panelled covers and an unusually large number of bands on the spine.

3. Dockets for two grants made to Clarendon were issued on the 17th – one of Cornbury Park, Oxon., and the other of the offices of Bailiff and Ranger of Whichwood Forest, Oxon.: *CSPD 1661–2*, pp. 65, 66.

ordinary man to one that had not known him. Here I stayed, till at last hearing that my Lord Privy Seale hath not the seal here, Mr. Moore and I hired a coach and went to Chelsy and there at an alehouse sat and drank and passed the time till my Lord Privy Seale came to his house;[1] and so we to him and examined and sealed the thing, and so homewards; but when we came to look for our coach, we find it gone, so we were fain to walk home afoot and saved our money.

We met with a companion that walked with us; and coming among some trees near the neate-houses,[2] he begun to whistle, which did give us some suspicion; but it proved that he that answered him was Mr. Marsh (the Lutenist)[3] and his wife; and so we all walked to Westminster together, in our way drinking a while at my cost; and had a song of him, but his voice is quite lost.

So walked home; and there I find that my Lady doth keep the children at home and lets them not come any more hither at present – which a little troubles me, to lose their company. This day my aunt Fenner dyed.

20. At the office in*a* the morning. And all the afternoon at home to put my papers in order. This day we came to some agreement with Sir R. Ford for his house to be added to the office to enlarge our Quarters.[4]

21. This morning by appointment ⟨I went to⟩ my father, and*b* after a morning draught, he and I went to Dr. William's; but he not within, we went to Mrs. Terry, a daughter of Mr. Wheately's, who lately offered a proposal of her sister for a wife for my brother Tom; and with her we discoursed about and agreed to go to her mother's this afternoon to speak with her. And in the meantime went to Wll. Joyces, and to an alehouse and drank a good while together – he being very angry that his

a repl. 'again'   *b* repl. 'came to me'

---

1. Danvers House: see below, pp. 187–8.
2. Market-gardeners' houses and houses of entertainment on the river-bank opposite Vauxhall. (R).

3. Alphonso Marsh, Gentleman or the Chapel Royal, and lutenist and singer in the King's service. (E).
4. See above, p. 143 & n. 4.

father Fenner will give him and his brother no more for mourning then their father did give him and my aunt at their mother's death. And a very troublesome fellow I still find him to be – that his company ever wearys me.

From hence about 2 a-clock to Mrs. Wheately's, but she being going to dinner, we went to White-hall and there stayed till past 3. And here I understand by Mr. Moore that my Lady Sandwich is brought to bed yesterday of a young Lady[1] and is very well.

So to Mrs. Wheatly again and there were well received; and she desirous to have the thing go forward; only, is afeared that her daughter is too young and portion not big enough, but offers 200*l* down with her. The girl is very well favoured, and a very child; but modest, and one I think[a] will do very well for my brother.[2] So parted till she hears from Hatfield from her husband, who is there. But I find them very desirous of it, and so am I.

Thence home to my father's; and I to the Wardrobe, where I supped with the ladies and hear their mother is well and the young child; and so home.

22. To the Privy Seale and sealed. So home at noon and there took my wife by coach to my Uncle Fenners; where there was, both at his house and the Sessions,[3] great deal of company, but poor entertainment, which I wonder at. And the house so hot that my Uncle Wight, my father and I were fain to go out and stay at an alehouse awhile to cool ourselves. Then back again and to church,[4] my father's family being all in mourning, doing him the greatest honour, the world believing[b] that he did give us it.

a MS. 'thing'   *b* repl. 'how'

1. Named Catherine (after the new Queen whom her father was now to bring over from Portugal); tenth child and fourth daughter.

2. This proposal was still alive two years later, but came to nothing. Wheatley appears to have been a tradesman and may have been a distant relative of Pepys.

3. The Sessions House, in the Old Bailey, where the family had presumably hired accommodation for the funeral.

4. St Sepulchre-without-Newgate, where Aunt Fenner was buried in the church.

So to church and stayed out the sermon; and then with my aunt Wight, my wife, and Pall and I, to her house by coach. And there stayed and supped upon a Westphalia ham; and so home and to bed.

23. This morning I went to my father's and there find him and my mother in a discontent, which troubles me much. And endeed, she is become very simple and unquiet. Hence he and I to Dr. Williams, and find him within – there we sat and talked a good while; and from him to Tom. Trices to an alehouse near and there sat and talked; and finding him fair – we examined my Uncles Will before him and Dr. Williams, and had them sign the*a* Copy; and so did give T. Trice the Originall to prove; so he took my father and I to one of the Judges of the Court,[1] and there we were Sworne; and so back again to the alehouse and drank, and parted.

Dr. Williams and I to a Cookes, where we eat a bit of mutton and away – I to W. Joyces, where by appointment my wife was; and I took her to the Opera and showed her *The Witts* (which I had seen already twice)[2] and was most highly pleased with it.

So with my wife to the Wardrobe to see my Lady; and then home.

24. At the office in the morning and did business. By and by we are called to Sir W. Battens to see the strange creature that Captain Holmes hath brought with him from Guiny; it is a great baboone, but so much like a man in most things, that (though they say there is a Species of them) yet I cannot believe but that it is a monster got of a man and she-baboone.[3] I do believe it already understands much english; and I am of the mind it might be tought to speak or make signs.

Hence the Comptroller and I to Sir Rd. Fords and viewed

a repl. 'it'

---

1. The Archbishop's Prerogative Court, where the will was proved this day before Dr William Merick. Tom Trice was an advocate of the Court. He had withdrawn his caveat, presumably after the discussion on 21 July. For the dispute, see above, p. 134 & n. 2.

2. On 15 and 17 August. (A).

3. Robert Holmes had in July returned from W. Africa. The creature was presumably a chimpanzee or gorilla. Stories about miscegenation were common.

the house again; and are come to a complete end with him, to give him 200 per annum for it.

Home; and there met Captain Isham[1] enquiring for me to take his leave of me, he being upon his voyage to Portugall, and for my letters to my Lord – which are not ready. But I took him to the Miter and gave him a glass of sack, and so Adieu. And then I straight to the Opera and there saw *Hamlet Prince of Denmarke*, done with Scenes very well.[2] But above all, Batterton did the Prince's part beyond imagination.[3]

Thence homeward, and met with Mr. Spong and took him to the Sampson in Pauls churchyard and there stayed till late; and it rained hard, so we were fain to get home wet. And so to bed.

25. *Lords=day.* At church in the morning; and dined at home alone with my wife very comfortably; and so again to church with her, and had a very good and pungent sermon of Mr. Mills concerning the necessity of Restitucion.[4]

Home, and I find my Lady*a* Batten and her daughter to look something askew upon my wife, because my wife doth not buckle to them and is not sollicitous for their acquaintance, which I am not troubled at at all.

By and by comes in my father (he intends to go into [the] country tomorrow); and he and I, among other discourse, at last called Pall up to us and there in great anger told her before my father that I would keep her no longer; and my father, he said he

---

a repl. 'wife'

---

1. Henry Isham, a relative of Sandwich.

2. Shakespeare wrote his first version of this tragedy c. 1600, and a garbled edition was published in 1603. Better texts appeared in 1604, 1611 and 1623. What Pepys saw on this occasion (at the LIF) was an adaptation by Davenant, in which Shakespeare's text was severely cut and some of his diction changed for the worse. This adaptation was published in 1676. The cast listed by Downes (p. 21) includes Betterton as Hamlet, Lilliston as Claudius, Harris as Horatio, Mrs Davenport as Gertrude and Mrs Sanderson as Ophelia. (A).

3. Hamlet was one of Betterton's greatest interpretations. There is an eye-witness description of it in Colley Cibber's *Apology*, ch. iv. Downes claims (p. 21) that Betterton's interpretation derived, *via* Davenant, from Joseph Taylor, who was 'instructed by the author *Mr. Shakespear*', which may be true, though Taylor did not join the King's Men until 1619, three years after the death of Shakespeare. (A).

4. Cf. Acts, iii. 21.

would have nothing to do with her.   At last, after we had brought down her high spirit, I got my father to yield that she should go into the country with my mother and him and stay there a while, to see how she will demean herself.   That being done, my father and I to my Uncle Wights and there supped, and he took his leave of them.   And so I walked with [him] as far as Pauls and there parted, and I home – my mind at some rest upon this making an end with Pall, who doth trouble me exceedingly.

26.   This morning before I went out I made even with my mayd Jane, who hath this day been my maid three yeares and is this day to go into the country to her mother.[1]   The poor girl cried, and I could hardly forbear weeping to think of her going; for though she be grown lazy and spoiled by Palls coming, yet I shall never have one to please us better in all things, and so harmlesse, while I live.   So I paid her her wages and gave her 2s-6d over, and bade her Adieu[a] – with my mind full of trouble for her going.

Thence to my father;   where he and I and Tho. together, setting things even[2] and casting up my father's account;   and upon the whole, I find that all he hath in money of his owne due to him in the world is but 45l.;   and he owes about the same Summ.   So that I cannot but think in what a condition had he left my mother if he should have died before my Uncle Robt. ⟨Hence to Tom. Trice for the probate of the Will and had it done to our minds;   which did give my father and me good content.⟩[b]

From hence to my Lady's at the Wardrobe and dined;   and thence to the Theatre and saw *The Antipodes*,[3] wherein there is much mirth but no great matter else.

Thence with Mr. Bostock, whom I met there (a clerk formerly

a repl. symbol rendered illegible   *b* addition crowded between paragraphs

---

1. Jane Birch twice returned to Pepys's service, in March 1662, for almost a year, and in March 1666, until in 1669 she married his man-servant, Tom Edwards. She always remained a favourite with the Pepyses.

2. An inventory of the goods left in the house in Salisbury Court on loan by John Pepys, sen., to his son Thomas is in Rawl. A 182, f.311r in the hand of Thomas Pepys; dated 25 August, and witnessed by Pepys and William Hewer; (printed in *Family Letters*, pp. 13–15).

3. A comedy by Richard Brome, first acted in 1638 and published in 1640. (A).

of Mr. Phelps's)[1] to the Divell tavern and there drank; and so away, I to my uncle Fenners, where my father was with him at an alehouse. And so we three went by ourselfs and sat talking a great while about a brokers daughter that he doth propose for a wife for Tom, with a great portion; but I fear it will not take, but he will do what he can. So we broke up; and going through the street, we met with a mother and some friends of my father's man Ned's, who are angry at my father's putting him away – which troubled me and my father, but all will be well as to that.

We have news this morning of my Uncle Tho. and his son Tho being gone into the country without giving notice thereof to anybody; which puts us to a stand, but I fear them not.

At night at home I find a letter from my Lord Sandwich, who is now very well again of his feaver but not yet gone from Alicante, where he lay sick and was twice let blood;[2] his letter dated the 22. July. last – which puts me out of doubt of his being ill. In[a] my coming home, I called in at the Three Crane tavern at the Stockes by appointment, and there met and took leave of Mr. Fanshaw,[3] who goes tomorrow, and Captain Isham, toward their voyage to Portugall. Here we drank a great deal of wine, I too much and Mr. Fanshaw till he could hardly go. So we took leave one of another.

27. This morning to the Wardrobe and there took leave of my Lord Hinchingbrooke and his brother and saw them go out by Coach toward Rye in their way to France; whom God blesse.[4] Then I was called up to my Lady's bedside, where we talked an houre about Mr. Edwd. Mountagus disposing of the 5000*l* for my Lord's preparation for Portugall, and our fears that he will not do it to my Lord's honour, and less to his profit; which I am to enquire a little after.

a preceded by '27' in margin crossed out

1. In the Exchequer.
2. Pepys's reply (29 August) is in Carte 73, f.585*r* (printed in *Letters*, pp. 20-1) and refers to Sandwich's letters from Alicante of 22 and 28 July. For Sandwich s illness, see above, p. 153, n. 1.
3. Lyonel Fanshawe, secretary to his cousin Sir Richard Fanshawe, now

going to Lisbon to prepare for the visit of Sandwich, who was to bring Charles II's bride to England.
4. Cf. above, p. 114 & n. 1. The Abbé Walter Mountagu (who was to take charge of them in France) had sent a man to conduct them on the journey: Carte 73, f.581*r*.

Thence to the office and there sat till noon. And then my wife and I by Coach to my Cosen Tho. Pepys the Executor[1] to dinner; where some ladies and my father and mother – where very merry; but methinks he makes but poor dinners for such guests, though there was a poor venison=pasty.[2]

Thence my wife and I to the Theatre and there saw *The Joviall Crew*,[3] where the King, Duke and Duchesse, and Madam Palmer were; and my wife, to her great content, had her full sight of them all, all the while. The play full of mirth. Thence to my father's and there stayed to talk a while; and so by foot home by mooneshine.

In my way and at home, my wife making a sad story to me of her brother Balty's condition, and would have me to do something for him; which I shall endeavour to do, but am afeared to meddle therein for fear I shall not be able to wipe my hands of him again when I once concern myself for him.[4] I went to bed, my wife all the while telling me his case with teares, which troubled me.

28. At home all the morning, setting papers in order. At noon to the Change and there met with Dr Williams by appointment and with him went up and down to look for an atturny, a friend of his, to advise with about our bond of my Aunt Pepys's of 200*l*;[5] and he tells me absolutely that we shall not be forced to pay interest for the money; yet I do doubt it very much. I spent the whole afternoon drinking with him – and so home. ⟨This day I counterfeited a letter to Sir W. Pen, as from the thiefe that stole his tankard lately, only to abuse and laugh at him.⟩[a]

---

a addition crowded into end of line

---

1. A Westminster business man. From here onwards in the diary he is often given this title to distinguish him from the other Thomas Pepyses. Possibly he was made executor of one or more of Pepys's early wills. After 1663, when he moved to Hatcham, Surrey, he is also called 'Hatcham Pepys'.

2. On 5 January 1660 he had served to his guests a venison pasty which was 'palpable beef': above, i. 9.

3. See above, p. 141 & n. 1. (A).

4. Balthasar St Michel seems to have been feckless and improvident at this time, although in Pepys's opinion he improved later. Pepys had him appointed muster-master in 1666, and he rose in the service of the navy to become Commissioner at Deptford and Woolwich, 1686–8.

5. See above, p. 134, n. 2.

29. At the office all the morning. And at noon my father, mother, and my aunt Bell (the first time that ever she was at my house) came to dine with me; and did and were very merry. After dinner the two women went to visit my aunt Wight, &c., and my father*a* about other business; and I abroad to my bookeseller and there stayed till 4 a-clock; at which time by appointment I was to meet my father at my uncle Fenners. So thither I went, and with him to an alehouse; and then came Mr. Evans the Taylor, whose daughter we have a mind to get for a wife for Tom, and then my father. And there we sat a good while and talked about the business; in fine, he told us that he hath not to except against us or our motion, but that the estate that God hath blessed him with is too great to give where there is nothing in present possession but a trade and house. And so we friendly ended. Then parted, my father and I together, and walked a little way. And then at Holborne he and I took leave of one another, he being to go to Brampton (to settle things against my mother comes) tomorrow morning.

So I home.

30. At noon my wife and I met at the Wardrobe and there dined with the children; and after dinner up to my Lady's bed-side and talked and laughed a good while. Then my wife and I to Drury lane to the French Comedy,[1] which was so ill done and the Scenes and company and everything else so nasty and out of order and poor, that I was sick all the while in my mind to be there. Here my wife met with a son of my Lord Somersett whom she knew in France, a pretty [man];[2] but I showed him no great countenance, to avoyd further acquaintance. That done,

a MS. 'me another'

---

1. At the Cockpit Theatre, Drury Lane; probably *Le mariage d'orphée et d'Eurydice* (completed by Chapoton, 1648), presented by a French company under Jean Channoveau. This is the first record of a performance by foreign actors after the Restoration. W. J. Lawrence in *Eliz. Playhouse* (1912), pp. 139–40. Cf. Evelyn, iii. 306 & n. 5. (A).

2. This was probably Thomas, second son of Lord John Somerset, who was second son of the 1st Marquess of Worcester, the wealthy royalist. Elizabeth Pepys as a young girl had lived in Paris, c. 1648–53.

there being nothing pleasant but the foolery of the Farce,¹ we went home.

31. At home and the office all the morning; and at noon comes Luellin to me and he and I to the taverne, and after that to Bartlemew faire;² and there, upon his motion, to a pitiful ale-house, where we had a dirtyᵃ slut or two come up that were whores; but my very heart went against them, so that I took no pleasure but a great deal of trouble at being there and getting from thence, for fear of being seen.   From thence he and I walked toward Ludgate and parted.   I back again to the fair all alone and there met with my ladies Jémimah and Paulina, with Mr. Pickering and Madamoiselle,³ at seeing the Monkys dance, which was much to see what they could be brought to do; but it troubledᵇ me to sit among such nasty company.   After that, with them into Christs: Hospitall, and there Mr. Pickering bought them some fairings and I did give every of them a bauble, which was the little globes of glass with things hanging in them, which pleased the ladies very well.

After that, home with them in their Coach; and there was called up to my Lady, and she would have me stay to talk with her, which I did, I think a full houre.   And the poor lady did with so much innocency tell me how Mrs. Crispe had told her that she did entend, by means of a lady that lies at her house, to get the King to be godfather to theᶜ young lady that she is in childbed now of.⁴   But to see in what a manner my Lady told it me, protesting that she sweat in the very telling of it, was the

---

a repl. 'wench'   *b* MS. 'was troubled'   *c* repl. 'her'

---

1. A humorous playlet presented after the main entertainment. (A).

2. In W. Smithfield; at this time only an amusement fair and held for about a fortnight beginning on 23 August (St Bartholomew's Eve); reduced in the 1690s to its original length of three days; in disuse after the 1830s. See H. Morley, *Memoirs*

Barth. fair. Pepys, for all his love of shows, generally found it 'nasty' or 'dirty'. Cf. his remarks in a letter of 16 September 1692: *Priv. Corr.*, i. 62.

3. Mlle le Blanc, the young ladies' governess.

4. The King was not a godfather: below, p. 171.

greatest pleasure to me in the world, to see the simplicity and harmelessnesse of a lady.

Then down to supper with the ladies, and so home; Mr. Moore (as he and I cannot easily part) leading me as far as Fanchurch-street to the Miter, where we drank a glass of wine; and so parted and I home – and to bed.

———

Thus ends the month. My mayde Jane newly gone, and Pall left now to do all the work till another mayde comes; which shall not be till she goes away into the country with my mother.*a* Myself and wife in good health. My Lord Sandwich in the Straits and newly recovered of a great sickness at Alicante. My father gone to settle at Brampton. And myself under much business and trouble for to settle things in the estate to our content. But which is worst, I find myself lately too much given to seeing of plays and expense and pleasure, which makes me forget my business, which I must labour to amend.

No money comes in, so that I have been forced to borrow a great deal of money for my own expenses and to furnish my father, to leave things in order. I have some trouble about my Brother Tom, who is now left to keep my father's trade, in which I have great fears that he will miscarry – for want of brains and care.

at Court things are in very ill condition, there being so much æmulacion, poverty, and the vices of swearing, drinking, and whoring, that I know not what will be the end of it but confusion. And the Clergy so high,* that all people that I meet with, all do*b* protest against their practice.[1] In short, I see no content or satisfaccion anywhere in any one sort of people.

The Benevolence proves so little, and an occasion of so much discontent everywhere, that it had better it had never been set up.

a repl. 'father and'   *b* MS. 'to'

———

1. For anti-clerical feeling at this time, see the Commons' debates of July in *Parl. Hist.*, iv. 82+; P. Bar- wick, *Life of Dr J. Barwick* (1903 ed.), p. 177. Cf. below, iv. 372.

I think to subscribe 20*l*.[1] We are at our office quiet; only, for lack of money, all things go to wrack. Our very bills offered to be sold upon the Exchange at 10 per cent losse. We are upon getting Sir R. Fords house added to our office. But I see so many difficultys will fallow, in pleasing of one another in the dividing of it and in becoming bound personally to pay the rent of 200*l* per annum – that I do believe it will yet scarce come to pass.[2]

The season very sickly everywhere of strange and fatall feavers.[3]

1. For the grant of this 'free gift', see above, p. 111 & n. 4. There was some objection to it as unconstitutional, since the method had been condemned by the Petition of Right (1628). Moreover, Royalists accused Presbyterians of having voted it in order to impose on them the greater part of the burden: HMC, *Rep.*, 5/145, 203–4. In September the Treasurer complained that contributions from the city of London had been 'few and small': *CTB*, i. 286. By Michael-mas of this year it had produced only c. £47,000; in the end, two years later, contributions totalled c. £230,000: C. D. Chandaman, 'Engl. public revenue, 1660–88' (unpub. thesis, Univ. London, 1954), p. 401. The maximum Pepys could have contributed was £200. The diary has no record of his subscribing anything; nor have the (very incomplete) records of the tax in the PRO.

2. It did not; cf. below, iv. 319.

3. See above, p. 131, n. 4.

SEPTEMBER

1. *Lords=day*. Last night being very rainy, [the rain] broke into my house (the gutter being stopped) and spoiled all my ceilings almost. At church in the morning. And dined at home with my wife. After dinner to Sir W. Battens, where I find Sir W. Penn and Captain Holmes. Here we were very merry with Sir W. Penn about the loss of his tankard, though all be but a cheate and he doth not yet understand it. But the tankard was stole by Sir W. Batten, and the letters as from the thief wrote by me; which makes very good sport.

Here I stayed all the afternoon; and then Captain Holmes and I by Coach to White-hall. In our way, I find him by discourse to be a great friend of my Lord's, and told me that there was many did seek to remove him; but they were old Seamen, such as Sir J. Mennes[1] (but he would name no more, though I do believe Sir W. Batten) is one of them that do envy him; but he says he knows that the King doth so love him, and the Duke of York too, that there is no fear of him. He seems to be very well acquainted with the King's mind and with all the several faccions at Court, and spoke all with so much frankenesse that I do take him to be my Lord's good friend, and one able to do him great service, being a cunning fellow, and one (by his own confession to me) that canne*a* put on two several faces and look his enemies in the face with as much love as his friends. But good God, what an age is this and what a world is this, that a man cannot live without playing the knave and dissimulacion. At White-hall we parted; and I to Mrs. Pierces, meeting her and Madam Clifford in the street, and there stayed talking and laughing with them a good while; and so back to my mother's and there supped; and so home and to bed.

2. In the morning to my Cosen Tho. Pepys, Executor,[2] and there talked with him about my uncle Tho. his being in the country; but he could not advise me to anything therein, not

a l.h. repl. s.h. 'doth'

1. Cf. below, pp. 216–17.　　　2. See above, p. 164, n. 1.

knowing what the other hath done in the country; and so we parted.

And so to White-hall; and there my Lord Privy Seale, who hath been out of town this week, not being yet come, we can have no seal. And therefore, meeting with Mr. Battersby the apothecary in Fanchurch-street, to the Kings apothecary's chamber in White-hall and there drank a bottle or two of wine; and so he and I by water toward London. I landed at Black-fryers, and so to the Wardrobe and dined; and then back to White-hall with Captain Ferrers and there walked; and thence to Westminster-hall, where we met with Mr. Pickering; and so all of us to the Rhenish wine-house (Priors), where the master of the house is laying out some money in making a cellar with an arch in his yard, which is very convenient for him. Here we stayed a good while; and so Mr. Pickering and I to Westminster-hall again and there walked an houre or two, talking. And though he be a fool, yet he keeps much company and will tell all he sees or hears, and so a man may understand what the common talk of the towne is. And I find by him that there is endeavours to get my Lord out of play at sea, which I believe Mr. Coventry and the Duke do think will make them more absolute; but I hope, for all this, they will not be able to do it. He tells me plainly of the vices of the Court, and how the pox is as common there, and so I hear of all hands, that it is as common as eating and swearing. From him, by water to the bridge and then to the Miter, where I met my uncle and aunt Wight, come to see Mrs. Rawlinson (in her husband's absence out of town); and so I stayed with them and Mr. Lucas and other company, very merry; and so home – where my wife hath been busy all the day making of pies; and hath been abroad and bought things for herself, and tells me that she met at the change with my young ladies of the Wardrobe[1] and there helped them to buy things, and also with Mr.*ᵃ* Somersett,[2] who did give her a bracelet of rings; which did a little trouble me, though I know there is no hurt yet in it, but only for fear of further acquaintance.

So to bed. This night I sent another letter to Sir W. Penn to offer him the return of his tankard upon his leaving of 30s at a place where that should be brought – the issue which I am to expect.

a MS. 'Mrs.'

---

1. Sandwich's daughters.   2. See above, p. 165 & n. 2.

3. This day some of us Commissioners went down to Detford to pay off some ships, but I could not go – but stayed at home all the morning setting papers to right. And this morning Mr. Howell our turner sent me two things to file papers on, very handsome. Dined at home; and then with my wife to the Wardrobe, where my Lady's child was christened (my Lord Crew and his Lady and my Lady Mountagu, my Lord's mother-in-law,[1] were the witnesses), and named Katharine (the Queene=elect's name); but to my and all our trouble, the parson of the parish[2] christened her, and did not sign the child with the sign of the cross.[3] After that was done, we had a very fine banquet, the best I ever was at; and so (there being but very little company) we by and by broke up, and my wife and I to my mother – who I took a liberty to advise about her getting things ready to go this week into the country to my father; and she (being become nowadays very simple) took it very ill and we had a great deal of noise and wrangling about it. So home by coach.

4. In the morning to the Privy Seale to do some things of the last month's, my Lord Privy Seale having been some time out of towne. Then my wife came to me to White-hall and we went and walked a good while in St. James's parke to see the brave alterations;[4] and so to Wilkinsons the Cook's to dinner, where we sent for Mrs. Sarah[5] and there dined – and had oysters, the first I have eat this year, and were pretty good. After dinner, by agreement to visit Mrs. Symonds, but she is abroad, which I wonder at; and so missing her, my wife and I again to my mother's (calling at Mrs. Pierces, who we find brought to bed of a girl last night) and there stayed[a] and drank; and she resolves to be going tomorrow without fayle. Many friends came in to take their leave of her. But a great deal of stir I had again tonight about getting her to go to see my Lady Sandwich before she goes; which she says she will do tomorrow. So I home.

5. To the Privy Seale this morning about business – in my

a MS. 'state'

---

1. Lady (Ann) Mountagu, step-mother of the Earl of Sandwich.

2. [?John] Seabrook, Rector of St Andrew-by-the-Wardrobe.

3. Puritan parsons did not use the sign of the cross in baptism.

4. Cf. above, p. 156 & n. 2.

5. Sandwich's housekeeper.

way taking leave of my mother, who goes to Brampton today. But doing my business at the Privy Seale pretty soon, I took boat and went to my uncle Fenners; and there I find my mother and my wife and Pall (of whom I had this morning at my own house taken leave, and given her 20s. and good counsel how to carry herself to my father and mother); and so I took them, it being late, to Beards,[1] where they were stayed for; and so I put them into the Waggon and saw them going presently – Pall crying exceedingly. Then in with my wife, my aunt Bell and Charles Pepys, whom we met there, and drank; and so to my uncle Fenners to dinner (in my way meeting a French footman with feathers, who was in quest of my wife and spoke with her privately; but I could not tell what it was; only, my wife promised to go to some place tomorrow morning, which doth trouble my mind how to know whither it was), where both his sons and daughters were; and there we were merry and dined.

After dinner, news was brought that my aunt Kite, the buchers widow in London[2] is sick, ready to die; and sends for my uncle and I to come to take charge of things and to be entrusted with the care of her daughter. But I, through want of time to undertake such a business, I was taken up by Antony Joyce; which came at last to very high words, which made me very angry, and I did not think that he would ever have[a] been such a fool to meddle with other people's business, but I saw he spoke worse to his father then to me and therefore I bore it the better. But all the company was offended with him. So we parted angry, he and I; and so my wife and I to the fair,[3] and I showed her the Italian dancing the ropes and the women that do strange tumbling tricks. And so by foot home.

Vexed in my mind about Ant. Joyce.

6. This morning my uncle Fenner by appointment came and drank his morning draught with me; and from thence, he and I to see my aunt Kite (my wife holding her resolution to go this

a repl. ? 'is'

1. The Huntingdon carrier.
2. Julian Clarke, of Wentworth St, Stepney, widow of Elias (? Ellis) Clarke. Her first husband (d. 1652) had been William Kite, a White-

chapel butcher and brother of Pepys's mother.

3. Bartholomew Fair: see above, p. 166, n. 2.

morning as she resolved yesterday; and though there could not
be much hurt in it, yet my owne Jealousy put a hundred things
into my minde which did much trouble me all day); whom we
find in bed and not like to live as we think; and she told us her
mind was that if she should die, she did give all she had to her
daughter; only, 5*l* apiece to her second husbands children in case
they live to come out of their apprenticeships; and that if her
daughter should die before marriage, then 10*l*. to be divided
between Sarah Kites children, and the rest as her own daughter
shall dispose of it.   And this I set down, that I may be able to
swear, in case there should be occasion.[1]

From thence to an alehouse while it rained; which keeped us
there I think above two houres; and at last we were fain to go
through the rainy streets home, calling on his sister Utbert and
drank there.   Then I home to dinner all alone; and thence, my
mind being for my wife's going abroad much troubled and unfit
for business, I went to the Theatre and saw *Elder Brother*,[2] ill acted.
That done, meeting here with Sir G. Askue, and Sir Theoph.
Jones, and another Knight, with Sir W. Pen we to the Ship taverne
and there stayed and were merry till late at night; and so got a
coach and Sir Wm. and I home.   Where my wife hath been
long come home, but I seemed very angry, as endeed I am, and
did not all night show her any countenance, neither before nor in
bed; and so slept and rise discontented.

7.   At the office all the morning.   At noon Mr. Moore dined
with me; and then in comes Wll. Joyce to answer a letter of mine
I writ this morning to him about a mayde of his that my wife had
hired; and she sent us word that she was hired to stay longer
with her master.   Which mistake he came to clear himself of,
and I took it very kindly.   So I having appointed the young
ladies at the Wardrobe[3] to go with them to a play today, I left

1. She died on the 12th.   Her will
(7 September, proved 20 November)
is summarised in Whitear, p. 143:
Pepys was made an executor.   There
were three sons of her second marriage.   The daughter (of the first
marriage) was Margaret (Peg); Sarah
was a niece married to Thomas Giles.
2. A comedy by John Fletcher,

probably revised by Philip Massinger;
written c. 1625, published in 1637;
now at the TR, Vere St.   The cast
listed by Downes (p. 6) includes Burt
as Charles, Kynaston as Eustace, and
Mrs Rutter and Mrs Boutel as the
leading ladies.   (A).

3. Sandwich's daughters.

him and my brother Tom, who came along with him to dine; and my wife and I to them and took them to the Theatre, where we seated ourselfs close by the King and Duke of Yorke and Madam Palmer (which was great content; and endeed, I can never enough admire her beauty); and here was *Barthlemew fayre*, with the Puppet Shewe, acted today, which had not been these forty years (it being so satyricall against puritanisme, they durst not till now; which is strange they should already dare to do it, and the King to countenance it); but I do never a whit like it the better for the puppets, but rather the worse.[1]

Thence home with the ladies, it being, by reason of our staying a great while for the King's coming and the length of the play, near 9 a-clock[2] before it was done; and so in their Coach home and, still in discontent with my wife, to bed;[a] and rose so this morning also.

8. *Lords day.*[b]
To church, it being a very wet night last night and today. Dined at home. And so to church again with my wife in the afternoon. And coming home again, find our new mayde Doll asleep that she could not hear to let us in, so that we were fain to send the boy in at a window to open the door to us.[3]

So up to my chamber all alone. And troubled in mind to think how much of late I have addicted myself to expense and pleasure, that now I can hardly reclaime myself to look after my great business of settling Gravely business,[4] till it is now almost too late. I pray God give me grace to begin now to look after my business; but it always was, and I fear will ever be, my foible,

a MS. 'wife'   *b* followed by blot between lines

1. The puppet show in Act V of Ben Jonson's *Bartholomew Fair* ('The Modern history of Hero and Leander') had been omitted from the performances which Pepys had seen on 8 and 27 June 1661. In this production two of the Puritans in the play were made up to resemble Richard Baxter and Edmund Calamy, two leading Puritan divines. The King, the Earl of Manchester, and the Bishop of London attended a performance: see R. F. Bosher, *Making of Restoration settlement*, pp. 238-9. (A).

2. Most performances in public theatres were over before 6.30 p.m. (A).

3. She was dismissed on 27 November.

4. See above, p. 136.

that after I am once got behindhand with business, I am hard to set to it again to recover it.

In the evening I begun to look over my accounts; and upon the whole, I do find myself, by what I can yet see, worth near 600*l.*; for which God be blessed – which put me into great comfort. So to supper and bed.

9. To the Privy Seale in the morning, but my Lord did not come. So I went with Captain Morrice[1] at his desire into the King's Privy Kitchin to Mr. Sayres the Master-Cooke, and there we had a good slice of beef or two to our breakfast. And from thence he took us into the wine-cellar; where by my troth we were very merry, and I drank too much wine – and all along had great and perticular kindness from Mr. Sayre. But I drank so much wine that I was not fit for business; and therefore, at noon I went and walked in Westminster-hall a while; and thence to Salsbury Court play-house, where was acted the first time *Tis pitty shee's a Whore* – a simple* play and ill acted;[2] only, it was my fortune to sit by a most pretty and most ingenious lady, which pleased me much.

Thence home and find Sir Wms. both, and much more company, gone to the Dolphin to drink the 30*s.* that we got the other day of Sir W. Pen about his tankard. Here was Sir R. Slingsby, Holmes, Captain Allen, Mr. Turner, his wife and daughter – my Lady Batten and Mrs. Martha &c. and an excellent company of fidlers; so we exceeding merry, till late. And then we begun to tell Sir W. Penn the business; but he hath been drinking today and so is almost gone that we could not make him understand it, which caused us more sport. But so much the better; for I believe when he doth come to understand it, he will be angry;

1. Robert Morris, Upholsterer-Extraordinary to the King's Household.

2. As Davenant had transferred his troupe, the Duke of York's Company, from the Salisbury Court Theatre to his new playhouse in Lincoln's Inn Fields in June (see above, p. 130), the performance seen by Pepys on this occasion may have been given by a company under the management of George Jolly, a veteran actor to whom the King had given a licence for the organisation of performances in September 1660. This licence was subsequently revoked, leaving Davenant and Thomas Killigrew with a clear monopoly of professional performances in London. The play was the tragedy by John Ford, written c. 1629, and published in 1633. (A).

he hath so talked of the business himself and the letters, up and down, that he will be ashamed to be found abused in it. So home and to bed.

10. At the office all the morn. Dined at home. Then my wife into Woodstreet to buy a chest; and thence to buy other things at my uncle Fenners[1] (though by reason of rain, we had ill walking); thence to my brother Toms and there discoursed with him about business; and so to the Wardrobe to see my Lady and after supper with the young ladies, bought a linke and carried it myself till I met one that would light me home for the link. So he light me home with his own, and then I did give him mine. This night I find Mary, my Cosen W. Joyces maid, come to me to be my Cooke mayde; and so my house is full again.[2]

So to bed.

11. earely to my Cosen Tho. Trice to discourse about our affairs. And he did make demand of the 200*l* and the interest thereof. But for the 200*l*, I did agree to pay him; but for the other, I did desire to be advised. So from him to Dr. Williams, who did carry me into his garden, where he hath abundance of grapes. And did show me how a dog that he hath doth kill all the Cattes that come thither to kill his pigeons, and doth afterwards bury them. And doth it with so much care that they shall be quite covered, that if but the tip of the tail hangs out, he will take up the cat*a* again and dig the hole deeper – which is very strange. And he tells me he doth believe that he hath killed above 100 cats. After he was ready, we went up and down to enquire about my affairs. And then parted – and to the Wardrobe and there took Mr. Moore to Tom. Trice, who promised to let Mr. Moore have copys of the bond and my aunts deed of

a   MS. 'dog'

---

1. Thomas Fenner was a freeman of the Blacksmiths' Company, and may have sold ironware. This is the only occasion in the diary on which Pepys mentions buying anything from him.

2. She left on 16 October.

gift.[1] And so I took him home to my house to dinner. Where I find my wife's brother Balty, as fine as hands could make him, and his servant, a Frenchman, to wait on him; and came to have my wife to visit a young lady which he is a servant* to[a] and hath hope to trapan and get for his wife. I did give way for my wife to go with him, and so after dinner they went. And Mr. Moore and I out again, he about his business and I to Dr. Williams to talk with him again; and he and I walking through Lincolne's= Inn fields, observed at the Opera a new play, *Twelfth night,*[2] was acted there, and the King there. So I, against my own mind and resolution, could not forbear to go in, which did make the play seem a burthen to me, and I took no pleasure at all in it. And so after it was done, went home with my mind troubled for my going thither, after my swearing to my wife that I would never go to a play without her. So that what with this and things going so crosse to me as to matters of my uncles estate, makes me very much troubled in my mind. And so to bed. My wife was with her brother to see his mistress today, and says she is young, rich, and handsome, but not likely for him to get.[3]

12. Though it was an office day, yet I was forced to go to the Privy Seale; at which I was all the morning. And from thence to my Lady's to dinner at the Wardrobe. And in my way, upon the Thames I saw the King's new pleasure-boat, that is come now for the King to take pleasure in above bridge[4] – and also two fine Gundalo's that are lately brought,[5] which are very rich and fine.

a MS. 'do'

1. In the deed of gift (made during an illness, 17 September 1648) Anne Pepys had made over to her son Thomas Trice (to be employed as she might appoint) the £200 which Robert Pepys had assigned to her in 1630: see above, p. 134, n. 2. She died in October 1661. The copies here mentioned were sold at Sotheby's on 11 April 1919, and are printed in Whitear, App. C.

2. Shakespeare's comedy; acted in 1602 and published in 1623. For the usual cast, see Downes, p. 23. (A).

3. Possibly this was the same person (Esther Watts) whom Balty married in 1662: see below, iii. 277.

4. This became known as the '*Bezan*' (*bezaan*, Du.; mizzen sail). It was a smaller variety of the *Mary* yacht presented to the King by the Dutch (q.v. above, i. 222 & n. 1). Pepys sailed in her and used her as a floating office on several journeys down river from the Bridge in 1665.

5. Gondolas presented by the Doge and Senate of Venice and meant for the canal in St James's Park. They had arrived on the 6th: *CSPVen. 1661–4*, p. 42.

After dinner I went into my Lady's chamber; where I find her up now, out of her child=bedd, which I was glad to see.   And after an hour's talk with her I took leave.   And to Tom. Trice again and sat talking and drinking with him about our business a great while; and do find that I am likely to be forced to pay interest for the 200*l*.   By and by in comes my Uncle Thomas; and as he was alway a close cunning fellow, so he carries himself to me and says nothing of what his endeavours are; though to my trouble, I know that he is about recovering of Gravely.   But neither I nor he begun any discourse of that business.   From thence to Dr. Williams again (at the little blind alehouse in Shooelane, at the Grid Iron, a place I am ashamed to be seen to go into); and there, with some bland*a* counsel of his, we discourse our matters.   But I find men of so different minds, that by my troth I know not what to trust to.

It being late, I took leave and by Linke home.   And called at Sir W. Battens and there hear that Sir W. Penn doth take our jest of the tankard very ill – which I am sorry for.

13.   This morning I was sent for by my uncle Fenner to come and advise about the buriall of my aunt the Butcher[1] – who died yesterday.   And from thence to the Anchor by Doctors Commons; and there Dr. Williams and I did write a letter for my purpose to Mr. Sedgewick of Cambridge[2] about Gravely business.   And after that I left him and an attorney with him and went to the Wardrobe, where I find my wife; and thence she and I to the water to spend the afternoon in pleasure; and so we went to old Georges[3] and there eat as much as we would of a hott shoulder of mutton.   And so to boat again and home.   So to bed – my mind very full of business and trouble.

14.   At the office all the morning.   At noon to the Change and then home again – to dinner, where my uncle Fenner by appointment came and dined with me, thinking to go together to my aunt Kites that is dead.   But before we had dined, comes

a   MS. 'blend'

---

1. See above, p. 172, n. 2.   Thomas Fenner was her brother-in-law.
2. Steward of Graveley manor.
3. At or near Lambeth.

Sir R. Slingsby and his Lady and a great deal of company to take my wife and I out by barge to show them the Kings and Dukes Yachts. So I was forced to leave my uncle and brother Tom at dinner and go forth with them; and we had great pleasure seeing all*a* four Yachts, *viz.* those two and the two duch ones.[1] And so home again. And I, after writing letters by post – to bed.

15. *Lords=day*. To my aunt Kites in the morning – to help my uncle Fenner to put things in order against anon, for the burial. And at noon home again; and after dinner to church, my wife and I. And after sermon with my wife to the buriall of my aunt Kite – where besides us and my uncle Fenners family, there was none of any Quality, but poor rasckally*b* people. So we went to church[2] with the Corps and there had service read at the grave; and back again with Pegg Kite – who will be, I doubt, a troublesome carrion to us Executors. But if she will not be ruled, I shall fling up my Executorship.[3] After that home – and Will. Joyce along with me – where we sat and talked and drunk and eat an hour or two; and so he went away. And I up to my chamber, and then to prayers and to bed.

16. This morning I was busy at home to take in my part of our fraight of Coles, which Sir G. Carteret, Sir R. Slingsby and myself sent for – which is 10 Chalderon – eight of which I took in, and with the other two repaid Sir W. Pen what I borrowed of him a little while ago. So that from this day I shall see how long 10 chalderon of coals will serve my house, if it please the Lord to let me live to see them burned.

In the afternoon, by appointment to meet Dr. Williams and his atturny, and they and I to Tom. Trice and there got him in discourse to confess the words that he had said, that his mother did desire him not to sue my Uncle about her 200*l* bond while she was alive. Here we were at high words with T. Trice – and

a l.h. repl. s.h. 'the'   *b* l.h. repl. s.h. 'rase'-

---

1. The *Catherine* was the King's yacht; the *Anne* the Duke's. The Dutch yachts (given to the King by the Dutch) were the *Mary* and the *Bezan*.

2. ? St Dunstan's, Stepney. (R).

3. On 20 November probate of the will was granted to Thomas Fenner alone. Cf. below, iii. 161.

then parted; and we to Standings in Fleetstreete, where we sat and drunk and talked a great while – about my going down to Gravely Court,[1] which will be this week; whereof the Doctor had notice in a letter from his sister this week. In the middle of our discourse, word was brought me from my brother's that there is a fellow come from my father out of the country on purpose to speak with me. So I went to him and he made a story how he had lost his letter, but he was sure it was for me to come into the country. Which I believed, and thought it might be to give me notice of Gravely Court; but I afterward find that it was a rogue that did use to play such tricks to get money of people; but he got none of me. At night I went home and there find letters from my father informing me of the Court, and that I must come down and meet him at Impington – which I presently resolved to do. And the next morning got up, telling my wife of my journy; and she with a few words got me to hire her a horse to go along with me.

《17.》 So I went to my Lady's and elsewhere to take leave. And of Mr. Townsend did borrow a very fine side-saddle for my wife; and so after all things were ready, she and I took coach to the end of the towne toward Kingsland;[2] and there got upon my horse and she upon her pretty mare that I hired her. And she rides very well; by the mare at one time falling, she got a fall but no harm. So we got to ware and there supped and to bed, very merry and pleasant.

18. The next morning, up early and begun our march. The way about Puckrige very bad; and my wife in the very last dirty place of all got a fall but no hurt, though some dirt. At last she begun, poor wretch, to be tired, and I to be angry at it; but I was to blame, for she is a very good companion as long as she is well.

In the afternoon we got to Cambrige, where I left my wife at my Cosen Angiers, while I went to Christ College and there find my brother in his chamber – and talked with him; and so to the barbers and then to my wife again and remounted for

---

1. The manorial court of Graveley, Cambs., the manor in which Pepys's copyholds were held: above, p. 136.

2. An area on the borders of Islington and Hackney. (R).

Impington. Where my Uncle[1] received me and my wife very kindly. And by and by, in comes my father. And we supped and talked and were merry; but being weary and sleepy, my wife and I to bed without talking with my father anything about our business.

19. Up early; and my father and I alone into the garden and there talked about our business and what to do therein. So after I had talked and advised with my Cosen Claxton and then with my uncle by his bedside, we all horsed away and to Cambrige, where my father and I, having left my wife at the[a] Beare[2] with my brother, went to Mr. Sedgewicke the steward of Gravely. And there talked with him, but could get little hopes from anything that he would tell us; but at last I did give him a fee, and then he was free to tell me what I asked; which was something, though not much comfort.

From thence to our horses and with my wife went and rode through Sturbrige[b] fayre;[3] but the fair was almost done, so we did not light there at all, but went back to Cambridge and there at the beare had some herings, we and my brother; and after dinner set out for Brampton, where we come in very good time and find all things well; and being somewhat weary, after some talk about tomorrow's business with my father, we went to bed.

20. Will Stankes and I set out in the morning betimes for Gravely, where to an alehouse and drank; and then going toward

a repl. 'my Cosen Angiers' ('my' in s.h.)   *b* l.h. repl. s.h. 'the' l.h. 'f'-

---

1. Talbot Pepys, his great-uncle.
2. There were two Bear Inns in Cambridge: the Black Bear, off Sidney St, opposite Holy Trinity Church (part of its yard surviving as Market Passage), and the White Bear off Trinity St (on the site of the modern Whewell's Court of Trinity College). The former was usually known as 'The Bear': *Proc. Camb. Antiq. Soc.*, 17(1914)/81 n. 1; VCH, *Cambs.*, iii. 115.
3. Once the greatest of all English fairs; abolished in 1934; still, in 1681, according to Thomas Baskerville, 'the greatest mart or fair we have in England': HMC, *Rep.*, 13/2/272-3. It was held by the corporation of Cambridge borough in fields about two miles east of the market-place, and at this period ran from 24 August to 28 September. Contemporary description in Baskerville, loc. cit.; see also C. H. Cooper, *Annals of Cambridge*, iv. 275+; T. D. Atkinson and J. W. Clark, *Cambridge Described*, ch. ix.

the Court=house, met my Uncle Thomas and his Son Tho., with Bradly (the rogue that had betrayed us) and one Young, a cunning fellow who guides them. There passed no unkind words at all between us, but I seemed* fair and went to drink with them: I said little till by and by that we came to the Court – which was a simple meeting of a company of country rogues, with the Steward and two Fellows of Jesus College, that are lords of the towne.¹ Where the Jury were sworne; and I producing no surrender (though I told them I was sure there is and must be one some-where), they find my Uncle Tho. heire-at-law, as he is; and so though I did tell him and his son that they would find themselfs abused by these fellows and did advise them to forbear being admitted this Court (which they would have done but that these rogues did persuade them to do it now), my uncle was admitted; and his son also, in reversion after his father, which he did well in to secure his money. The father paid a year and half for his fine,* and the son half a year; in all 48*l*., besides about 3*l* fees. So that I do believe the charges of his journys and what he gives his two rogues, and other expenses herein, cannot be less then 70*l* – which will be a sad thing for them if a surrender be found.

After all was done, I openly wished them joy in it. And so rode to Offord with them and there parted fairly, without any words. I took occasion to bid them money for their half acre of land; which I have a mind to do, that in the surrender I might secure Piggotts, which otherwise I shall be forced to lose.²

So with Stankes home and supped; and after telling my father how things went, I went to bed with my mind in good temper, because I saw the matter and manner of the Court and the bottom of my business, wherein I was before and should always have been ignorant.

21. All the morning pleasing myself with my father; going up and down the house and garden with my father and my wife,

---

1. Jesus College owned both manor and advowson: VCH, *Cambs.*, iii. 428. For the dispute, see above, p. 135 & n. 2.

2. For the Pigott mortgage, see above, p. 137, n. 4. Pepys had been bequeathed land in Offord, Hunts. The half-acre went by the custom of the manor to the heir-at-law, i.e. Thomas Pepys: below, iii. 222.

contriving some alterations.[1] After dinner (there coming this morning my aunt Hanes[2] and her son from London, that is to live with my father), I rode to Huntington; where I met Mr. Philips and there put my Bugden matters[3] in order against the Court. And so to Hinchingbrooke, where Mr. Barnwell showed me the condition of the house, which is yet very backward and I fear will be very darke in the Cloyster when it is done.[4] So home and to supper and to bed – very pleasant and quiet.

22. *Lords=day.* Before church time, walking with my father in the garden, contriving. So to church, where we had common prayer[5] and a dull sermon by one Mr. Case, who yet I heard sing very well. So to dinner; and busy with my father about his accounts – all the afternoon; and people come to speak with us about business.

Mr. Barnwell at night came and supped with us. So after setting matters even with my father and I, to bed.

23. Up, and sad to hear my father and mother wrangle as they used to do at London, of which I took notice to both; and told them that I should give over care for anything unless they would spend what they have with more love and quiet. So (John Bowles coming to see us before we go) we took horse and got early to Baldwick; where there was a fair,[6] and we put in and eat a mouthful of porke, which they made us pay 14*d* for, which vexed us much. And so away to Stevenage and stayed till a showre was over; and so rode easily to Welling – where we supped well and had two beds in the room and so lay single; and must remember it that, of all the nights that ever I slept in my life, I never did pass a night with more epicurisme of sleep – there being now and then a noise of people stirring that

1. For their completion, see below, iii. 94.

2. Lettice Haines, a sister of Pepys's mother.

3. Robert Pepys had left land and houses at Buckden, Hunts. Lewis Phillips was a lawyer.

4. For the rebuilding of the house, see above, p. 49 & n. 1.

5. Use of the prayer-book was not enforced by law until 24 August 1662 after the passing of the Act of Uniformity on 19 May 1662: see below, iii. 97 & n. 2. The parson was probably Thomas Case (a namesake of the well-known Presbyterian) who took his B.A. at Oxford in 1631.

6. For Baldock fair, see VCH, *Herts.*, iii. 67.

waked me; and then it was a very rainy night; and then I was a little weary,^a that what between waking and then sleeping again, one after another, I never had so much content in all my life. And so my wife says it was with her.

24.   We rose and set forth; but find a most sad alteration in the roade by reason of last night's rains, they being now all dirty and washy, though not deep.   So we rode easily through and only drinking at Halloway at the sign of a woman with Cakes in one hand and a pot of ale in the other,[1] which did give good occasion of mirth, resembling her to the mayd that served us; we got home very timely and well.   And finding there all well, and letters from Sea that speak of my Lord's being well and his accion, though not considerable of any side, at Argier,[2] I went straight to my Lady and there sat and talked with her; and so home again; and after supper, we to bed somewhat weary – hearing of nothing ill since my absence but my Brother Tom, who is pretty well though again.

25.   By Coach with Sir W. Pen to Covent garden.   By the way, upon my desire, he told me that I need not fear any refleccion upon my Lord for their ill successe at Argier, for more could not be done then was done.   I went to my Cosen Tho. Pepys there and talked with him a good while about our country business, who is troubled at my Uncle Tho. his folly, and so we parted; and then meeting Sir R. Slingsby in St. Martin-lane, he and I in his coach through the Mewes (which is the way that now all coaches are forced to go because of a stop at Charing-cross, by

a   repl. 'sleepy'

---

1. The Mother Redcap; a well-known house on the Great North Road.

2. John Creed to Pepys, Lisbon, 31 August/10 September (partly in Latin); Edward Shipley to Pepys, Lisbon, 1/11 and 2/12 September: BM, Add. 38849, ff. 8-9, 14-15. The former is printed in HMC, *Eliot Hodgkin*, pp. 158-60. The letters report Sandwich's bombardment of Algiers, 5-8 August, which had been broken off by bad weather. Sandwich had thereupon left a squadron under Lawson plying before the harbour, and had set sail for Lisbon. See Sandwich, pp. 91+; Harris, i. 200-1. A treaty was made with Algiers in the following spring: below, iii. 89.

reason of digging of a drayne[1] there to clear the streets) to White-hall; and there to Mr. Coventry and talked with him. And thence to my Lord Crewes and dined with him; where I was used with all imaginable kindness, both from him and her. And I see*a* that he is afeared that my Lord's reputacion will a little suffer in common talk by this late successe.* But there is no help for it now.

The Queene of England (as she is now owned and called) I hear, doth*b* keep open Court and distinct at Lisbone.[2]

Thence, much against my nature and will (yet such is the power of the Devil over me I could not refuse it) to the Theatre and saw *The Merry Wifes of Windsor*, ill done.[3] And that ended, with Sir W. Pen and Sir G. Ascue to the Taverne and so home with him by coach.

And after supper to prayers and to bed – in full quiet of mind as to thought, though full of business, blessed be God.

26. At the office all the morning. So dined at home, and then abroad with my wife by coach to the Theatre to show her *King and no King*[4] – it being very well done. And so by coach, though hard to get, it being rainy, home. So to my chamber to write letters and the Journall for these six last days past.

27. By coach to White-hall with my wife (where she went to see Mrs. Pierce, who was this day churched, her month of child-bed being out): I went to Mr. Mountagu and other businesses. And at noon met my wife at the Wardrobe – and there dined, where we find Captain Country (my little Captain that I loved, who carried me to the Sound)[5] come with some Grapes and

a l.h. repl. s.h. 'fear'   *b* l.h. repl. s.h. 'is'

1. Either one of the sewers carrying away surface water or a street gutter. (R).

2. Until now the Infanta Catherine had lived in strict seclusion under the guardianship of her mother the Queen Regent. But Charles II had declared her Queen on 22 June and signed the marriage treaty on the day after. They were not married until 21 May 1662.

3. Cf. above, i. 310 & n. 1. (A).

4. A tragicomedy by Beaumont and Fletcher; see above, p. 54. (A).

5. Richard Country had left Lisbon on 13 September with letters for the Duke of York: Sandwich, p. 99. In May 1659 he had carried Pepys in the *Hind* to the Baltic with private letters to Mountagu. Pepys was in 1676 to be the means of having him preferred to the sinecure position of gunner on the *Royal Charles*: Cat., iii. 311.

Millons from my Lord at Lisbone – the first that ever I saw any. And my wife and I eat some, and took some home. But the grapes are rare things. Here we stayed; and in the afternoon comes Mr. Edw. Mountagu (by appointment this morning) to talk with my Lady and me about the provisions fit to be bought and sent to my Lord along with him. And told us that we need not trouble ourselfs how to buy them, for the King would pay for all, and that he would take care to get them – which put my Lady and me into a great deal of ease of mind. Here we stayed and supped too; and after my wife had put up some of the grapes in a basket for to be sent to the King, we took coach and home – where we find a hampire of Millons sent to me also.

28. At the office in the morning. Dined at home; and then Sir W. Penn and his daughter and I and my wife to the Theatre and there saw *Fathers owne Sonn*,[1] a very good play, and the first time I ever saw it. And so at night to my house, and there sat and talked and drank and merrily broke up, and to bed.

29. *Lords=day*. To church in the morning and so to dinner; and Sir W. Pen and daughter, and Mrs. Poole his kinswoman, Captain Pooles wife, came by appointment to dinner with us. And a good dinner we had for them, and were very merry. And so to church again and then to Sir W. Pens and there supped; where his Brother,[2] a traveller and one that speaks Spanish very well, and a merry man, supped with us; and when at dinner and supper, I drank, I know not how, of my owne accord, so much wine, that I was even almost foxed and my head aked all night. So home, and to bed without prayers, which I never did yet since I came to the house of a Sonday night: I being now so out of order that I durst not read prayers, for fear of being perceived by my servants in what case I was. So to bed.

30. This morning up by mooneshine; at 5 a-clock to White-hall to meet Mr. Moore at the Privy Seale; but he not being come

1. Probably John Fletcher's comedy, *Monsieur Thomas*, published in 1639 and reissued c. 1661 under the title *Father's own son*. Now at the TR, Vere St. (A).

2. George Penn, twenty years older than Sir William; once a merchant in Seville.

as appointed, I went into King-Streete to the Red Lyon to drink my morning draught and there I heard of a fray between the two Embassadors of Spaine and France; and that this day being the day of the entrance of an Embassador from Sweden, they were entended to fight for the precedence.[1]   Our King, I heard, hath ordered that no Englishman should meddle in the business, but let them do what they would;[2] and to that end, all the Souldiers in the town were in arms all the day long, and some of the train-bands in the City and a great bustle through the City all the day.   Then I to the Privy Seale; and there, Mr. Moore and a gentleman being come with him, we took coach (which was the business I came for) to Chelsy to my Lord Privy Seale and there got him to seal that business.   Here I saw by day-light two very fine pictures in the gallery,[3] that a little while ago I saw by night. And did also go all over the house, and find it to be the prettiest

1. The Great Powers were from time to time involved in such disputes, until in 1815 they adopted the rule that the order of precedence should be fixed at each capital according to the seniority (by appointment) of their ambassadors there. In this period it was based on the supposed seniority (by foundation) of the monarchies themselves. France and Spain contested for first place among the secular powers: their ambassadors had quarrelled over it at The Hague in 1657. The dispute which Pepys reports occurred on the occasion of the state entry of the new Swedish ambassador, Brahe. He was to travel this afternoon by water from Westminster to the Tower, where he would enter a coach provided by the King and, at the head of a procession, ride to the court. Later he would be given his first public audience. The French and Spanish ambassadors (d'Estrades and Vatteville) were both determined to get the place next after the King's coach. Pepys's story is in part an eye-witness account, and be-

cause of the diplomatic disputes that followed, of special value. Pepys retained in his library Sir John Finett's *Finetti Philoxenis* (1656; PL 556), an account of similar disputes in England in the early 17th century.

2. This was after he had failed to persuade the French and Spanish ambassadors not to take part in the procession at all. Everyone expected trouble.

3. Little is known of the pictures collected by Lord Robartes. His son, the 2nd Earl of Radnor (d. 1723), lived in a house in St James's Park which contained pictures by artists popular in Pepys's time and later, such as Vanzoon, Roestraeten, Danckerts, Griffier, Van de Velde and Schalcken. It is not clear whether these painters had been employed by the first Earl or by his son; or which of them had collected the Italian and Flemish pictures included in the second Earl's sale, 28 April 172(?)3: G. Vertue, *Notebooks*, i. 132. (OM).

contrived house that ever I saw in my life.[1] So to coach back again. And at White-hall light and saw the soldiers and people running up and down the streets. So I went to the Spanish Embassadors and the French,[2] and there saw great preparations on both sides; but the French made the most noise and vaunted most, the other made no stir almost at all; so that I was afeared the other would have had too great a conquest over them.

Then to the Wardrobe and dined there; and then abroad, and in Cheapeside hear that the Spaniard hath got the best of it and killed three of the French coach-horses and several men[3] and is gone through the City next to our King's coach. At which it is strange to see how all the City did rejoice. And endeed, we do naturally all love the Spanish and hate the French.[4]

But I, as I am in all things curious, presently got to the water-side and there took oares to Westminster-palace, thinking to have seen them come in thither with all the coaches; but they being come and returned, I[a] run after them with my boy after me, through all the dirt and the streets full of people; till at last at the mewes[5] I saw the Spanish coach go, with 50[b] drawne swords at least to guard it and our soldiers shouting for joy. And so I fallowed the coach, and then met it at Yorke-house,[c] where the Embassador lies; and there it went in with great state.

a repl. 'and'   *b* repl. '100'   *c* repl. 'Arundel-house' ('house' in s.h.)

---

1. The house (Danvers House) is described in Randall Davies, *Chelsea Old Church*, pp. 104+ ; plans in the John Thorpe collection, Soane Museum, London. It was a substantial house of 26 hearths, at the s.-e. end of Danvers St, opposite Crosby Hall. Aubrey (c. 1691) wrote of it: 'The house is very elegant and ingeniose but not according to that staid perfection of Roman architecture now in vogue' (qu. Davies, pp. 138–9).

2. York House and Exeter House, on the s. and n. sides of the Strand respectively.

3. There had been a running fight from Tower Wharf to Crutched Friars; and, according to the French ambassador, six Frenchmen had been killed and 33 wounded.

4. Probably because the French were more commonly to be seen in London and were more serious competitors for jobs with the Londoners. Cf. Edward Browne, *Journal of a visit to Paris in . . . 1664* (ed. Keynes), p. 11. D'Estrades's footmen had had a scuffle with watermen a few days before, with some fatalities: *CSPVen. 1661–4*, p. 55. In 1669 an Italian traveller remarked that Londoners were 'proud, arrogant, and uncivil to foreigners . . . especially the French': Magalotti, pp. 396–7.

5. The Royal Mews, Charing Cross.

So then I went to the French house, where I observe still that there is no men in the world of a more insolent spirit where they do well or before they begin a matter, and more abject if they do miscarry,*a* then these people are. For they all look like dead men and not a word among them, but shake their heads.

The truth is, the Spaniards were observed not only to fight most desperately, but also they did outwitt them; first in lining their owne harnesse with chains of iron, that they could not be cut – then in setting their coach in the most advantageous place, and to appoint men to guard every one of their horses, and others for to guard the coach, and others the coachmen. And above all, in setting upon the French horses and killing them, for by that means the French were not able to stir.

There were several men slain of the French, and one or two of the Spaniards, and one Englishman by a bullett – which is very observable, the French were at least four to one in number.[1] And had near 100 case of pistolls among them, and the Spaniards had not one gun among them; which is for their honour for ever, and the others disgrace.

So having been very much dawbed with dirt, I got a coach and home – where I vexed my wife in telling of her this story and pleading for the Spaniard against the French.

So ends this month. Myself and family in good condition of health. But my head full of my Lord's and my own and the office business – where we are now very busy about the business of sending forces to Tanger.[2] And the fleet to my Lord of Sandwich, who is now at Lisbone to bring over the Queene – who doth now keep a Court as Queen of England.

The business of Argier[3] hath of late troubled me, because my Lord hath not done what he went for, though he did as much as any man in the world could have done.

The want of money puts all things, and above all things the Navy, out of order; and yet I do not see that the King takes care to bring in any money, but thinks of new designs to lay out money.

a l.h. repl. s.h. 'carry'

---

1. Evelyn put the numbers at 150 Frenchmen and 40 Spaniards.

2. By a council order of 30 September, 1000 foot soldiers and a troop of 100 horse were to be raised and transported: PRO, PC 2/55, pp. 386–7. A Governor (Peterborough) had just been appointed: see below, p. 202 & n. 1.

3. See above, p. 184 & n. 2.

1. This morning my wife and I lay long in bed; and among other things, fell in talk of Musique and desired that I would let her learn to sing – which I did consider and promised her she should: so before I rose, word was brought me that my singing[a] master Mr. GoodGroome was come to teach me; and so she rise and this morning begun to learn also.

To the office, where busy all day. So to dinner and then to the office again till night; and then to my study at home to set matters and papers in order – which, though I can hardly bring myself to do, yet doth please me much when it is done. So eat a bit of bread and cheese and to bed.

2. All this morning at Pegg Kites with my uncle Fenner and two friends of his, prising her goods that her mother hath left. But the slut is like to prove so troublesome that I am out a heart with troubling myself in her business. After we had done, we all went to a cook's shop in Bishops=gate-street and dined; and then I took them to the taverne and did give them a Quart of Sack, and so parted. I home and there took my wife out; and in a coach of a Gentlewomans that had been to visit my Lady Batten and was going home again our way, we went to the Theatre; but coming late and sitting in an ill place, I never had so little pleasure in a play in my life; yet it was the first time that I ever saw it, *Victoria Corombona*[1] – methinks a very poor play. And then at night troubled to get my wife home, it being very dark; and so we were forced to have a coach. So to supper and to bed.

3. At the office all the morning. Dined at home. And in the afternoon Mr. Moore came to me and he and I went to tower hill to meet with a man; and so back all three to my

---

a repl. 'sing'-

1. Correctly, *Vittoria Corombona*, part of the sub-title of John Webster's tragedy, *The white devil*, which was first acted c. 1609, published in 1612, and, despite Pepys's unfavourable reaction to it, was one of the principal stock plays of the King's Company at the TR, Vere St. (A).

house, and there I signed a bond to Mr. Battersby,[1] a friend of Mr. Moores, who lends me 50*l* – the first money that ever I borrowed upon bond for my own occasions; and so I took them to the Miter, and a portugall millon with me; there sat and discoursed in matters of religion till night, with great pleasure. And so parted. And I home, calling at Sir Wm. Batten's – where his Son and his wife was,[2] who had yesterday been at the play where we was; and it was good sport to hear how she talked of it with admiration, like a fool. So home; and my head was not well with the wine that I drank today.

4. By coach to White-hall with Sir W. Pen. So to Mr. Mountagu, where his man Monsieur Eschar makes a great complaint against the English, that they did help the Spaniard against the french the other day, and that their Embassador doth demand justice of our King, and that he doth resolve to be gone for France the next week – which I and all that I meet with, all are very glad of.[3] Thence to Paternoster row, where my Will did receive the 50*l* I borrowed yesterday. I to the Wardrobe to dinner and there stayed most of the afternoon, very merry with the ladies. Then Captain Ferrers and I to the Theatre, and there came too late; so we stayed and saw a bit of *Victoria*, which pleased me worse then it did the other day. So we stayed not to see it out but went out and drank a bottle or two of China=ale, and so I home – where I find my wife vexed at her people for grumbling to eate Suffolk cheese[4] – which I also am vexed at. So to bed.

5. At the office all the morning; then dined at home, and so

1. A clergyman: below, p. 215. It was by no means unknown for clergymen to lend money at interest.

2. See above, p. 30, n. 3.

3. For the dispute, see above, p. 187 & n. 1. D'Estrades left on 8 October, and returned on the following 14 January. Nothing came of the French demand that Charles should dismiss the Spanish ambassador from the country and punish the Londoners alleged to have taken part in the affray. But the Spanish King was forced to recall his ambassador from London, and to give not only an apology for this incident but a promise to yield precedence to the French in the future. The two monarchies did not reach an agreement about rules of precedence until 1761. In England the incident led to a ruling by Charles II that in future only British subjects should take part in state entries: *CSPD 1661–2*, p. 104.

4. A very hard variety.

stayed at home all the afternoon, putting up my Lord's Modell of the *Royall James*, which I borrowed of him long ago to hang up in my room.[1] And at night Sir W. Pen and I alone to the Dolphin and there eat some bloat-herrings[2] and drank good sack. Then came in Sir W. Warren and another and stayed[a] a while with us; and then Sir Arnld. Brames, with whom we stayed late and till we had drank too much wine; so home and I to bed, pleased at my afternoon's work in hanging up the Shipp. So to bed.

6. *Lords day.*   To church in the morning; Mr. Mills preached, who I expect should take it in Snuffe that my wife did not come to his child's christening the other day.[3]   The winter coming on, many of parish ladies are come home and appear at church again; among others, the three sisters of the Thornburys,[4] very fine, and the most zealous people that ever I saw in my life; even to admiration, if it were true zeal.   There was also my pretty black girl, Mrs. Dekins.   And Mrs. Margaret Pen this day came to church in a new flowered satin suit that my wife helped to buy her the other day.

So home to dinner.   And to church that afternoon to St. Gregorys by Paul's; where I saw Mr. Moore in the gallery and so went up to him and hear a good sermon of Dr. Buck[5] – one I never heard before, but a very able man.   So home; and in the evening I went to my valentine,[6] her father and mother being out of town, to fetch her to supper to my house; and then came Sir W. Penn and would have her to his; so with much sport I got them all to mine and we were merry; and so broke up and to bed.

7.   Up in the morning and to my Uncle Fenners, thinking to have met Pegg. Kite about her business,[7] but she comes not; and

---

a   MS. 'state'

---

1. See above, p. 121.
2. Pepys seems to have been fond of bloaters: *Priv. Corr.*, i. 199, 204; ii. 44.
3. His daughter Anna had been baptised on 3 October: *Harl. Soc. Reg.* 46/68.
4. Mrs Thornbury had been one

of the godparents.
5. James Buck, later Rector of St James Garlickhithe and St Peter's Cornhill, and preacher at the Temple.
6. Martha Batten.
7. See above, p. 179.

so I went to Dr. Williams's, where I find him sick in bed, and was sorry for it. So about business all day, troubled in my mind till I can hear from Brampton how things go at Sturtlow at the Court; which I was cleared in at night by a letter which tells me that my Cosen Tom. was there, to be admitted in his father's name as heire-at-law; but that he was opposed and I was admitted by proxy[1] – which put me out of great trouble of mind.

8. At the office all the morning. After office done, went and eat some Colchester oysters with Sir W. Batten at his house and there with some company dined. And stayed there talking all the afternoon; and late after dinner took Mrs. Martha out by Coach and carried her to the Theatre in a frolique, to my great expense; and there showed her part of *The Beggars bush*[2] without much pleasure, but only for a frolique; and so home again.

9. This morning, went out about many affairs; among others, to put my Theorbo out to be mended; and then at noon home again, thinking to go with Sir Wms. both to dinner by invitacion to Sir W. Riders; but at home I find Mrs. Pierce *la=belle* and Madam Clifford, with whom I was forced to stay, and made them the best welcome I could; and I was (God knows) very well pleased with their beautiful company. And after dinner took them to the theatre and showed them *The Chances*.[3] And so saw them both at home and back to the Fleece tavern in Covent-garden, where Luellin and Blurton and my old friend Franke Bagg was to meet me. And there stayed till late, very merry. Fra. Bagg tells me a story of Mrs. Pepys that lived with my Lady Harvy (Mr. Mountagu's sister), a good woman; that she hath been very ill and often asked for me. That she is in good condition and that nobody could get her to make her Will; but that she did still enquire for me. And that now she is well, she desires to have a chamber at my house. Now do not I

1. Pepys had possession of Robert Pepys's surrender for the Sturtlow land: above, p. 138.
2. A comedy by John Fletcher and others (see above, i. 297 & n. 2); now at the TR, Vere St. (A).

3. A comedy by John Fletcher; now at the TR, Vere St; see above, p. 89 & n. 1. (A).

know whether this is a trick of Baggs or a good will of hers to do something for me; but I will not trust her,[1] but told him I should be glad to see her and that I would be sure to do all that I could to provide a place for her.   So by Coach home late.

10.   At the office all the morning.   Dined at home; and after dinner, Sir W. Pen and my wife and I to the theatre (she first going into Covent-garden to speak a word with a woman to enquire of her mother, and I in the meantime with Sir W. Penn's coach, staying at W. Joyces), where the King came today; and there was *The Traytor*[2] most admirably acted – and a most excellent play it is.   So home and entended to be merry, it being my sixth wedding night;[3] but by a late bruise in one of my testicles I am in so much pain that I eat my supper and in pain to bed;[4] yet my wife and I pretty merry.

11.   All day in bed with a cataplasme to my Codd; and at night rise a little and to bed again, in more ease then last night. This noon there came my brother and Dr. Tom.[5] and Snow to dinner, and by themselfs were merry.

12.   In bed the greatest part of this day also, and my swelling in some measure gone.   I received a letter this day from my father that Sir R. Bernard doth a little fear that my Uncle hath

1. Probably a slip for 'him'.   This Mrs Pepys has not been identified. Nothing came of all this.

2. A tragedy by James Shirley (see above, i. 300 & n. 1); at the TR, Vere St.   (A).

3. This statement has to be interpreted in conjunction with the entry in the register of St Margaret's, Westminster, which establishes that the civil marriage took place on 1 December 1655 before Richard Sherwin, Justice of the Peace.   The most likely explanation is that the Pepyses insisted on a religious ceremony (on the preceding 10 October and at a place now unknown) as well as the civil marriage required by the act of 1653. The diary shows that they reckoned the years of their married life from the October ceremony.   For further discussion of this question, see *Comp.*: 'Pepys, Elizabeth.'

4. Dr C. E. Newman writes: 'Probably not a bruise, but an attack of inflammation derived from infection left after his operation for the stone, and precipitated by a temporary obstruction caused possibly by his sitting with his legs crossed.'

5. Dr Thomas Pepys, physician.

not observed exactly the Custome of Brampton[1] and in [his] Will about his lands there, which puts me to a great trouble in mind; and at night I wrote to him and to my father about it, being much troubled at it.

13. *Lords=day.* Did not stir out all day, but rose and dined below. And this day left off half-shirts and put on a waste-coate* and my false taby waistcoat with gold lace. And in the evening there comes Sir W. Batten to see me and sat and supped very kindly with me; and so to prayers and to bed.

14. This morning I ventured by water abroad to Westminster, but lost my labour and [time], for Mr. Mountagu was not in towne. So to the Wardrobe and there dined with [my] Lady, which is the first time that I have seen [her] dine abroad since her being brought to bed of my Lady Katherine.[2] In the afternoon Captain Ferrers and I walked abroad to several places; among others, to Mr. Pim's my Lord's taylours and there he went out with us to the Fountaine taverne and did give us store of wine; it being the Duke of Yorkes birth day, we drank the more to his health. But Lord, what a sad story he makes of his being abused by a Doctor of Physique who is in one part of the tenement where-in he dwells. It would make one laugh, though I see he is[a] under a great trouble in it. Thence home by Linke. And find a good answer from my father, that Sir Rt. Bernard doth clear all things as to us and our title to Brampton – which puts my heart in great ease and quiet.

15. At the office all the morning. And so dined at home. And in the afternoon to Paul's churchyard to a blind place, where Mrs. Goldsborough was to meet me (who dare not be known where she lives) to treat about the difference which remains between my uncle and her.[3] But Lord, to hear how she

a symbol blotted

---

1. The custom of the manor, by which the descent of the copyhold tenures was controlled.
2. On 20 August: above, p. 159.
3. She owed £10 to the estate of Robert Pepys, and presumably did not want her address to be known for fear of arrest. There was also some dis-pute about the mortgage on her estate: below, iii. 232; iv. 203.

talks and how she rails against my uncle would make one mad. But I seemed* not to be troubled at it; but would endeed gladly have an agreement with her. So I appoint Mr. Moore and she another against Friday next, to look into our papers and to see what can be done to conclude the matter. So home in much pain; by walking too much yesterday I have made my testicle to swell again, which much troubles me.

16. In bed till 12 a-clock. This morning came several maids to my wife to be hired; and at last she pitched upon one Nell, whose mother, an old woman, came along with her; but would not be hired under half a year, which I am pleased at their drolenesse.[1] This day dined by appointment with me Dr. Tho. Pepys and my Cosen Snow and my brother Tom, upon a Fin of Ling and some Sounds, neither of which did I ever know before, but most excellent meat they are both, that in all my life I never eat the like fish. So after dinner came in W. Joyce and eat and drank and were merry. So up to my chamber and put all my papers at rights. And in the evening our maid Mary (who was with us upon triall for a month) did take her leave of us, going as we suppose to be married, for the maid liked us and we her; but all she said was that she had a mind to live in a tradesmans house where there was but one maid. So to supper and to bed.

17. At the office all the morning. At noon, my wife being gone to my Cosen Snow's with Dr. Tho. Pepys and my brother Tom. to a venison pasty《*which proved a pasty of salted porke》,[2] by appointment I went with Captain David Lambert to the Exchange; and from thence, by appointment, he and I were to meet at a Cookes shop to dine. But before I went to him, Captain Cock[3] (a merchant I have not long known) took me off to the Sun taverne and gave me a glass of Sack. And being a man of great observation and repute, did tell me that he was confident that the parliament, when it comes the next month to sit again, would bring trouble with it and enquire how the King hath disposed of offices and money, before they will raise any more; which I

1. Nell proved 'a simple slut' and left after one half-year: below, p. 233; iii. 57.

2. Cf. above, i. 9.

3. George Cocke, hemp merchant, of London and Greenwich, who was to become an important associate of Pepys; always full of political news.

fear will bring all things to ruin again. Thence to the cook's, and there dined with Captain Lambert and his father-in-law and had much talk of Portugall from whence he is lately come, and he tells me that it is a very poor dirty place – I mean the City and Court of Lisbone.[1] That the King[2] is a very rude and simple fellow; and for reviling of somebody a little while ago and calling of him cuckold, was run into the cods with a sword, and had been killed had he not told them that he was their king. That there is there no glass windows, nor will have any;[3] which makes sport among our merchants there, to talk of a English factor that being newly come thither, he writ into England that glasse would be a good commodity to send thither, &c. That the King hath his meat sent up by a dozen of lazy guards and in pipkins sometimes to his own table – and sometimes nothing but fruits and now and then half a hen. And that now the Infanta is become our Queene, she is come to have a whole hen or goose to her table – which is not ordinary. So home and to look over my papers that concern the difference between Mrs. Goldsbrough and us; which cost me much pains, but contented me much after it was done. So at home all the evening and to supper and bed.

18. To White-hall to Mr. Mountagu's, where I met with Mr. Pierce the purser to advise about the things to be sent to my Lord

---

1. David Lambert was Captain of the *Norwich*, a frigate just home from Sandwich's Mediterranean fleet. He had been in Lisbon during August: BM, Sloane 505, f.66r. Thomas Fisher's account of Lisbon at this same time is more complimentary than Lambert's: see ib., ff. 15+. He thought the palace (rebuilt in the previous reign but never finished) rather simple, with its whitewashed walls. English travellers usually found Portugal inferior to the worst parts of Spain; cf. John Jackson to Pepys, 21 May/1 June 1701: *Priv. Corr.*, ii. 218. Lady Anne Fanshawe thought Lisbon

in 1663 'old and decayed', but admired the churches: *Memoirs* (1829), pp. 169–71. The court was not frequented by the nobility except on festivals, and the King ate alone, without ceremony; *Description de . . . Lisbonne* (Paris, 1730), p. 80; cf. Fanshawe, pp. 153+.

2. The feeble-minded cripple, Afonso VI, deposed in 1667.

3. A common feature in Mediterranean countries. In Italy oiled paper was sometimes used. Pepys later found that at Tangier the windows had only shutters: *Tangier Papers*, p. 55.

for the Queenes provision,[1] and was cleared in it; and that now there is all haste made for the fleete's going.

At noon to my Lady's to dinner. And in the afternoon, leaving my wife there, Mr. Moore and I to Mrs. Goldsborough, who sent for a friend to meet with us, and so we were talking about the difference between [us] till 10 at night. I find it very troublesome, and have brought it into some hopes of an agreement – I offering her to forgive her 16l that is yet due, according to my uncle's accounts, to us. So we left her friend to advise about it; and I hope to hear of her – for I would not by any means go to law with a woman of so devilish a tongue as she is.

So to my Lady's, where I left my wife to lie with Madamoiselle[2] all night and I by link home and to bed. This night, lying alone and the weather cold and having this last seven or eight days beene troubled with a tumor in one of my stones, which is now abated by a poultice of a good handful of bran with half a pint of vinegar and a pint of water boiled till it be thick, and then a spoonful of honey put to it and so some spread in a cloth and laid to it. I first put on my wastecoate,* to lie in all night this year, and do not entend to pull it off again till spring. ⟨I met with complaints at home that my wife left no victuals for them all this day.⟩[a]

19. At the office all morning; and at noon Mr. Coventry, who sat with us all this morning, and Sir G. Carteret, Sir W. Penn and myself by coach to Captain Marshes[3] at Limehouse, to a house that hath been their ancestors for this 250 years – close by the Lime-house which gives the name to the place. Here they have a design to get the King to hire a docke for the herring=busses (which is now the great design on foote) to lie up in.[4] We had a

---

a addition crowded into end of line

1. On 2/12 September Edward Shipley had written to Pepys from Lisbon asking him to send by Pierce (about to sail to Portugal) neats' tongues, bacon, oil, anchovies, pickled oysters, Cheshire cheese, and butter: HMC, *Eliot Hodgkin*, p. 160.

2. Mlle le Blanc, the governess.

3. Richard Marsh, ordnance officer.

4. The establishment of the Royal Fishery Council on 22 August 1661 had been followed shortly afterwards by the issue of letters patent inviting subscriptions to a central fund by means of which a fleet of herring boats would be set out: *CSPD 1661-2*, p. 83. The scheme failed, like others before and after it. Pepys became a member of the Fishery Corporation of 1664.

very good and handsome dinner, and excellent wine. I not being neat in clothes, which I find a great fault in me, could not be so merry as otherwise and at all times I am and can be, when I am in good habitt; which makes me remember my father Osborne's rule for a gentleman, to spare in all things rather then in that.[1] So by coach home; and so to write letters by post, and so to bed.

20. *Lordsday.* At home in bed all the morning to ease my late tumour; but up to dinner, and much offended in mind at a proud trick my man Will: hath got, to keep his hatt on in the house; but I will not speak of it to him today, but I fear I shall be troubled with his pride and lazinesse, though in other things he is good enough. To church in the afternoon, where a sleepy presbyter preached. And then to Sir W. Batten, who is to go to Portsmouth tomorrow too, to wait upon the Duke of Yorke, who goes to take possession and to set in order the Garrison there.[2] Supped at home and to bed.

21. earely with Mr. Moore by coach to Chelsy to my Lord Privy Seale's but have missed of coming time enough; and having taken up Mr. Pargiter the goldsmith (who is the man of the world that I do most know and believe to be a cheating rogue), we drank our morning draught there together, of Cake and ale, and did make good sport of his losing so much by the King's coming in, he having bought much of Crowne lands, of which (God forgive me) I am very glad.[3] At White-hall at the privy

1. Francis Osborne, one of Pepys's favourite authors, had written in his *Advice to a son* (1658; pt i. 23): 'Weare your *Cloaths neat*, exceeding, rather than comming short of others of like fortune . . . *spare all other ways rather than prove defective in this.*'

2. The Duke had been appointed Governor of Portsmouth on 31 May 1661. He acted by means of a deputy.

3. Crown and church lands were now, after the confiscations of the revolution, restored to their legal owners without compensation to their purchasers. The goldsmith was John Pargiter, sen., who had purchased Crown lands in Buckinghamshire: S. J. Madge, *Domesday of Crown lands*, p. 403. He was several times fined by the Goldsmiths' Company for bad workmanship, and in March 1668 his name was removed by the Court of Aldermen from the list of nominees for the office of alderman. He may have been the Pargiter prosecuted in 1669 for coin clipping: PRO, SP 29/256, no. 17.

Seale, did with Sir W. Penn take advice about passing of thing[s] of his there that concern his matters of Ireland.[1]   Thence to the Wardrobe and dined.   So against my judgment and conscience (which God forgive, for my very heart knows that I offend God in breaking my vowes herein) to the opera, which is now newly begun to act again after some alteration of their Scene, which doth make it very much worse.   But the play, *Love and honour*,[2] being the first time of their acting it, is a very good plot and well done.   So on foot home;   and after a little business done in my study and supper, to bed.

22.   At the office all the morning, where we had a Deputacion[3] ⟨from the Duke⟩ in his absence (he being gone to Portsmouth) for us to have the whole dispose and ordering of the fleet.   In the afternoon, about business up and down;   and at night to visit Sir R. Slingsby, who is fallen sick of this new disease, an ague and fever.[4]   So home after visiting my aunt Wight and Mrs. Norbury (who continues still a very pleasant lady);   and to supper and so to bed.

23.   To White-hall and there to drink our morning [draught], Sir W. Pen and I, at a friend's lodging of his (Collonell Treswell); and at noon he and I dined together alone at the Legg in King's-

1. A grant of c. 12,000 acres of land in co. Cork made to Penn under the terms of the Irish land settlement of November 1660, in compensation for the loss of lands he had gained in the Cromwellian settlement and which were now returned to their former owner, the Earl of Clancarty. See the order (28 October 1661) in *CSP Ireland 1660–2*, p. 449. Disputes over the grant continued until 1669: W. Penn, *My Irish journal* (ed. Grubb), pp. 11+, 95+.

2. A tragicomedy by Davenant, first acted in 1634, and published in 1649; now at the LIF. Downes (pp. 21–2) lists a cast which includes Betterton as Alvaro, Harris as Prospero, Price as Lionel and Mrs Davenport as Evandra. He also notes (p.

21) that this production was 'Richly c[l]oath'd' because Betterton, Harris and Price were permitted to wear the coronation suits of the King, the Duke of York and the Earl of Oxford respectively. It was an exceptionally popular production, as Pepys's subsequent visits on 23 and 25 October attest. The alteration to which Pepys refers was probably some adjustment in the system of movable wings and rear flats used to provide scenic backgrounds in Restoration theatres; see above, p. 131 & n. 2.   (A).

3. Dated 21 October: PRO, Adm. 106/5, f.423r.

4. For the 'new disease', see above, p. 131 & n. 4.   Slingsby died a week later.

street; and so by coach to Chelsey to my Lord Privy Seales about business of Sir Wms.; in which we had a fair admittance to talk with my Lord, and had his answer; and so back to the Opera and there I saw again *Love and Honour*, and a very good play it is; and thence home, calling by the way to see Sir Robt: Slingsby, who continues ill. And so home.

This day all our office is invited against Tuesday next, my Lord Majors day, to dinner with him at Guild hall. This evening Mr. Holliard[1] came and sat with us and gave us both directions to observe.

24. At the office all morning. At noon Luellin dined with me; and then abroad to Fleetstreet, leaving my wife at Tom's while I went out and did a little business. So home again, and went to see Sir Robt: who continues ill and this day hath not spoke at all, which makes them all afeared of him. So home.

25. To White-hall; and so to dinner at the Wardrobe, where my wife met me; and there we met with a venison pasty, and my Lady very merry and very handsome methought. After dinner, my wife and I to the Opera and there saw again *Love and Honour*, a play so good that it hath been acted but three times and I have seen them all, and all in this week; which is too much, and more then I will do again a good while. Coming out of the house, we met Mrs. Pierce and her comrade, Mrs. Clifford; and I seeming willing to stay with them to talk, my wife grew angry; and whether she be jealous or no I know not, but she loves not that I should speak of Mrs. Pierce. Home on foot, very discontentedly. In my way, I calling at the Instrument-maker's, Hunts, and there saw my Lute, which is now almost done, it being to have a new neck to it and to be made to double Strings.[2] So home and to bed. This day I did give my man Will a sound lesson about his forbearing to give us[a] the respect due to a master and mistress.

a repl. 'me'

---

1. The surgeon.
2. This was his theorbo: see below, p. 203. The instrument was to be provided with two strings, instead of the usual one, per course,

and perhaps with more diapason strings. Additional strings would have required more pegs and thus a new neck. (E).

26. This morning Sir W. Pen and I should have gone out of town with my Lady Batten to have met Sir Wm. coming back from Portsmouth at Kingston; but could not, by reason that my Lord of Peterborough (who is to go Governor of Tanger)[1] came this morning with Sir G. Carteret to advise with us about completing of the affairs and preparacions for that place. So at the office all the morning. And in the afternoon Sir Wm. Pen, my wife and I to the Theatre and there saw *The Country Captaine*,[2] the first time that it hath been acted this 25 years – a play of my Lord Newcastles, but so silly a play as in all my life I never saw, and the first that ever I was weary of in my life. So home again; and in the evening news was brought that Sir R. Slingsby our Comptroller (who hath this day been sick a week) is dead; which put me into so great a trouble of mind, that all the night I could not sleep, he being a man that loved me and had many Qualitys that made me to love him above all the officers and Comissioners in the Navy. Coming home, we called at Dan. Rawlinson's and there drank good sack; and so home.

27. *Lords day.* At church in the morning; where in the pew, both Sir Wms. and I had much talk about the death of Sir Rbert. which troubles me much, and them in appearance; though I do not believe it, because I know that he was a Cheque to their ingrossing the whole trade of the navy-office. Home to dinner; and in the afternoon to church again, my wife with me (whose mourning is now grown so old[3] that I am ashamed to go to church with her); and after church, to see my uncle and aunt Wight, and there stayed and talked and supped with them and were merry as we could be in their company. Among other things, going up into their chamber to see their two pictures, which I am forced to commend against my judgment – and also she showed us her Cabinett, where she had very pretty medalls and good Jewells. So*ᵃ* home and to prayers and to bed.

a repl. 'he'

---

1. Henry Mordaunt, 2nd Earl, Governor of Tangier 1661-2; appointed on 16 September: Routh, p. 17.
   2. A comedy by the Marquess of Newcastle, first acted c. 1640 and

published in 1649. James Shirley may have helped him to write it; see Wood, *Ath. Oxon.* (ed. Bliss), iii. 739-40. Now at the TR, Vere St. (A).
   3. See below, p. 203 & n. 3.

28. At the office all the morning, and dined at home; and so to Pauls churchyard to Hunts, and there find my Theorbo done. Which pleases me very well, and costs me 26*s* to the altering – but now he tells me it is as good a Lute as any is in England, and is worth well 10*l*. Hither I sent for Captain Ferrers to me, who comes with a friend of his [1] and they and I to the Theatre and there saw *Argalus and Parthenia;*[2] where a woman acted Parthenia and came afterward on the Stage in man's clothes, and had the best legs that ever I saw; and I was very well pleased with it. Thence to the Ringo=ale house, and thither sent for a belt-maker and bought of him a handsome belt for second mourning,[3] which cost me 24*s* and is very neat. So home and to bed.

29. This day I put on my half-Cloth black stockings and my new Coate of the fashion, which pleases me well; and with my beaver I was (after office was done) ready to go to my Lord Mayors feast, as we are all invited; but the Sir Wms. were both loath to go because of the Crowd, and so none of us went; and I stayed and dined with them, and so home; and in the evening, by consent, we met at the Dolphin, where other company came to us and would have been merry; but their wine was so naught and all other things out of order, that we were not so; but stayed long at night and so home and to bed. My mind not pleased with the spending of this day, because I had proposed a great deal of pleasure to myself this day at Guild hall.

This Lord Mayor, it seems, brings up again the Custome of Lord Mayors going the day of their installment to Pauls, and walking round about the Crosse and offering something at the alter.[4]

30. All the morning at the office. At noon played on my Theorbo and much pleased therewith – as it is now altered with a new neck. In the afternoon Captain Lambert called me out by

---

1. ? the German, Luffe, mentioned below, p. 228.

2. See above, p. 27 & n. 3. (A).

3. It was some three months since Pepys's Uncle Robert had died.

4. For this ceremony, now revived after the Interregnum, see *Liber Albus* (ed. H. T. Riley), i. 26–7; *Diary of Henry Machyn . . . 1550–63* (ed. Nichols, 1848), pp. 48, 156, 271, 294; J. Tatham, *Londons Tryumphs* (1661), p. 19; Sharpe, i. 35, ii. 397. It took place after the banquet, and afterwards the mayor was escorted to his home. The Lord Mayor was Sir John Frederick.

appointment and we walked together to Deptford; and there in his ship the *Norwich* I got him to show me every hole and corner of the ship, much to my informacion and the purpose of my going. So home again; and at Sir W. Battens heard how he had been already at Sir R. Slingsby's (as we were all invited and I entended this night to go); and there*a* he finds all things out of order and no Such thing done tonight; but pretending that the Corps stinks, they will bury it tonight privately, and so will unbespeake all their Guests and there shall be no funerall – which I am sorry for, that there should be nothing done for the honor of Sir Robt.; but I fear he hath left his family in great distraction. Here I stayed till late at Cards with my Lady and Mrs. Martha, and so home. I sent for a bottle or two of wine thither.

At my coming home, I am sorry to find my wife displeased with her maid Doll:, whose fault is that she cannot keep her peace, but will alway be talking in an angry manner, though it be without any reason and to no purpose. Which I am sorry for – and do see the inconvenience that doth attend the increase of a man's fortune, by being forced to keep more servants, which brings trouble.

Sir Henery Vane, Lambert, and others are lately sent suddenly away from the tower, prisoners to Scilly; but I do not think there is any plot as is said; but only a pretence, as there was once pretended often against the Cavaleers.[1]

31. This morning comes Prior of Brampton to me about the houses that he hath to buy of me;[2] but I was forced to be at the

a 'and there' repeated

---

1. The prisoners were shipped on the 25th – Vane to the Scillies, Lambert to Guernsey, Corbet and Waller to Jersey: *CSPD 1661–2*, p. 118. The scare was caused by the Worcestershire or Yarranton Plot; for the evidence about it, see *AHR*, 14/507–8. Pepys again expresses his scepticism about plots below, at 1 December.

2. The property included a 'little house' or 'cottage' (part of Robert Pepys's Brampton estate), occupied by one Barton, which Pepys was to sell with some land to William Prior a year later: below, iii. 31, 223. The sale provoked some difficulties with Pepys's uncle Thomas who had a reversionary interest in the estate: below, iii. 221. There would appear to have been further difficulty (not resolved by 1676) in determining Robert Pepys's title – if this is the 'Barton's business' referred to in *Family Letters*, pp. 12, 42, 45. Prior paid £268 in instalments by 1664.

office all the morning – and so could then not talk with him. And so after the office was done and dined at home, I went to my Brother Tom's and there met him. He demanded some abatement, he having agreed with^a my father for Barton's house^b at a price which I told him I would not meddle with; but as for anything to secure his title to them, I was ready. And so we parted. I thence to Sir Robt. Bernard and as his Client, did ask his advice about my uncle Thomas's case and ours as to Gravely and ours; and in short, he tells me that there is little hopes of recovering it or saving his annuity – which doth trouble me much, but God's will be done.

Thence, with my mind full of trouble, to my Uncle Fenner's; where at the alehouse, I find him drinking and very Jolly and youthsome, and as one that I believe will in a little time get a wife.[1] So home.

a repl. ? 'attended'   *b* MS. 'houses'

---

1. His first wife had died in August. He was married again with- in a few months to an 'old and ugly' midwife: below, iii. 13.

NOVEMBER.

1. I went this morning with Sir Wm. Pen by coach to West-minster; and having done my business at Mr. Mountagu's, I went back to him at White-hall; and from thence with him to the Three Tun taverne at Charing-cross, and there sent for up the Maister of the house's dinner[1] and dined very well upon it; and afterwards had him and his fayre Sister (who is very great with Sir W. Batten and Sir W. Penn in mirth) up to us, and looked over some medalls that they showed us of theirs; and so went away to the Theatre to *The Joviall=Crew*[2] and from thence home; and at my house we were very merry till late, having sent for his Son, Mr. Wm. Pen, lately come from Oxford.[3]   And after supper parted and to bed.

2. At the office all the morning; where Sir John Minnes our new Comptroller was fetched by Sir Wm. Pen[a] and myself from Sir W. Battens and led to his place in the office – the first time that he hath come hither.   And he seems a good fair-condition[ed] man and one that I am glad hath the office.[4]

After the office done, I to the Wardrobe and there dined; and in the afternoon had an hour or two's talk with my Lady with great pleasure; and so with the two young ladies by Coach to my house and gave them some entertainment; and so late at night sent them home with Captain Ferrers by Coach.

This night my boy Wainman, as I was in my chamber, [I] over-heard him let off some Gunpouder; and hearing my wife chide him below for it, and a noise made, I call him up and find that it was powder that he had put in his pocket, and a mach carelessly with it, thinking that it was out; and so the match did give fire

a   repl. 'Batten'

---

1. The *table d'hôte* dinner.
2. See above, p. 141 & n. 1.   (A).
3. William Penn (later the Quaker leader) had been sent down from Christ Church in October for his part in a 'riot' against the reintroduction of

surplices: T. Clarkson, *Mem. W. Penn* (1813), i. 10–11.
4. His patent was dated 28 November; his pay ran from 30 October. Pepys's opinion soon changed.

to the powder and had burned his side, and his hand that he put into his pocket to put out the fire. But upon examination, and finding him in a lie about the time and place that he bought it, I did extremely beat him. And though it did trouble me to do it, yet I thought it necessary to do it. So to write by the post, and to bed.

3. *Lords day*. This day I stirred not out, but took physique and it did work very well; and all the day, as I was at leisure, I did*a* read in Fuller's *Holy Warr* (which I have of late bought)[1] and did try to make a Song[2] in the prayse of a Liberall genius (as I take my own to be) to all studies and pleasures; but it not proving to my mind, I did reject it and so proceeded not in it. At night my wife and I had a good supper by ourselfs, of a pullet= hashed; which pleased*b* me much to see my condition come to allow ourselfs a dish like that. And so at night to bed.

4. In the morning, being very rainy, by Coach with Sir W. Penn and my wife to White-hall; and sent her to Mrs. Hunts, and he and I to Mr. Coventry about business; and so sent for her again, and all three home[3] again; only, I to the Miter (Mr. Rawlinson's), where Mr. Pierce the purser had got us*c* a most rare Chine of beef and a dish of marrow bones. Our Company, my Uncle Wight, Captain Lambert, one Captain Doves, and purser Barber, Mr. Rawlinson, and ourselfs – and very merry. After dinner*d* I took Coach and called my wife at my brother's, where I left her; and to the Opera, where we saw *The Bondman*,[4] which of old we both did so doate on, and do so still; though, to both our thinking, not so well acted here (having too great expectacions) as formerly at Salsbury Court – but for Baterton; he is called by us both the best actor in the world.[5] So home by coach,

a l.h. repl. s.h. 'ded' *b* MS. 'plead' *c* repl. 'me'
d preceded by small blot

---

1. Thomas Fuller, *The historie of the holy warre*; a history of the Crusades, first published in 1639. PL 2095 (Cambridge, 1651, 4th ed.).

2. Possibly write verses. He 'begun to compose songs' on 11 February 1662. (E).

3. Sc. 'homewards', Mrs Pepys being dropped at Tom's in Salisbury Court on the way.

4. See above, p. 47 & n. 2. (A).

5. Mrs Pepys had a dog named Betterton in 1664 (*Shorthand Letters*, p. 22) – perhaps so-called because of his acting.

I lighting by the way at my uncle Wights and stayed there a little, and so home after my wife. And to bed.

5. At the office all the morning. At noon came my brother Tom and Mr. Armiger^a to dine with me; and did, and we were very merry. After dinner and having drunk a great deal of wine, I went away, seeming* to go about business with Sir W. Pen to my Lady Battens (Sir W. being at Chatham); and there sat a good while and then went away (before I went, I called at home to see whether they were gone, and find them there and Armiger inviting my wife to go to a play; and like a fool would be courting her, but he is an asse; and lays out money with Tom,¹ otherwise I should not think him worthy half this respect I show him) to the Dolphin, where he and I and Captain Cocke sat late and drank much, seeing the boys in the street fling their Crackers – this day being keeped all the day very stricktly in the City.² At last broke^b up and called at my Lady Battens again; and would have gone to Cards, but Sir W. Penn was so fuddled that we could not woo him to play; and therefore we parted, and I home and to bed.

6. Going forth this morning, I met Mr. Davenport³ and a friend of his, one Mr. Furbisher, to drink their morning draught with me; and I did give it them in good wine and anchoves, and pickled oysters; and took them to the Sun in fishstreete and there did give them a barrel of good ones and a great deal of wine, and sent for Mr. W. Bernard (Sir Robts. son, a grocer thereabouts) and were very merry; and cost me a good deal of money. And at noon left them, with my head full of wine; and being invited by a note from Luellin that came to my hand this morning in bed, I went to Nick. Osborne's at the Victualling Office and there saw his wife, who he hath lately married, a good sober woman and new-come to their house. We had a good dish or two of marrowbones and another of neats tongs to dinner; and that being done, I bid them adieu and hastened to White-hall

a repl. 'Pargiter'   *b* MS. 'brother'

1. William Armiger, who was related to the Pepyses, lodged at Tom's.

2. See *Comp.*: 'Gunpowder Treason Day'.

3. Of Brampton, Hunts.

(calling Mr. Moore by the way) to my Lord Privy Seale, who will at last force the Clerkes to bring in a table of their Fees, which they have so long denied.[1] But I do not joyne with them and so he is very respectful to me: so he desires me to bring in one which I observe in taking of Fees, which I will speedily do. So back again and endeavoured to speak with Tom. Trice (who I fear is haching some mischief); but could not, which vexed me; and so I went home and sat late with pleasure at my lute; and so to bed.

7. This morning came one Mr. Hill (sent by Mr. Hunt the instrument maker) to teach me to play on the Theorbo; but I do not like his play nor singing, and so I found a way to put him off. So to the office and then to dinner; and got Mr. Pett the Commissioner to dinner with mee, he and I alone, my wife not being well; and so after dinner, parted. And I to Tom. Trice; who in short, showed me a Writt he hath ready for my father and I, and I promised to answer it. So I went to Dr. Williams (who is now pretty well got up after his sickness) and after that to Mr. Moore to advise; and so returned home late on foot, with my mind cleared, though not satisfyed. I met with letters at home from my Lord from Lisbone, which speak of his being well; and he tells me he had seen at the Court there, the day before he wrote this letter, the *huego de Toro*.[2] So fitted myself for bed.

Coming home, I called at my Uncle Fenners, who tells me that Pegg Kite hath now declared that she will have the beggarly rogue, the Weaver; and so we are resolved neither to meddle nor make with her.[3]

8. This morning, up early and to my Lord Chancellors with a letter to him from my Lord, and did speak with him; and he

---

1. The Lord Privy Seal received one-fifth of all fees, and a fixed tariff would facilitate his check on the clerks' accounts as well as protect the public. No official table appears to have survived among the papers of the Privy Seal Office. There are some fee-accounts (from 1717 on) in PRO, PSO 4/1, 22(9).

2. Sandwich wrote a description of the bull-fight in his *Journal*, pp. 100–1 (30 September); printed also in Harris, i. 203–4.

3. This marriage has not been traced. Cf. below, p. 231 & n. 5.

did ask me whether I was son to Mr. Talbot Pepys or no (with whom he was once acquainted in the Court of Requests),[1] and spoke to me with great respects. Thence to Westminster-hall (it being tearme time) and there met with Commissioner Pett; and so at noon he and I by appointment to the Sun in new fish-street,[2] where Sir J. Minnes, Sir Wm. Batten and we all were to dine at an invitation of Captain Stoakes and Captain Clerke, and were very merry; and by discourse I find Sir J. Mennes a fine gentleman and a very good scholler.

After dinner to the Wardrobe and thence to Dr. Williams, who went with me (the first time that he hath been abroad a great while) to the Six Clerkes Office to find me a Clerke there able to advise me in my business with Tom. Trice;[3] and after I had heard them talk and had given me some comfort, I went to my brother Tom's and took him with me to my Cosen Turner[4] at the Temple, and had his opinion that I shall not pay more then the principall 200*l*: with which I was much pleased; and so home.

9. At the office all the morning. At noon Mr. Davenport, Phillips and Mr. Wm. Bernard and Furbisher came by appointment and dined with me, and we were very merry. After dinner, I to the Wardrobe and there stayed talking with my Lady all the afternoon, till late at night. Among other things, my Lady did mightily urge me to lay out money upon my wife, which I perceived was a little more earnest then ordinary; and so I seemed to be pleased with it and do resolve to bestow a lace[5] upon her – and what with this and other talk, we were exceeding merry. So home at night.

10. *Lordsday.* At our own church in the morning, where Mr. Mills preached. Thence alone to the Wardrobe to dinner with my Lady – where my Lady continues upon yesterday's

1. Talbot Pepys was Pepys's great-uncle. The Court of Requests (in which he had practised as a barrister) had been abolished in 1641.

2. Fish St Hill in Bridge Ward. (R).

3. See below, p. 215, n. 1.

4. John Turner; a Bencher of the Middle Temple since February.

5. Of gold- or silver-thread; later made into a handkerchief: see below, pp. 212, 214. Pepys did not give his wife a dress allowance until 1669.

discourse still, for me to lay out money upon my wife. Which I think it is best for me to do, for her honour and my owne. Last night died Archiball, my Lady's butler and Mrs. Sarahs brother, of a dropsy, which I am troubled at.

In the afternoon went and sat with Mr. Turner in his pew at St. Gregory's,[1] where I hear our Queene Katharine, the first time by name as such, publicly prayed for – and heard Dr. Buck upon "Woe unto thee, Corazin" &c;[2] where he started a difficulty which he left to another time to answer, about why God should give means of grace to those people which he knew would not receive them, and deny to others which he himself confesses, if they had had them, would have received them, and they would have been effectuall too. I would I could hear him explain this when he doth come to it. Thence home to my wife and took her to my aunt Wights and there sat a while with her (my uncle being at Katharine hill),[3] and so home. And I to Sir W. Batten's, where Captain Cock was; and we sent for two bottles of Canary to the Rose, which did do me a great deal of hurt and did trouble me all night; and endeed, came home so out of order that I was loath to say prayers tonight, as I am used ever to do on Sundays; which my wife took notice of and people of my house, which I was sorry for.

11. To the Wardrobe, and with Mr. Townsend and Moore to the Saracens-head to a barrel of oysters. And so Mr. Moore and I to Tom. Trices, with whom I did first set my hand to answer to a writt of his this tearme.[4] Thence to the Wardrobe to dinner; and there by appointment met my wife, who hath by my direction brought some laces, for my Lady to choose one for her; and after dinner I went away and left my wife and Lady together, and all their work was about this lace of hers.

Captain Ferrers and I went out together; and he carried me, the first time that ever I saw any gaming house,[5] to one entering

---

1. John Turner lived in the parish of St Bride's, Fleet St; St Gregory's was his father's parish. (R).

2. *Recte* 'Chorazin': Matt., xi. 21; Luke, x. 13.

3. Near Guildford, Surrey, where in 1672 he died.

4. See below, p. 215 & n. 1.

5. As a child in arms Pepys had been taken to see the gaming at one of the Temple halls: below, ix. 3.

into Lincolnes Inn fields at the end of bellyard – where strange
the folly of men, to lay and lose so much money; and very glad
I was to see the manner of a gamsters life – which I see is very
miserable, and poor and unmanly.

And thence he took me to a dancing Schoole in Fleetstreete,
where we saw a company of pretty girles dance, but I do not in
myself like to have young girles exposed to so much vanity.[1]

So to the Wardrobe, where I find my Lady hath agreed upon
a lace for my wife, of 6l., which I seemed much glad of that it
was no more, though in my mind I think it too much, and I
pray God keep me so to order myself and my wife's expenses
that no inconvenience in purse or honour fallow this my pro-
digality.   So by coach home.

12.   At the office all the morning.   Dined at home alone.
So abroad with Sir W. Pen, my wife and I, to *Barthlemew fayre*,
with puppets (which I have seen once before,[2] and the play without puppets often); but though I love the play as much as ever I
did, yet I do not like the puppets at all, but think it to be a lessening
to it.   Thence to the Grayhound in Fleetstreete, and there drank
some Raspbury Sack and eat some Sasages; and so home very
merry.

This day Holmes came to towne and we do expect hourely to
hear what usage he hath from the Duke and the King about this
late business of letting the Swedish Embassador go by him without
striking his flag.[3]

1. Cf. Magalotti ([1669], p. 314):
'Dancing is a very common and
favorite amusement of the ladies in
this country [England]; every evening there are entertainments at different places [in London], at which
many ladies and citizens' wives are
present, they going to them alone, as
they do to the rooms of the dancing
masters, at which there are frequently
upwards of forty or fifty ladies.'
2. See above, p. 117 & n. 1. (A).
3. Sailing for Sweden, the ambassador (Nils Nilsson Brahe) had refused to lower his flag on meeting the
Royal Charles in the mouth of the

Thames.   Capt. Robert Holmes had
fired three shots to make the Swedes
heave to, but they had escaped under
cover of night while Holmes was
waiting for confirmation of the
ambassador's story that he had acted
with Charles II's express permis-
sion.   Holmes was examined by the
Council on 27 November, deprived
of his command and committed to the
Tower.   He was pardoned and re-
leased a few days later.   Below,
pp. 222-3, 229; PRO, PC 2/55, pp.
459, 460; *CSPVen. 1661-4*, pp. 69,
71, 74; HMC, *Rep.*, 11/7/3; T. W.
Fulton, *Sovereignty of sea*, pp. 455-6.

13. By appointment, we all went this morning to wait upon the Duke of Yorke, which we did in his chamber as he was dressing himself in his riding-suit to go this day by sea to the Downes (he is in mourning for his Wifes grandmother,[1] which is thought a great piece of fondness*). After we had given him our letter relating the bad condition of the Navy for want of mony, he referred it to his coming back and so parted.[2] And I to Westminster-hall and to see *La belle* Pearce; and so on foot to my Lord Crews, where I find him come to his new house, which is next to that he lived in last.[3] Here I was well received by my Lord and Sir Thomas[4] – with whom I had great talk; and he tells me in good earnest that he doth believe the parliament (which comes to sit again the next week) will be troublesome to the Court and Clergy, which God forbid. But they see things carried so by my Lord Chancellor and some others, that get money themselfs, that they will not endure it. From thence to the Theatre and there saw *Father's owne Sonn*[5] again. And so it raining very hard, I went home by Coach, with my mind very heavy for this my expenseful life; which will undo me I fear, after all my hopes, if I do not take up[a] – for now I am coming to lay out a great deal of money in clothes upon my wife, I must forbear other expenses.

To bed, and this night begin to lie in the little green Chamber where the maids lie; but we could not a great while get Nell to lie there, because I lie there and my wife; but at last, when she saw she must lie there or sit up, she with much ado came to bed.

14. At the office all the morning. At noon I went by appointment to the Sun in Fish=street to a dinner of young Mr. Bernards for myself, Mr. Phillips, Davenport, Weaver, &c:,

a blot over symbol

---

1. Anne, widow of Sir Thomas Aylesbury, Bt, who was buried this day in Westminster Abbey.
2. On the 9th the Duke had written asking for a statement of money owing: PRO, Adm. 2/1745, f.15r.
3. The new house was probably what we now call the former 52 Lincoln's Inn Fields (rebuilt in 1912), where he was living in 1667. (R).

4. Sir Thomas Crew, son of Lord Crew; M.P. for Brackley, Northants., and a critic of the government.
5. Probably Fletcher's comedy, *Monsieur Thomas*; q.v. above, p. 186 & n. 1. (A).

where we had a most excellent dinner, but a pie of such pleasant variety of good things as in all my life I never tasted. Hither came to me Captain Lambert to take his leave of me, he being this day to set sail for the Straights. We drank his farewell and a health to all our friends; and were very merry and drank wine[a] enough. Hence to the Temple to Mr. Turner about drawing up my bill in Chancery against T. Trice. And so to Salsbury Court, where Mrs. Turner is come to towne tonight, but very ill still of an ague, which I was sorry to see.[1] So to the Wardrobe and talked with my Lady, and so home. And to bed.

15. At home all the morning. And at noon with my wife to the Wardrobe to dinner; and there did show herself to my Lady in the hankercher that she bought the lace for the other day; and endeed, it is very handsome. Here I left my wife, and went to my Lord Privy Seale to White-hall and there did give him a copy of the fees of the office as I have received them, and he was well pleased with it.[2] So to the Opera, where I met my wife and Captain Ferrers and Madamoiselle la Blanc, and there did see the second part of *The Siege of Rhodes*[3] very well done. And so by coach set her home; and the coach driving down the hill through Thames-street (which I think never any coach did before from that place to the bridge-foot); but going up Fish-street hill, his horses were so tired that they could not be got to go up the hill, though all the street boys and men did beat and whip them. At last I was fain to send my boy for a link, and so light out of the coach till we got another at the corner of Fan-church-street; and so home. And to bed.

16. At the office all the morning. Dined at home; and so about my business in the afternoon to the temple, where I find

a MS. 'wife'

---

1. This was a long illness: for her recovery, see below, iii. 30.
2. Cf. the accounts of receipts from Privy Seal fees dated 1 October, and covering 15 March – 1 July 1661 in Rawl. A 174, ff. 259+ (in an unidentified clerk's hand).
3. See above, p. 130 & n. 2. (A).

my chancery bill drawn against T. Trice;[1] which I read, and like it. And so home.

17. *Lords day.* To our own church. And at noon by invitation Sir W. Penn dined with me and I took Mrs. Hester (my Lady Batten's kinswoman) to dinner from church with me – and we were very merry. So to church again and heard a simple fellow upon the praise[a] of church musique, and exclaiming against men's wearing their hats on in the church.[2] But I slept part of the sermon, till later prayer and blessing; and all was done without waking, which I never did in my life. So home; and by and by comes my Uncle Wight and my aunt and Mr. Norbury and his lady. And we drank hard and were very merry till supper time; and then we parted, my wife and I being invited to Sir Pen's where we also were very merry; and so home to prayers and to bed.

18.[b] By coach with Sir W. Penn – my wife and I toward Westminster; but seeing Mr. Moore in the street, I light and he and I went to Mr. Battersby's the Minister (in my way, I putting in at St. Pauls, where I saw the Quiristers in their Surplices going to prayers, and a few idle poor people and boys to hear them, which is the first time I have seen them, and am sorry to see things done so out of order); and there I received 50*l* more, which makes up a 100*l* that I now have borrowed of him;[3] and so I did tear the old bond for 50*l*; and paying him the use of it, did make a new bond for the whole 100*l*. Here I dined and had a good dinner, and his wife a good pretty woman. There was a young parson at the table that had got[c] himself drunk before dinner, which troubled me to see.

After dinner to Mr. Bow[y]ers at Westminster for my wife,

a MS. 'prise'   *b* repl. '16'   *c* MS. 'god'

---

1. Dated 23 November: with Trice's answer of 3 December it is in PRO, C 10, 63/77; printed in Whitear, pp. 152+. The bill was filed in order to stop an action at common law which Trice had begun for the recovery of the £200 in which the bond of 1630 was secured: above, p. 134, n. 2. The dispute dragged on till 1663 and was finally settled out of court. Cf. Whitear, pp. 148–50.

2. Archbishop Laud had condemned the habit.

3. See above, p. 191.

and brought her to the Theatre to see *Philaster*[1] (which I never saw before), but I find it far short of my expectation. So by coach home.

19. At the office all the morning; and coming home, find Mr. Hunt with my wife in the chamber alone; which God forgive me, did trouble my head; but remembering that it was washing-day and that there was no place else with a fire for him to be in, it being also cold weather, I was at ease again. He dined with us; and after dinner took coach and carried him with us as far as my Cosen Scotts (where we set him down and parted) and my wife and I stayed there at the christening of my Cosens boy – where my Cosen, Sam. Pepys of Ireland, and I were godfathers.[2] And I did name the child Samuell. There was a company of pretty women there in the chamber; but we stayed not, but went with the Minister[3] into another room and eat and drank. And at last, when most of the women were gone, Sam and I went into my Cosen Scott, who was got off her bed; and so we stayed and talked and were very merry (my she-Cosen Stradwick being godmother); and then I left my wife to go home by coach, and I walked to the Temple about my law business; and there receiving a Subpoena for T. Trice, I carried it myself to him at the usual house at Doctors Commons and did give it him; and so home and to bed. ⟨It cost me 20s between the midwife and the two nurses today.⟩[a]

20. To Westminster-hall by water in the morning, where I saw the King going in his barge to the parliament-house, this being the first day of their meeting again. And the Bishops I hear do take their places in the Lords' house this day.[4] I walked long in the Hall, but hear nothing of newes but what Ned. Pickering tells me, which I am troubled at, that Sir J. Mennes should send word to the King that if he did not remove all my Lord Sandwichs

---

[a] addition crowded into end of page

1. A tragicomedy by Beaumont and Fletcher, first acted c. 1611, and published in 1620. Now at the TR, Vere St. (A).

2. Benjamin Scott, citizen and pewterer of St Sepulchre's, Holborn, had married Judith, daughter of Sir

Richard Pepys (d. 1659), Lord Chief Justice of Ireland. Samuel Pepys of Ireland, a clergyman, was her brother.

3. Thomas Gouge.

4. The act of 1642 excluding them had been repealed in July.

Captaines out of this fleet, he believed the King would not be master of the fleet at its coming home again – and so doth endeavour to bring disgrace upon my Lord. But I hope all that will not do, for the King loves him.

Hence by water to the Wardrobe and dined with my Lady, my Lady Wright being there too (whom I find to be a witty but very conceited woman and proud);[1] and after dinner Mr. Moore and I to the Temple, and there he read my bill and likes it well enough. And so we came back again, he with me as far as the lower end of Cheapside; and there I gave him a pint of Sack and parted. And I home, and went seriously to look over my papers touching T. Trice, and think I have found some that will go near to do me more good in this difference of ours then all I have before. So to bed, with my mind cheery upon it; and lay long reading Hobbs his *liberty and necessity*,[2] and a little but a very shrewd piece. And so to sleep.

21. In the morning, again at looking over the last night's papers; and by and by comes Mr. Moore, who finds that my papers may do me[a] much good. He stayed and dined with me, and we had a good surloyne of roast beef (the first that ever I had of my own buying since I kept house); and after dinner he and I to the Temple and there showed Mr. Smallwood[3] my papers, who likes them well; and so I left them with him and went with Mr. Moore to Grayes Inne to his chamber; and there he showed me his old Cambdens *Brittannia*,[4] which I entend to buy of him and so took it away with me and left it at St. Pauls churchyard to be bound; and so home and to the office all the afternoon, it being the first afternoon that we have sot (which we are now to do always, so long as the Parliament sits, who this day have

a s.h. repl. l.h. 'mee'

---

1. Anne, wife of Sir Henry Wright and sister of Lady Sandwich. She wrote sprightly letters to Sandwich, sometimes in French: e.g. Carte 73, ff. 254r, 573r.

2. Thomas Hobbes, *Of libertie and necessitie*, first published in 1654; PL 47 (1676 ed.).

3. William Smallwood or the Middle Temple, Trice's lawyer.

4. William Camden, *Britannia*; first published in Latin in 1586, several times re-issued; translated by Philemon Holland in 1610. The only copy in the PL is Edmund Gibson's 1695 edition in English (PL 2807), which contains contributions by Pepys on the dockyards and arsenals of the Royal Navy: cf. *Times Lit. Supp.*, 3 May 1934, p. 322.

voted the King 120000*l*[1] to be raised to pay his debts); and after the office, with Sir W. Batten to the Dolphin and drank and left him there, and I again to the Temple about my business; and so on foot home again.   And to bed.

22.   Within all the morning; and at noon with my wife by appointment to dinner at the Dolphin; where Sir W. Batten and his Lady and daughter Matt, and Captain[a] Cock and his lady, a Germane lady but a very great beauty; and we dined together at the spending of some wagers won and lost between him and I. And there we had the best Musique and very good songs, and were very merry and danced.   But I was most of all taken with Madam Cock and her little boy, which in mirth his father hath given to me.   But after all[b] our mirth, comes a Reckoning of 4*l*, besides 40*s* to the Musique; which did trouble us, but it must be paid; and so I took leave and left them there about 8 at night; and on foot went to the Temple and there took my Cosen Turners man Roger, and went by his advice to Serjeant Fountaine[2] and told him our case, who gives me good comfort in it, and I gave him 30*s* fee.   So home again.   And to bed.   ⟨This day a good pretty mayd[3] was sent my wife by Mary Bowyer, which my wife hath hired.⟩[c]

23.   To Westminster with my wife (she to her father's); and about 10 a-clock, back again home; and there I to the office a little and thence by coach with Comissioner Pett to Cheapeside to one Savill a painter, who I entend shall do my picture and my wife's.[4]   Thence I to dinner to the Wardrobe, and so home to the office and there all the afternoon till night; and then both Sir Wms. to my house; and in comes Captain Cock, and they to

a l.h. repl. l.h. 'Dr.'   *b* repl. 'all' (blurred)
        c addition crowded into end of line

1. *Recte* £1,200,000: *CJ*, viii. 317.
2. John Fountaine of Lincoln's Inn; a distant relative of Pepys by marriage.
3. Sarah.   She started work on 28 November; Mrs Pepys dismissed her in December 1662.
4. Nothing is known of the *œuvre* of Savill.   He is perhaps the Mr Savile, 'picture-maker', who was associated in 1677 with the Painter-Stainers'

Company: GL, MS. 5667/2, f.213r. The portraits of Pepys and his wife were hung in Pepys's dining-room on 22 February 1662 and varnished there by the artist on 11 June 1662.   They are no longer extant.   (For a contrary view concerning Pepys's portrait, see D. Pepys Whiteley in *Country Life*, 1961, pp. 778.+)   (OM).

Cards. By and by Sir Wm. Batten and Cock, after drinking a good deal of wine, went away; and Sir W. Penn stayed with my wife and I to supper, very pleasant; and so good-night. This day I had a Chine of beefe sent home, which I bespoke to send and did send it, as a present to my uncle Wight.

24. ⟨*Lords:day.*⟩

Up earely and by appointment to St. Clements lane to church;[1] and there to meet Captain Cock, who hath often commended Mr. Alsopp their Minister to me, who is endeed an able man but as all things else, did not come up to my expectation. His text was that all good and perfect gifts are from above.[2]

Thence Cock and I to the Sun taverne behind the Exchange and there met with others that are come from the same church, and stayed and drank and talked with them a little; and so broke up and I to the Wardrobe and there dined; and stayed all the afternoon with my Lady alone, talking. And thence to see Madam Turner; who, poor lady, continues very ill, and I begin to be afeared of her. Thence homewards; and meeting Mr. Yong the Upholster, he and I to the Miter and with Mr. Rawlinson sat and drank a Quart of sack; and so I to Sir W. Batten's and there stayed and supped; and so home – where I find an invitacion sent my wife and I to my Uncle Wights on Tuesday next, to the Chine of beef which I presented them with yesterday.

So to prayers and to bed.

25. To Westminster-hall in the morning with Captain Lambert – and there he did at the Dogg give me, and some other friends of his, his foy, he being to set sail today toward the Streights. Here we had oysters and good wine. Having this morning met in the hall with Mr. Sanchy, we appointed to meet at the play this afternoon. At noon, at the rising of the House, I met with Sir W. Pen, and with him and Major-Generall Massy (who I find by discourse to be a very ingenious man, and among other things, a great master in the Secresys of powder and fireworkes)[3] and another Knight to dinner at the Swan in the Palace yard, and our meat brought from the Legg. And after dinner

1. St Clement's, Eastcheap.
2. Jas., i. 17.
3. Maj.-Gen. Sir Edward Massey (M.P. for Gloucester) had been an expert on siege warfare in the Civil War.

Sir W. Pen and I to the Theatre and there saw *The Country Cap-tain*,[1] a dull play; and that being done, I left him with his Torys[2] and went to the Opera and saw the last act of *The Bondman*;[3] and there find Mr. Sanchy and Mrs. Mary Archer, sister to the fair Betty, whom I did admire at Cambrige.[4] And thence took them to the fleece in Covent Garden, there to bid good-night to Sir W. Penn, who stayed for me. But Mr. Sanchy could not by any argument get his lady to trust herself with him into the taverne, which he was much troubled at; and so we returned immediately into the city by Coach, and at the Miter in Cheapside there light and drank, and then set her at her uncles in the Old Jury. And so he and I back again thither and drank till past 12 at night, till I had drank something too much – he all the while telling me his intentions to get this girle, who is worth 1000*l.* And many times we had her sister Betty's health, whose memory I love. At last parted, and I well home; only, have got cold and was hoarse, and so to bed.

26. Not well in the morning and lay long in bed. At last rise and at noon with my wife to my Uncle Wights, where we met Mr. Cole, Mr. Rawlinson, Norbury and his wife and her daughter, and other friends to the Chine of beef that I sent them the other day, and eat and were merry. By and by I am called to the office, whither I went and there we sat late; and after the office done, Sir Wms both and I and Captain Cock and Mr. Bence (who being drunk, showed himself by his talk a bold foole, and so we were fain to put him off and get him away) we sat till 9 a-clock by ourselfs in the office, talking and drinking three or four bottles of wine. And so home and to bed. My wife and her mayde Dorothé falling out, I was troubled at it.

---

1. See above, p. 202 & n. 2. (A).
2. Irishmen; only in the late 1670s was the word used politically. Penn had estates in Ireland and was Gover-nor of Kinsale.
3. See above, p. 47 & n. 2. At this time playgoers claimed the right to see the fourth or fifth act of a play without paying for admission and Pepys probably availed himself of the

privilege on this occasion. The pri-vilege was prohibited by the Lord Chamberlain on 7 December 1663, but nevertheless continued. (A).
4. Clement Sankey was a Fellow of Magdalene. He married Mary Archer (of Bourn, Cambs.) in 1669, when he was Rector of St Clement's, Eastcheap, and a Canon of York.

27. This morning our maid Dorothy and my wife parted – which though she be a wench for her tongue not to be borne with, yet I was loath to part with her. But I took my leave kindly of her; and went out to Savill's the painter and there sat the first time for my face with him.[1] Thence to dinner with my Lady. And so after an hour or two's talk in Divinity with my Lady – Captain Ferrers and Mr. Moore and I to the Theatre and there saw *Hamlett*, very well done.[2] And so I home and find that my wife hath been with my aunt Wight and Ferrers to wait on my Lady today, this afternoon, and there danced and were very merry; and my Lady very fond, as she is alway of my wife. So to bed.

28. At home all the morning. At noon Will brought me from White-hall, whither I had sent him, some letters from my Lord Sandwich from Tanger – where he continues still, and hath done some execution upon the Turks – and retaken an Englishman from them, of one Mr. Parker's, a merchant in Markelane.[3]
In the afternoon Mr. Pett and I met at the office. There being none more there then we two, I saw there was not the reverence due to us observed; and so I took occasion to break up, and took Mr. Gawden along with me; and he and I (though it rained) were resolved to go, he to my Lord Treasurers and I to the Chancellers with a letter from my Lord today. So to a taverne at the end of Marke-lane, and there we stayed till with much ado we got a Coach; and so to my Lord Treasurers and lost our labours; then to the Chancellors, and there I met with Mr. Dugdale and with him and one Mr. Simons (I think that belongs to my Lord Hatton) and Mr. Kipps and others to the Fountaine

1. See above, p. 218 & n. 4. (OM).
2. By 'Theatre', Pepys usually means the Theatre Royal in Vere St managed by Thomas Killigrew. Here, however, it probably refers to the Lincoln's Inn Fields playhouse managed by Davenant, because on 12 December 1660 Davenant had been given the exclusive right to stage *Hamlet*. See Nicoll, pp. 352–3; also above, p. 161 & n. 2. (A).
3. Sandwich had gone to Tangier from Lisbon on 3 October. These letters were written to Pepys on 28 October and referred to the exploits of the *Princess* and the *Fairfax*, commanded by Lawson. A Turkish (Algerian) man-of-war had been chased, forced ashore near Malaga, and its crew of 150 captured; and a small English trader, richly laden with silks from Italy worth £11,000, had been rescued: Sandwich, pp. 103–5.

tavern and there stayed till 12 at night, drinking and singing, Mr. Simons and one Mr. Agar singing very well.[1] Then Mr. Gawden, being almost drunk, had the wit to be gone; and so I took leave too, and it being a fine moone shine night, he and I footed it all the way home; but though he was drunk, he went such a pace as I do admire how he was able to go. When I come home, I find our new mayde Sarah come, who is a tall and a very well favoured wench, and one that I think will please us. So to bed.

29. I lay long in bed, till Sir Wms. both sent me word that we were to wait upon the Duke of Yorke today and that they would have me to meet them at Westminster-hall at noon; so I rose and went thither[a] and there I understand that they are gone to Mr. Coventrys lodgings in the old palace-yard to dinner (the first time I knew that he hath any); and there I met them two and Sir G. Carteret, and had a very fine dinner and good welcome and discourse; and so by water after dinner to White-hall to the Duke, who met us in his Closett; and there he did discourse to us the business of Holmes,[2] and did desire of us to know what hath been the common practice about making of forrayne ships to strike sail to us:[3] which they did all do as much as they could, but I could say nothing to it, which I was sorry for; so endeed, I was forced to study a lie: and so after we were gone from the Duke, I told Mr. Coventry that I had heard Mr. Selden often say that he could prove that in Henry the 7ths time he did give com-

a repl. incorrect symbol for 'thither'

1. John Dugdale (son of William, herald and antiquary) was chief gentleman-usher to the Chancellor; Thomas Kipps (once in Sandwich's service and an old friend of Pepys) was his purse-bearer; Thomas Agar was Deputy-Clerk of the Crown Office. Lord Hatton was the 1st Baron, whose patent as Governor of Guernsey (22 May 1662) may have been in negotiation now. He had married a Mountagu – the daughter of Sir Charles, of Boughton, Northants. – and was an old friend of the Dugdales.

2. See above, p. 212 & n. 3.

3. On 21 January 1662 the Duke issued an order on the subject: BM, Add. 5439, ff. 76-7. The Holmes incident and others led to the elaboration of English claims: below, ix. 397 & n. 3; T. W. Fulton, *Sovereignty of sea*, esp. pp. 472+. The limits of territorial waters were not yet established, and treaties on the subject left many points ambiguous. Pepys later gathered some material about the precedents: *Naval Minutes*, pp. 53, 55, 56, 66.

mission to his Captains to make the King of Denmark's ships to strike to him in the Baltique.[1]

From thence Sir W. Pen and I to the Theatre but it was so full that we could hardly get any room; so he went up to one of the boxes, and I into the 18*d* places and there saw *Love at first sight*,[2] a play of Mr. Killigrews, and the first time that it hath been acted since before the troubles; and great expectation there was, but I find the play to be a poor thing; and so I perceive everybody else do. So home, calling at Pauls churchyard for a *Mare Clausum*,[3] having it in my mind to write a little matter, what I can gather about the business of Striking sayle and present it to the Duke, which I now think will be a good way to make myself known. So home and to bed.

30. In the morning to the Temple – Mr. Philips's and Dr Williams about my several law matters; and so to the Wardrobe to dinner. And after dinner stole away, my Lady not dining out of her chamber; and so home and there to the office all the afternoon; and that being done, Sir W. Batten and I and Captain

1. John Selden, the great legal authority, was the author of the semi-official *Mare Clausum* (1635), which put English claims at their highest, claiming for Britain the sovereignty over the seas around her, and interpreting their limits as extending well out into the Atlantic and to the opposite shores of the Channel and North Sea. But he never laid claim for Britain to the Baltic. Selden had died in November 1654 when Pepys was 21. Pepys may have known of him not only by reputation but also through Selden's friendship with John Langley, Pepys's schoolmaster. Possibly Pepys's visit to the Baltic in 1659 inspired the invention of this story. It was a most unlikely one, since Denmark and Sweden successfully claimed sovereignty over the Baltic. Pepys was in later life sceptical about all such extravagant

claims: *Naval Minutes*, pp. 330, 373.

2. The 18*d*. places were in the middle gallery, between the boxes and the top gallery. Pepys often sat in this part of the auditorium during his earlier years of theatregoing. *The Princess, or Love at first sight*, a tragi-comedy by Thomas Killigrew, was first acted c. 1637, but not published until 1663. Now at the TR, Vere St. (A).

3. Selden's treatise; in Latin (with sprinklings of Greek and Hebrew); first published in 1635; PL 2048. It was probably the translation of 1652 which Pepys now bought (cf. below, iv. 105). It was replaced by that of 1663 (PL 2131). Pepys was later critical of the work: *Naval Minutes*, pp. 53, 275. Nothing is known of the 'little matter' which Pepys here thought of writing; he may not have written it.

Cock got a bottle of sack into the office, and there we sat late and drank and talked. And so home and to bed.[a]

I am this day in very good health, only got a little cold. The Parliament hath sat a pretty while. The old condemned Judges of the late King have been brought before the Parliament, and like to be hanged.[1] I am deep in Chancery against Tom Trice;[2] God give a good issue. And my mind under great trouble for my late great expending of money vainly, which God stop for the future. This is the last day for the old State's Coyne to pass in common payments, but they say it is to pass in public payments to the King three months still.[3]

a   followed by long diagonal line

1. These were the group of regicides who had been tried and condemned in October 1660, but whose sentences had been suspended until confirmed by act of parliament, on the grounds that they had obeyed an order to surrender, and could adduce other extenuating facts. There were 19 of them, only 12 of whom could appear in parliament. The bill to have them executed was introduced on 22 November and had on the 26th been committed, after second reading. It was never passed, however, and the condemned men lived out their lives in prison. *CJ*, viii. 317, 319, 320.

2. See above, p. 134, n. 2.

3. By a proclamation of 7 September 1661 all gold and silver coins issued by the usurpers were demonetised from 30 November. Further proclamations of 7 December and the following 23 January extended their validity for tax payments to 1 May 1662: Steele, nos 3326, 3342, 3351; Sir J. Craig, *The Mint*, p. 157.

DECEMBER

1. Lords=day.

In the morning at church and heard Mr. Mills. At home
dined, and with me by appointment Mr. Sanchy, who should
have brought his mistress, Mrs. Mary Archer of Cambrige,
but she could not come. But we had a good dinner for him;
and so in the afternoon my wife went to church, and he and I
stayed at home and drank and talked and he stayed with me till
night and supped with me – when I expected to have seen Jack
Cole and Lem. Wagstaffe, but they did not come.

We this day cut a brave Coller of Brawne from Winchcombe,
which proves very good. And also opened the glass of Girkins
which Captain Cock did give my wife the other day, which are
rare things.

So at night to bed.

There hath lately been great Clapping up of some old states-
men,* such as Ireton, Moyer and others; and they say upon a
great plot, but I believe no such thing;[1] but it is but justice that
they should be served as they served the poor Cavaliers and I
believe it will oftentimes be so as long as I live, whether there be
cause or no.

This evening my Brother Tom: was with me and I did talk
again to him about Mr. Townsends daughter, and I do entend to
put the business in hand; I pray God give a good end to it.

---

[1]. This was the Yarranton or
Baxter Plot. John Ireton had been
Lord Mayor in 1658-9, and Samuel
Moyer a member of Cromwell's
Council of State. The warrant for
Moyer's arrest was issued on 25
November: HMC, *Rep.*, 11/7/3.
The government claimed to have
prevented an uprising and to have
uncovered a most important rebel
organisation. See the proclamation
of 28 November (*CSPD 1661-2*,
p. 161); Clarendon's speech to parliament on 19 December (*Parl. Hist.*,
iv. 226); a letter (19 December)
describing the rebels' organisation
(HMC, *Rep.*, 12/9/51). But the re-
view of the evidence in M. P. Ashley,
John Wildman (p. 172) reaches the
same conclusion as Pepys. Cf.
Pepys's scepticism at 30 October
1661. He was himself to suffer
similarly as a victim of the Popish
Plot in 1679.

2.   To Savills the painter's; but he not being well, I could do nothing there and so I returned home, and in my way met Mr. Moore and took him with me home; where we stayed and talked all the morning and he dined with me.   And after dinner went away to the Privy Seale, this being our first day this month. By and by called on by Mr. Sanchy and his mistress, and with them by coach to the Opera to see *The Madd Lover*;[1] but not much pleased with the play.   That done, home all to my house, where they stayed and supped and were merry; and at last, late, bade good-night, and so we to bed.

3.   To the paynters and sat and had more of my picture done; but it doth not please me, for I fear it will not be like me.   At noon from thence to the Wardrobe; where dinner not being ready, Mr. Moore and I to the Temple about my little business at Mr. Turner's[2] and so back again; and dinner being half-done, I went in to my Lady, where my Lady Wright was at dinner with her.   And all our talk about the great happiness that my Lady Wright says there is in being in the fashion and in variety of fashions, in scorn of others that are not so, as citizens wifes and country-gentlewomen – which though it did displease me enough, yet I said nothing to it.   Thence by water to the office through bridge, being carried by him in oares that the other day rowed in a scull faster then my oares to the Tower, and I did give him 6*d*.: at the office all the afternoon, and at night home to read in *Mare Clausum* till bedtime; and so to bed.   But had a very bad night by dreams of my wife's riding with me, and her horse throwing her and breaking her leg.   And then I dreamt that I had one of my testicles swelled, and in such pain that I waked with it; and had a great deal of pain there a very great while, till I fell asleep again; and such apprehensions I had of it that when I rose and trussed up myself, thinking that it had been no dream – till in the daytime I found myself very well at ease and remembered that I did dream so; and did dream that Mr. Creed was with me and that I did complain to him of it, and he said he had the same pain in his left which I had in my right stone – which pleased me much to remember.

1. See above, p. 34 & n. 3; at the LIF. (A).

2. The legal dispute with Trice: cf. above, p. 216.

4. To Westminster-hall with both Sir Wms:; then by water (where I saw a man lie dead upon Westminster-stairs that had been drowned yesterday) to the Temple; and thence to Mr. Phillips and got my Copy of Sturtlow lands.[1] So back to the Three Tons at Charing-Crosse and there met the two Sir Wms. and Collonell Treswell and Mr. Falconer and dined there at Sir W. Penn's cost. And after dinner, by water to Cheapside to the painter's and there find my wife; and having sat a little, she and I by Coach to the Opera and Theatre;[2] but coming too late to both, and my mind being a little out of tune, we returned and I settled to read in *Mare Clausum* till bedtime; and so to bed.

5. This morning I went early to the painter's and there sat for my picture[3] the fourth time; but it doth not yet please me, which doth much trouble me. Thence to the Treasury Office,[4] where I find Sir Wm. Batten come before me, and there we set to pay off the *St. George*.[5] By and by came Sir Wm. Pen and he and I stayed while Sir W. Batten went home to dinner; and then he came again, and Sir W. Penn and I went and dined at my house, and had two mince-pies sent thither by our order from the messenger, Slater, that had dressed some victuals for us. And so we were very merry; and after dinner rode out in his Coach, he to White-hall and my wife and I to the Opera and saw *Hamlett*[6] well performed. Thence to the Temple and Mrs. Turners (who continues still very ill); and so home and to bed.

6. Lay long in bed; and then to Westminster-hall and there walked; and then with Mr. Spicer, Hawly, Washington, and little Mr. Ashwell (my old friends at the Exchequer) to the dogg and there gave them two or three Quarts of wine. And so away to White-hall; where at Sir G. Carterets, Sir Wms. both and I dined very pleasantly. And after dinner, by appointment

---

1. Cf. above, p. 193 & n. 1.
2. I.e. to the LIF and the TR, Vere St; both in the Lincoln's Inn Fields district. (A).
3. See above, p. 218 & n. 4. (OM).
4. The office of the Treasurer of

the Navy in Leadenhall St. (R).
5. Her pay amounted to c. £2472. Thomas Turner and three other clerks attended. PRO, Adm. 20/2, nos 214, 1065.
6. See above, p. 161 & n. 2. (A).

came the Governors of the East=India Company to sign and seal the contract between us (in the King's name) and them.¹ And that done, we all went to the King's Closett and there spoke with the King and the Duke of Yorke, who promise to be very careful of the India=trade to the utmost. So back to Sir G. Carterets and ended our business; and so away homewards. But Sir W. Batten offering to go to the Three Tuns at Charing-Crosse, where the pretty maid the daughter of the house is, I was saying that that tickled Sir W. Pen. He² seemed to take these words very heinously and angrily. Which I saw, and seemed indifferent to go home in his Coach with them; and so took leave to go to the Council-chamber to speak with my Lord Privy Seale; which I did, but they did stay for me, which I was pleased at. But no words passed between him and me in all our way home. So home and to bed.

7. This morning came Captain Ferrers and the German, Emanuel Luffe (who goes as one of my Lord's footmen, though he deserves much a better preferment) to take their leave of me.³ And here I got the German to play upon my Theorbo, which he did both below and in my wife's chamber, who was in bed. He plays rarely. And I find by him that my lute is a most excellent lute. I did give them a mince-pie and Coller of brawn and some wine for their breakfast, and were very merry; and sent for Mr. Adams our neighbour to drink Mr. Sheply's health. At last we all parted. But within a Quarter of an houre after they were gone and my wife and I were talking about buying of a fine Scallop* which is brought her this morning by a woman to be sold, which is to cost her 45s, in comes the German back again, all of a goare blood; which I wondered at and tells me that he is afeared that the Captain is killed by the watermen at Tower stayres. So I presently went thither and find that upon some rude pressing of the watermen to ply the Captain, he struck one

---

1. Two contracts (6 December) arranged for the despatch of four royal ships to Bombay, just acquired under the terms of the marriage treaty with Portugal. The company agreed to pay for their manning and victualling and for freight charges on the return journey: *CSPD Add. 1660–85*, pp.

32–5; ib., *1661–2*, p. 168. The agreement later gave rise to a dispute: below, iv. 368 & n. 3.

2. Batten.

3. They went with the fleet which was to meet Sandwich at Lisbon and escort the new Queen.

of them with his Cane; which they would not take, but struck him again and then the German drow his sword and run at one of them. But they were both soundly beaten. The Captain is however got to the Hoy that carries him and the pages to the Downes, and I went into the alehouse at the Stairs and got them to deliver the Captains feathers, which one from the Captain was come to demand; and went home again and there find my wife dressing of the German's head and so did give him a Cravett for his neck and a Crowne in his purse, and sent him away again. Then came Mr. Moore and he and I to Westminster, and so to Worster-house to see Mr. Mountagu before he goes away (this night); but could not see him, nor do I think he hath a mind to see us, for fear of our demanding of money of him for anything. So back to White-hall and eat a bit of meat at Wilkinsons; and then to the Privy Seale and sealed there, the first time this month. And among other things that passed, there was a patent for Roger Palmer (Madam Palmer's husband) to be Earle of Castlemaine and Baron of Limbricke in Ireland. But the honour is tied up to the males got on the body of this wife, the Lady Barbary – the reason whereof everybody knows.[1] That done, by water to the office, where I find Sir W. Pen hath been alone all this night and was just rose; and so I to him, and with him I find Captain Holmes, who hath wrote his case and gives me a Copy,[2] as he hath many among his friends, and presented the same to the King and Councell – which I shall make use of in my attempt of writing something concerning the business of Striking Sayle which I am now about. But he doth cry out against Sir John Mennes as the veriest knave and rogue and Coward in the world. Which I was glad to hear, because he hath given out bad words concerning my Lord,[3] though I am sorry it is so. Here Captain Cox then came in, and he and I stayed a good while

---

1. The new Earl and his wife (the King's mistress) were not living together, and the intention was that the title should become extinct, as it did on the death of the Earl in 1705. The patent to which Pepys here refers was sealed on 11 December. Pepys briefly mentioned the grant in a letter to Sandwich of 9 December: Carte 73, f.641r. Three sons born later to Lady Castlemaine were all acknowledged as the King's bastards.

2. This concerned the dispute with the Swedes about striking sail: see above, p. 212 & n. 3. The paper does not appear to have survived among Pepys's MSS. For notices of another copy, see PRO, PC 2/55, pp. 459, 460.

3. Above, pp. 216–17.

and so good-night. Home, and wrote by the post to my father; and so to bed.

8. *Lords=day*. In bed all the morning, thinking to take Phisique; but it being a frost, my wife would not have me.[1] So to dinner at the Wardrobe; and after a great deal of good discourse with my Lady after dinner, and among other things, of the great Christening yesterday at Mr. Rumballs and Courtiers and pomp that was there (which I wonder at),[2] I went away, up and down into all the churches almost between that place and my house, and so home. And then came my brother Tom and stayed and talked with me; and I hope he will do very well – and get money. So to supper and to bed.

This morning as I was in bed, one brings me T. Trices answer to my bill in Chancery from Mr. Smallwood, which I am glad to see, though afeared it will do me hurt.[3]

9. ⟨To White-hall, and thence to the Renish wine-house; where I met Monsieur Shar[4] and there took leave of him, he being to go this night to the Downes towards Portugall, and Soe⟩ spent all the morning.[a] At noon to dinner to the Wardrobe – where my Lady Wright was, who did talk much upon the worth and the desert of gallantry; and that there was none fit to be Courtiers but such as have been abroad and know fashions; which I endeavoured to oppose and was troubled to hear her talk so, though she be a very wise and discreet lady in other things. From thence Mr. Moore and I to the Temple about my law business with my Cosen Turner, and there we read over T. Trices answer to my bill – and advised thereupon – what to do in his absence, he being to go out of town tomorrow. Thence he and I to Mr. Wallpoole my atturny, whom I never saw before, and we all to an alehouse hard by and there we talked of our business,

a The paragraph originally began 'At home all the morning'. The addition was inserted in the upper margin.

---

1. She probably thought his kidney trouble made him sensitive to cold.

2. William Rumbold, Clerk of the Wardrobe, was a favourite at Court because of his work as a royalist agent

under the Protectorate. The child was his son Charles.

3. See above, p. 215 & n. 1; below, iii. 7 & n. 2.

4. D'Esquier, Edward Mountagu's servant.

and he put me into great hopes; but he is but a young man, and so I do not depend so much upon his encouragement. So by Coach home and to supper and to bed – having stayed up till 12 at night writing letters to my Lord Sandwich and all my friends with him at Sea,[1] to send tomorrow by Monsieur Eshar, who goes tomorrow post to the Downes, to go along with the fleet to Portugall.

10. To White-hall; and there finding Monsieur Eschar to be gone, I sent my letters by a porter to the posthouse in Southwarke, to be sent by dispach to the Downes.[2] So to dinner to my Lord Crews by Coach, and in my way had a stop of above an houre and a half, which is a great trouble this Parliament time, but it cannot be helped.[3] However, I got thither before my Lord came from the House, and so dined with him; and dinner done, home to the office and there sat late, and so home.

11. My brother Tom and then Mr. Moore came to me this morning and stayed a while with me; and then I went out and in my way met Mr. Howell the Turner, who invited me to dine this day at Mr. Rawlinson's with some friends of his, officers of the tower, at a venison pasty which I promised him. And so I went to the old Bayly[4] and there stayed and drank with him, who told me the whole story how Pegg Kite hath married herself to a Weaver, an ugly fellow, to her undoing – of which I am glad that I have nothing to do in it.[5] From thence home and put on my velvet coat; and so to the Mitre to dinner according to my promise this morning; but going up into the room, I find at least twelve or more persons and knew not the face of any of them, and so I went down again; and though I met Mr. Yong the upholster, yet I would not be persuaded to stay, but went

1. The letter to Sandwich is in Carte 73, f.641r.

2. Thomas Barlow, postmaster, Southwark, was paid for many similar services to the Navy Board: cf. PRO, Adm. 20/3, p. 286.

3. Traffic-blocks in 17th-century London were at their worst in parliament time, when the town was full. Pepys was unable on this occasion to abandon his coach and take a boat, since his destination (Lincoln's Inn Fields) was not on the river.

4. A street running south from Newgate St, outside the walls. (R).

5. Pepys had probably already resigned the executorship of her mother's estate: above, p. 179. There were disputes ahead about her portion: below, iii. 161.

away. And walked to the Exchange and up and down, and was very hungry; and from thence home – where I understand Mr. Howell was come for me to go thither, but I am glad I was not at home. And my wife was gone out by Coach to ClerkenWell to see Mrs. Margaret Pen, who is at schoole there. So I went to see Sir W. Pen, who for this two or three days hath not been well; and he and I, after some talk, took a Coach and went to Moore fields; and there walked, though it was very cold, an houre or two and went into an alehouse; and there I drank some ale and eat some bread and cheese, but he would not eat a bit. And so being very merry, we went by coach home again. He to his lodgings and I by promise to Sir W. Batten's, where he and my Lady are gone out of towne and so Mrs. Martha was at home alone, and Mrs. Moore; and there I supped upon some good things left of yesterday's dinner there, where dined a great deal of company, Sir Rd. Browne and others. And by and by comes in Captain Cox, who promised to be here with me; but he stayed very late, and had been drinking somewhere and was very drunk, and so, very capricious – which I was troubled to see in a man that I took for a very wise and wary man. So I home and left him there, and so to bed.

12. We lay long in bed. Then up and made me ready; and by and by comes Will Bowyer and Mr. Gregory my old Ex-chequer friends to see me; and I took them to the Dolphin and there did give them a good morning draught, and so parted. And invited them and all my old exchequer acquaintance to come and dine with me there on Wednesday next.[1]

From thence to the Wardrobe and there dined with my Lady. Where her brother Mr. John Crew dined also, and a strange gentlewoman dined at the table as a servant of my Lady's; but I know her not, and so I was afeared that poor Madamoiselle was gone; but I since understand that she is come as housekeeper to my Lady, and is a married woman.[2] From thence to West-minster to the Lords house to meet my Lord Privy Seale, who appointed to Seale there this afternoon; but by and by word is brought that he is come to White-hall, and so we are fain to go

1. But see below, p. 241.
2. 'Madamoiselle' was the govern-ess, Mlle le Blanc. The house-

keeper was possibly Elizabeth Elton, who appears in Lady Sandwich's will (1673) as a servant.

thither to him; and there we stayed to seal, till it was so late, that though I got leave to go away before he had done, yet the office was done before I could get thither. And so I to Sir W. Pen's and there sat and talked and drank with him; and so home.

13. At home all the morning, being by the cold weather, which for these two days hath been frost, in some pain in my blather. Dined at home; and then with my wife to the painter's[1] and there she sat the first time to be drawn, while I all the while stood looking on a pretty lady's picture whose face did please me extremely. At last, he having done, I find that the dead colour of my wife is good, above what I expected, which pleases me exceedingly. So home and to the office about some special business, where Sir Wms both were. And from thence with them to the Steeleyard,[2] where my Lady Batten and others came to us; and there we drank and had Musique and Captain Coxes company. And he paid all; and so, late back again home by coach and so to bed.

14. All the morning at home, lying abed with my wife till 11 a-clock – such a habitt we have got this winter, of lying long abed. Dined at home. And in the afternoon to the office. There sat late; and so home and to bed.

15. *Lordsday.* To church in the morning, where our young Reader[3] begun the first day to read. Sir W. Penn dined with me, and we were merry. Again to church; and so home and all alone read till bedtime, and so to prayers and to bed.

I have been troubled this day about a difference between my wife and her maid Nell, who is a simple slut and I am afeared we shall find her a cross-grained wench. I am now full of study about writing something about our making of strangers strike

---

1. See above, p. 218, n. 4. (OM).
2. Sc. to the Rhenish winehouse at the entrance to the Steelyard.

3. Unidentified; he read from the Prayer Book.

to us at sea; and so am altogether reading Selden and Grotius and such other Authors, to that purpose.[1]

16. Up by 5 a-clock this morning by candlelight (which I have not been of many a day), being called up by one Mr. Bollen[a] by appointment, who hath business to be done with my Lord Privy Seale this morning.[2] And so by Coach, calling Mr. Moore at the Wardrobe, to Chelsy, and there did get my Lord to seal it. And so back again to Westminster-hall, and thence to my Lord Sandwiches lodgings, where I met my wife (who had been to see Mrs. Hunt, who was brought to bed the other day of a boy); and got a Joynt of meat thither from the Cookes and she and I and Sarah dined together; and after dinner to the Opera, where there was a new play (*Cutter of Colemanstreete*) made in the year 1658, with reflection much upon the late times.[3] And it being the first time, the pay was doubled; and so to save money, my wife and I went up into the gallery and there sat and saw very well;[4] and a very good play it is – it seems of Cowly's making. From thence by coach home. And to bed.

17. Up and to the painters to see how he went forward in our pictures. So back again to dinner at home. And then was sent

a repl. l.h. name rendered illegible

1. For this controversy, see above, p. 223, n. 1. The Dutch case had been stated in Hugo Grotius's *Mare Liberum* (first published in 1609), to which Selden's *Mare Clausum* (1635) had been a reply. Pepys did not retain a copy of the Grotius.

2. James Bollen was appointed Groom of the Privy Chamber in extraordinary by letters patent issued on 23 February 1662: PRO, LC 3/73, p. 43.

3. Pepys's description of this piece as 'a new play' is rather misleading. *The cutter of Coleman Street* is a comedy by Abraham Cowley, based upon an earlier play of his, *The*

Guardian, which had been acted before Prince Charles at Trinity College, Cambridge, in 1641, and published in 1650. In his revision of this earlier play, Cowley shifted the scene to London in 1658 and satirised the Puritans of that time and the type of cavalier who succumbed to their influence. A 'cutter' is a swaggerer. This is the first record of a public performance of the play. The cast listed by Downes (p. 25) includes Betterton as Col. Jolly, Harris as Trueman Junior, Sandford as Worm and Mrs Sanderson as Aurelia. (A).

4. When prices were doubled, a seat in the top gallery cost 2s. (A).

for to the Privy Seale, whither I was forced to go and stay so long and late that I was much vexed. At last we got all done; and then made haste to the office, where they were sat, and there we sat late; and so home and to supper and to Selden*ª* *Mare Clausum* and so to bed.

18. At the office upon business-extraordinary all the morning; then to my Lady Sandwichs to dinner, whither my wife (who had been at the painter's, came to me) and there dined. And there I left her and to the Temple, my brother's, and to see Mrs. Turner (who begins to be better) and so back to my Lady's, where much made of; and so took my wife home by Coach. And at home to my study till bed-time, and so to bed.

19. This morning my wife dressed herself fine to go to the christening of Mrs. Hunts child; and so she and I in the way in the morning went to the painter's; and there she sat till noon, and I all the while*ᵇ* looking over great variety of good prints which he hath. And by and by comes my boy to tell us that Mr. Hunt hath been at our house to tell us that the christening is not till Saturday next. So after the painter had done, I did like the picture pretty well. And my [wife] and I went by coach home. But in the way I took occasion to fall out with my wife very highly, about her ribbands being ill mached and of two Colours; and to very high words, so that I (like a passionate fool) did call her whore, for which I was afterward sorry. But I set her down at home and went myself by appointment to the Dolphin, where Sir Wm. Warren¹ did give us all a good dinner. And that being done, to the office and there sat late, and so home.

20. Lay long in bed. And then up and so to the Wardrobe to dinner; and from thence out with Mr. Moore toward my house; and in our way met with Mr. Swan (my old acquaintance) and we to a taverne – where we had enough of his old simple religious talk; and is still a Coxcomb in those things as he ever was. And tells me he is setting out a book called *The Unlawfull use of lawfull things.*² But a very simple fellow he is, and so I leave him. So we drank and at last parted; and Mr. Moore

a l.h. name blotted   *b* MS. 'way'

---

1. Timber merchant of Wapping.   2. Untraced; ? not published.

and I into Cornehill, it being dark night, and in the street and on the Exchange discoursed about the Dominion of the sea, wherein I am lately so much concerned. And so I home and sat late up, reading of Mr. Selden. And so to bed.

21. To White-hall to the Privy Seale, where my Lord Privy Seale did tell us he would seal no more this month, for that he goes 30 mile out of towne to keep his Christmas.[1] At which I was glad; but only, afeared lest any thing of the King's should force us to go after him to get a seal in the Country. Thence to Westminster-hall (having by the way drank with Mrs. Sarah and Mrs. Betty at my Lord's lodgings); and thence taken by some Exchequer men to the Dogg; where it being St. Thomas day, by Custome they have a general meeting, a dinner.[2] There I was and all very merry. And there I spoke to Mr. Falconberge to look whether[a] he could, out of Doomesday Book, give me anything concerning the Sea – and the Dominion thereof – which he says he will look after.[3]   Thence, taking leave, to my brother's; and there by appointment met with Prior of Brampton, who hath money to pay me; but desiring some advice, he stays till Monday. So by Coach home to the office, where I was vexed to see Sir Wms: both seem to think so much that I should be a little out of the way, saying that without their Register they were not a Comittee, which I take in some dudgeon and see clearly that I must keep myself at a little distance with them and not Crouch, or else I shall never keep myself up even with them. So home and write letters by[b] the post. This evening my wife came home from christening Mrs. Hunts Son, his name John.[4]   And a Merchant in Marke-lane came along with

a repl. 'whether'   *b* repl. 'and other things'

---

1. ? to Felsted, Essex (c. 48 miles from London), where he had an estate: P. Morant, *Essex* (1768), ii. 419.

2. Cf. above, i. 320 & n. 1.

3. A copy of Domesday Book (together with certain other public records) was kept in the Receipt of the Exchequer (of which Edward Falconberg was Deputy-Chamberlain) until in 1859 it was transferred to the Public Record Office. Pepys was mistaken in thinking that it might contain much about the sea or anything about the dominion of the sea. His friend in later life, Dr Thomas Gale, gave him a few notes on the subject: *Naval Minutes*, pp. 96–7, 177, 183, 299.

4. At St Margaret's, Westminster: *Harl. Soc. Reg.*, 64/10.

her, that was her partener. So after my business was done and read something in Mr. Selden, I went to bed.

22. *Lords day.* To church in the morning, where the Reader made a boyish young sermon. Home to dinner; and there I took occasion, from the blackness of the meat as it came out of the pot, to fall out with my wife and the maids for their sluttery; and so left the table and went up to read in Mr. Selden till church time; and then my wife and I to church and there in the pew, with the rest of the company, was Captain Holmes in his gold-laced suit; at which I was troubled, because of the old business which he attempted upon my wife.[1] So with my mind troubled, I sat still; but by and by I took occasion from the rain now holding up (it raining when*a* we came into the church) to put my wife in mind of going to the christening (which she was invited to) of N. Osbornes child. Which she did; and so went out of the pew and my mind was eased. So home after sermon, and there came by appointment Dr. T. Pepys, Will Joyce, and my brother Tom and supped with me; and very merry they were and I seemed to be, but I was not pleased at all with their company. So they being gone, we went to bed.

23. early up and by Coach (before daylight) to the Wardrobe and took up Mr. Moore; and he and I to Chelsy to my Lord Privy Seale and there sealed some things, he being to go out of town for all Christmas tomorrow. So back again to Westminster; and from thence by water to the Treasury Office, where I find Sir W. Penn paying off the *Sophia* and *Griffen*[2] and there I stayed with him till noon; and having sent for some Coller of beef and a minced-pie, we eat and drank, and so I left him there and to my brother's by appointment to meet Prior; but he came not, so I went and saw Mrs. Turner, who continues weak. And by and by word was brought me that Priors man was come to Tom's and so I went and told out 128*l* which I

a repl. 'where'

---

1. Nothing is known about this. Pepys repeats his suspicions at 6 January 1662.

2. PRO Adm. 20/2, p. 185: each was owed just over a year's pay.

am to receive of him;[1] but Prior not coming, I went away and left the money by his desire with my brother all night, and they to come to me tomorrow morning. So I took Coach; and lighting at my bookseller's in Pauls churchyard, I met there with Mr. Cromlom and the Second Master of Pauls school;[2] and thence I took them to the Starr and there we sat and talked; and I had great pleasure in their company, and very glad I was of meeting him so accidentally, I having omitted too long to go to see him. Here, in discourse of books, I did offer to give the Schoole what book he would choose of 5l.[3] So we parted; and I home and to Mr. Selden and then to bed.

24. Home all the morning and dined at home; and in the afternoon to the office; and so home.

25. *Christmas day.* In the morning to church; where at the door of our pew I was fain to stay, because that the Sexton had not opened the door. A good sermon of Mr. Mills. Dined at home all alone. And taking occasion, from some fault in the meat, to complain of my maid's Sluttery, my wife and I fell out, and I up to my Chamber in a discontent. After dinner my wife comes up to me and all friends again; and she and I to walk upon the Leads; and there Sir W. Pen called us and we went to his house and supped with him. But before supper, Captain Cock came to us half-drunck and begun to talk; but[a] Sir W. Pen, knowing his humour and that there was no end of his talking, drinks four great glasses of wine to him one after another, healths to the King &c., and by that means made him drunk, and so he went away; and so we sat down to supper and were merry; and so after supper home and to bed.

26. This morning Sir W. Pen and I to the Treasury office; and there we paid off the *Amity* (Captain Stokes's ship that was at

a MS. 'by'

---

1. For the purchase of a house or houses at Brampton: see above, p. 204 & n. 2.
2. Samuel Cromleholme, High Master, and Nathaniel Bull, Sur-

master, of St Paul's. The former was a considerable collector of books. The shop was Joseph Kirton's.
3. See below, p. 239 & n. 3.

Guinny) and another ship,[1] and so home; and after dinner Sir Wm. came to me, and he and his son and daughter and I and my wife by Coach to Moore fields to walk (but it was most foule weather); and so we went into an alehouse and there eat some cakes and ale; and a Washeall=bowle woman and girl came to us and sung to us;[2] and after all was done, I called my boy (Waynman) to us to eat some cake that was left, and the woman of the house told us that he had called for two Cakes and a pot of ale for himself, at which I was angry and am resolved to correct him for it. So home; and Sir W. Penn and his son and daughter to supper to me to a good Turkey, and were merry at Cards; and so to bed.

27.[a] In the morning to my bookesellers to bespeak a Stephens's *Thesaurus*,[3] for which I offer 4*l*, to give to Paul's Schoole. And from thence to Pauls church and there I heard Dr. Gunning preach a good sermon upon the day (being St. Johns day) and did hear him tell a story, which he did persuade us to believe to be true, that St. John and the Virgin Mary did appear to Gregory, a Bishopp, at his prayer to be confirmed in the fayth,[4] which I did wonder to hear from him. Here I met with Mr. Crumlum (and told him of my endeavours to get Stephens *Thesaurus* for[b] the schoole); and so home and after dinner comes Mr. Faulconberge to see me; and at his desire I sent over for his Kinsman, Mr. Knightly the Merchant, and so he came over and sat and drank with us; and at his request I went over with him, and there I

a repl. '26'   *b* MS. 'from'

---

1. The *Amity* was given a year's pay (c. £1530): PRO, Adm. 20/2, p. 185. The other ship was probably the *George*: ib., loc. cit. Thomas Turner and three other clerks were employed: ib., p. 31.

2. The wassail bowl would be carried from door to door to the accompaniment of carols in Christmas week.

3. The *Thesaurus Graecae linguae* of Henricus Stephanus (Henri Estienne, d. 1598), first published in 1572 in five volumes; the greatest lexicon of its day. Pepys eventually gave £4 10*s*. for it at another bookseller's: see below, iii. 290. The copy he presented to the school seems to have perished in the Great Fire.

4. This is said to be the first known instance of a record of a Marian apparition. The saint was St. Gregory Thaumaturgus (c.213–c.270): F. L. Cross, *Oxf. Dict. Christian Church* (Oxf. 1974), p. 601.

sat till the evening and till both Mr. Knightly and Mr. Falconberge (for whom I sent my boy to get a coach to carry him to Westminster) were both drunke; and so home, but better wine I never drank in all my life. So home; and finding my wife gone to Sir W. Pen's, I went thither; and there I sat and played at cards and supped, and so home. And to bed.

28. At home all the morning; and in the afternoon, all of us at the office upon a letter from the Duke for the making up of a speedy estimate of all the debts of the Navy[1] – which put into*a* good forwardness, I home and Sir W. Penn to my house, who with his*b* children stayed playing at Cards late. And so to bed.

29. *Lords=day*. Long in bed with my wife. And though I had determined to go to dine with my wife at my Lady's (chiefly to put off dining with Sir W. Penn today, because Holmes dined there), yet I could not get a coach time enough to go thither; and so I dined at home and my brother Tom with me. And then a coach came and I carried my wife to Westminster and she went to see Mrs. Hunt; and I to the Abby and there meeting with Mr. Hooper, he took me in among the Quire and there I sang with them their service.[2] And so that being done, I walked up and down till night, for that Mr. Coventry was not come to White-hall since dinner yet. At last I went thither and he was come; and I spoke with him about some business of the office and so took leave of him and sent for my wife and the coach; and so to the Wardrobe and supped and stayed very long talking with my Lady – who seems to dote every day more and more upon us. So home. And to prayers and to bed.

30. At the office about this Estimate. And so with my wife and Sir W. Penn to see our pictures – which do not much

a MS. 'into too'   *b* MS. 'us'

---

1. Dated 27 December, asking for estimates covering the period up to 31 January following: PRO, Adm. 106/6, f.97r; copy in Adm. 2/1745, f.64v. See below, p. 241 & n. 3; cf. *CSPD 1661-2*, p. 197.

2. Cf. the entry at 9 December 1660 when Pepys similarly sang in Whitehall Chapel. William Hooper was a minor canon of the Abbey. (E).

displease us. And so back again; and I stayed at the Miter, whither I had invited all my old acquaintance of the Exchequer to a good Chine of beefe – which with three barrels of oysters and three pullets and plenty of wine and mirth, was our dinner. There was about twelve of us. Among others, Mr. Bowyer the old man, and Mr. Faulconberge, Shadwell, Taylor, Spicer, Woodruffe (who by reason of some friend that dined with him, came to us after dinner), Servington, &c.; and here I made them a foolish promise to give them one this day twelvemonth, and so for ever while I live. But I do not entend it.

Here I stayed as long as I could keep them; and so home to Sir W. Penn, who with his children and my wife hath been at a play today and saw *D'Ambois*,¹ which I never saw. Here we stayed late at supper and playing at Cards; and so home and to bed.

31. My wife and I this morning to the paynters; and there she sat the last time and I stood by and did tell him some little things to do, that now her picture I think will please me very well. And after her, her little black dogg² sat in her lap and was drawn, which made us very merry. So home to dinner, and so to the office and there late, finishing our estimate of the debts of the Navy to this day; and it comes to near 37400*l*.³

So home; and after supper and my barber had trimmed me, I sat down to end my Journall for this year; and my condition at this time, by God's blessing, is thus:

My health (only upon ketching cold, which brings great pain in my back and making of water, as it use to be when I had the stone) very good, and so my wife's in all respects.

My servants, W. Hewer, Sarah, Nell, and Waynman. My house at the Navy Office. I suppose myself to be worth about 500*l* clear in the world, and my goods of my house my owne, and what is coming to me from Brampton when my father dies – which God defere. But by my uncles death, the whole care and

1. *Bussy D'Ambois*, a tragedy by George Chapman, first acted c. 1604, and published in 1607; now at the TR, Vere St. (A).

2. Possibly the dog given her by her brother on 8 February 1660. For the portrait (by Savill), see above, p. 218, n. 4.

3. This was the charge for the year, not the total debt: cf. above, p. 240 & n. 1; below, iv. 49. The estimates themselves have not been traced. A grant of £72,000 was made by the Treasury on 10 January: *CTB*, i. 349.

trouble of all and settling of all lies upon me; which is very great because of law-suits, especially that with T. Trice about the inter[e]st of 200*l* – which will I hope be ended soon.

My chiefest thoughts is now to get a good wife for Tom – there being one offered by the Joyces, a cousin of theirs, worth 200*l* in ready money. I am also upon writing a little treatise to present to the Duke, about our privilege in the seas as to other nations striking their flags to us. But my greatest trouble is that I have for this last half-year been a very great spendthrift in all manner of respects, that I am afeared to cast up my accounts, though I hope I am worth what I say above. But I will cast them up very shortly.

I have newly taken a solemne oath about abstaining from plays and wine, which I am resolved to keep according to the letter of the oath, which I keepe by me.[1] The fleete hath been ready to sail for Portugall, but hath lack[ed] wind this fortnight.[2] And by that means my Lord is forced to keep at sea all this winter till he brings home the Queen – which is the expectacion of all now – and the greatest matter of public talk.[a]

a followed by one blank page

---

1. It was sometimes the mere letter of the oaths which he kept: below, iv. 128–9, 354. He recorded his oaths, probably in a small book, which he often read at odd moments, particularly on Sundays, and occasionally in the open air: e.g. below, iv. 247 (in a wood at Epsom). From time to time, in his effort to keep them, he wrote out fair copies: e.g. below, iv. 3, 249. None of these MSS has been traced.

2. It did not set sail until 15 January: *CSPD 1661–2*, p. 257.

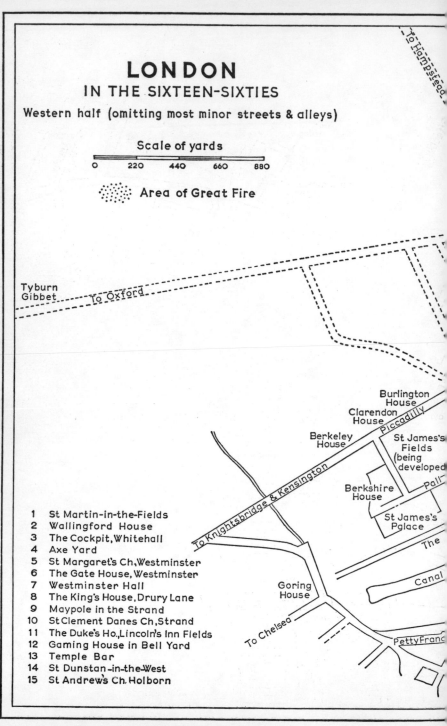

LONDON
IN THE SIXTEEN-SIXTIES
Western half (omitting most minor streets & alleys)

Scale of yards

| 0 | 220 | 440 | 660 | 880 |

⋯ Area of Great Fire

To Hampstead

Tyburn
Gibbet .... To Oxford ....

Burlington House
Clarendon House
Piccadilly
Berkeley House
St James's Fields (being developed)

Berkshire House
Pall

St James's Palace

The

To Knightsbridge & Kensington

Canal

Goring House

To Chelsea

PettyFranc

1 St Martin-in-the-Fields
2 Wallingford House
3 The Cockpit, Whitehall
4 Axe Yard
5 St Margaret's Ch, Westminster
6 The Gate House, Westminster
7 Westminster Hall
8 The King's House, Drury Lane
9 Maypole in the Strand
10 St Clement Danes Ch, Strand
11 The Duke's Ho., Lincoln's Inn Fields
12 Gaming House in Bell Yard
13 Temple Bar
14 St Dunstan-in-the-West
15 St Andrew's Ch. Holborn

Map prepared by the late Professor T. F. Reddaway

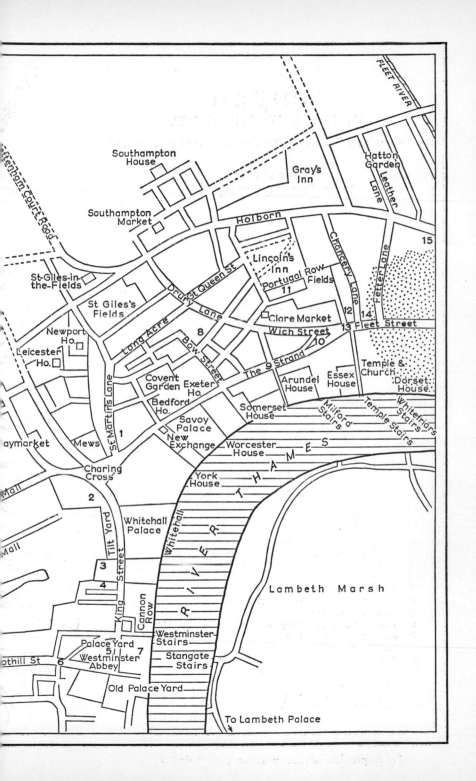

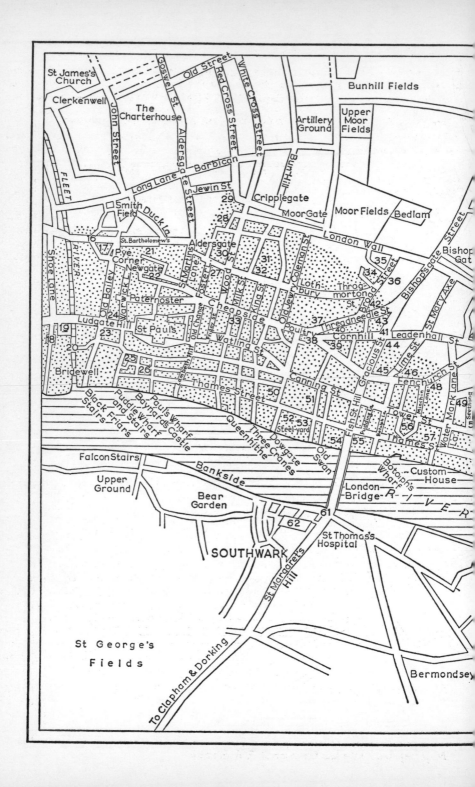

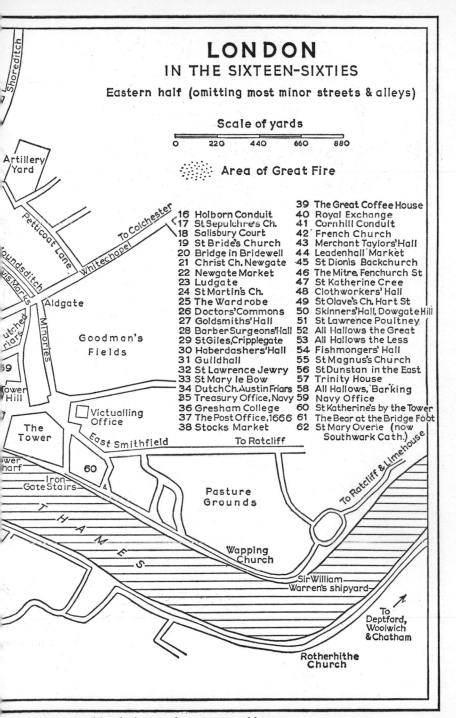

LONDON
IN THE SIXTEEN-SIXTIES
Eastern half (omitting most minor streets & alleys)

Scale of yards

0   220   440   660   880

Area of Great Fire

16 Holborn Conduit
17 St Sepulchre's Ch.
18 Salisbury Court
19 St Bride's Church
20 Bridge in Bridewell
21 Christ Ch. Newgate
22 Newgate Market
23 Ludgate
24 St Martin's Ch.
25 The Wardrobe
26 Doctors'Commons
27 Goldsmiths'Hall
28 Barber Surgeons'Hall
29 St Giles, Cripplegate
30 Haberdashers'Hall
31 Guildhall
32 St Lawrence Jewry
33 St Mary le Bow
34 Dutch Ch.Austin Friars
35 Treasury Office, Navy
36 Gresham College
37 The Post Office,1666
38 Stocks Market
39 The Great Coffee House
40 Royal Exchange
41 Cornhill Conduit
42 French Church
43 Merchant Taylors'Hall
44 Leadenhall Market
45 St Dionis Backchurch
46 The Mitre, Fenchurch St
47 St Katherine Cree
48 Clothworkers' Hall
49 St Olave's Ch. Hart St
50 Skinners'Hall, Dowgate Hill
51 St Lawrence Poultney
52 All Hallows the Great
53 All Hallows the Less
54 Fishmongers' Hall
55 St Magnus's Church
56 St Dunstan in the East
57 Trinity House
58 All Hallows, Barking
59 Navy Office
60 St Katherine's by the Tower
61 The Bear at the Bridge Foot
62 St Mary Overie (now
    Southwark Cath.)

Shoreditch

Artillery Yard

Petticoat Lane

To Colchester

Whitechapel

Houndsditch

vis Marks

Aldgate

Goodman's Fields

out ched friars

Minories

Tower Hill

Victualling Office

The Tower

East Smithfield

To Ratcliff

wer harf

Iron-Gate Stairs

60

T H A M E S

Pasture Grounds

To Ratcliff & Limehouse

Wapping Church

Sir William Warren's shipyard

To Deptford, Woolwich & Chatham

Rotherhithe Church

Map prepared by the late Professor T. F. Reddaway

SELECT LIST OF PERSONS

ADMIRAL, the: James, Duke of York, Lord High Admiral of England

ALBEMARLE, 1st Duke of (Lord Monke): Captain-General of the Kingdom

ARLINGTON, 1st Earl of (Sir Henry Bennet): Secretary of State

ASHLEY, 1st Baron (Sir Anthony Ashley Cooper, later 1st Earl of Shaftesbury): Chancellor of the Exchequer

ATTORNEY-GENERAL: Sir Geoffrey Palmer

BACKWELL, Edward: goldsmith–banker

BAGWELL, Mrs: Pepys's mistress; wife of ship's carpenter

BALTY: Balthasar St Michel; brother-in-law; minor naval official

BATTEN, Sir William: Surveyor of the Navy

BETTERTON (Baterton), Thomas: actor in the Duke's Company

BIRCH, Jane: maidservant

BOOKSELLER, my: Joseph Kirton (until the Fire)

BOWYER, my father: Robert Bowyer, senior Exchequer colleague

BRISTOL, 2nd Earl of: politician

BROUNCKER (Bruncker, Brunkard, Brunkerd), 2nd Viscount: Commissioner of the Navy

BUCKINGHAM, 2nd Duke of: politician

CARKESSE (Carcasse), James: clerk in the Ticket Office

CARTERET, Sir George: Treasurer of the Navy and Vice-Chamberlain of the King's Household

CASTLEMAINE, Barbara, Countess of: the King's mistress

CHANCELLOR, the: *see* 'Lord Chancellor'

CHILD, the: usually Edward, eldest son and heir of Sandwich

CHOLMLEY, Sir Hugh: courtier, engineer

COCKE, George: hemp merchant

COFFERER, the: William Ashburnham

COMPTROLLER (Controller), the: the Comptroller of the Navy (Sir Robert Slingsby, 1660–1; Sir John Mennes, 1661–71)

COVENTRY, Sir William: Secretary to the Lord High Admiral, 1660–7; Commissioner of the Navy

CREED, John: household and naval servant of Sandwich

CREW, 1st Baron: Sandwich's father-in-law; Presbyterian politician

CUTTANCE, Sir Roger: naval captain

DEANE, Anthony: shipwright

DEB: *see* 'Willet, Deborah'

DOWNING, Sir George: Exchequer official, ambassador to Holland and secretary to the Treasury Commission

DUKE, the: usually James, Duke of York, the King's brother; occasionally George (Monck), Duke of Albemarle

DUKE OF YORK: *see* 'James, Duke of York'

EDWARD, Mr: Edward, eldest son and heir of Sandwich

EDWARDS, Tom: servant

EVELYN, John: friend, *savant*; Commissioner of Sick and Wounded

FENNER, Thomas (m. Katherine Kite, sister of Pepys's mother): uncle; ironmonger

FERRER(s), Capt. Robert: army captain; Sandwich's Master of Horse

FORD, Sir Richard: Spanish merchant

FOX, Sir Stephen: Paymaster of the Army

GAUDEN, Sir Denis: Navy victualler

GENERAL(s), the: Albemarle, Captain-General of the Kingdom, 1660–70; Prince Rupert and Albemarle, Generals-at-Sea in command of the Fleet, 1666

GIBSON, Richard: clerk to Pepys in the Navy Office

GWYN, Nell: actress (in the King's Company) and King's mistress

HARRIS, Henry: actor in the Duke's Company

HAYTER, Tom: clerk to Pepys in the Navy Office

HEWER, Will: clerk to Pepys in the Navy Office

HILL, Thomas: friend, musician, Portuguese merchant

HINCHINGBROOKE, Viscount (also 'Mr Edward', 'the child'): eldest son of Sandwich

HOLLIER (Holliard), Thomas: surgeon

HOLMES, Sir Robert: naval commander

HOWE, Will: household and naval servant of Sandwich

JAMES, DUKE OF YORK: the King's brother and heir presumptive (later James II); Lord High Admiral

JANE: usually Jane Birch, maidservant

JOYCE, Anthony (m. Kate Fenner, 1st cousin): innkeeper

JOYCE, William (m. Mary Fenner, 1st cousin): tallow-chandler

JUDGE-ADVOCATE, the: John Fowler, Judge-Advocate of the Fleet

KNIPP (Knepp) Mrs: actress in the King's Company

LADIES, the young, the two, the: often Sandwich's daughters

LAWSON, Sir John: naval commander

LIEUTENANT OF THE TOWER: Sir John Robinson

L'IMPERTINENT, Mons.: [?Daniel] Butler, friend, ? clergyman

LORD CHAMBERLAIN: Edward Mountagu, 2nd Earl of Manchester; Sandwich's cousin

LORD CHANCELLOR: Edward Hyde, 1st Earl of Clarendon (often called Chancellor after his dismissal, 1667)

LORD KEEPER: Sir Orlando Bridgeman

LORD PRIVY SEAL: John Robartes, 2nd Baron Robartes (later 1st Earl of Radnor)

LORD TREASURER: Thomas Wriothesley, 4th Earl of Southampton

MARTIN, Betty (née Lane): Pepys's mistress; shopgirl

MENNES (Minnes), Sir John: Comptroller of the Navy

MERCER, Mary: maid to Mrs Pepys

MILL(E)S, Rev. Dr John: Rector of St Olave's, Hart St; Pepys's parish priest

MONCK (Monke), George (Lord): soldier. See 'Albemarle, 1st Duke of'

MONMOUTH, Duke of: illegitimate son of Charles II

MOORE, Henry: lawyer; officer of Sandwich's household

MY LADY: usually Jemima, wife of Sandwich

MY LORD: usually Sandwich

NELL, NELLY: usually Nell Gwyn

PALL: Paulina Pepys; sister (sometimes spelt 'pall')

PEARSE (Pierce), James: courtier, surgeon to Duke of York, and naval surgeon

PENN, Sir William: Commissioner of the Navy and naval commander (father of the Quaker leader)

PEPYS, Elizabeth (née St Michel): wife

PEPYS, John and Margaret: parents

PEPYS, John (unm.): brother; unbeneficed clergyman

PEPYS, Tom (unm.): brother; tailor

PEPYS, Paulina (m. John Jackson): sister

PEPYS, Capt. Robert: uncle, of Brampton, Hunts.

PEPYS, Roger: 1st cousin once removed; barrister and M.P.

PEPYS, Thomas: uncle, of St Alphege's, London

PETT, Peter: Commissioner of the Navy and shipwright

PICKERING, Mr (Ned): courtier, 1662-3; Sandwich's brother-in-law and servant

POVEY, Thomas: Treasurer of the Tangier Committee

PRINCE, the: usually Prince Rupert

QUEEN, the: (until May 1662) the Queen Mother, Henrietta-Maria, widow of Charles I; Catherine of Braganza, wife of Charles II (m. 21 May 1662)

RIDER, Sir William: merchant

ROBERT, Prince: Prince Rupert

RUPERT, Prince: 1st cousin of Charles II; naval commander

St MICHEL, Alexandre and Mary: parents-in-law

St MICHEL, Balthasar ('Balty'; m. Esther Watts): brother-in-law; minor naval official

SANDWICH, 1st Earl of: 1st cousin once removed, and patron; politician, naval commander and diplomat

SHIPLEY, Edward: steward of Sandwich's household

SIDNY, Mr: Sidney Mountagu, second son of Sandwich

SOLICITOR, the: the Solicitor-General, Sir Heneage Finch

SOUTHAMPTON, 4th Earl of: Lord Treasurer

SURVEYOR, the: the Surveyor of the Navy (Sir William Batten, 1660–7; Col. Thomas Middleton, 1667–72)

TEDDIMAN, Sir Thomas: naval commander

THE: Theophila Turner

TREASURER, the: usually the Treasurer of the Navy (Sir George Carteret, 1660–7; 1st Earl of Anglesey, 1667–8); sometimes the Lord Treasurer of the Kingdom, the Earl of Southampton, 1660–7

TRICE, Tom: half-brother; civil lawyer

TURNER, John (m. Jane Pepys, distant cousin): barrister

TURNER, Betty and Theophila: daughters of John and Jane Turner

TURNER, Thomas: senior clerk in the Navy Office

VICE-CHAMBERLAIN, the: Sir George Carteret, Vice-Chamberlain of the King's Household and Treasurer of the Navy

VYNER, Sir Robert: goldsmith–banker

WARREN, Sir William: timber merchant

WARWICK, Sir Philip: Secretary to the Lord Treasurer

WIGHT, William: uncle (half-brother of Pepys's father); fishmonger

WILL: usually Will Hewer

WILLET, Deborah: maid to Mrs Pepys

WILLIAMS ('Sir Wms. both'): Sir William Batten and Sir William Penn, colleagues on the Navy Board

WREN, Matthew: Secretary to the Lord High Admiral, 1667–72

SELECT GLOSSARY

A Large Glossary (of words, phrases and proverbs in all languages) will be found in the *Companion*. This Select Glossary is restricted to usages, many of them recurrent, which might puzzle the reader. It includes words and constructions which are now obsolete, archaic, slang or dialect; words which are used with meanings now obsolete or otherwise unfamiliar; and place names frequently recurrent or used in colloquial styles or in non-standard forms. Words explained in footnotes are not included. The definitions given here are minimal: meanings now familiar and contemporary meanings not implied in the text are not noted, and many items are explained more fully in *Companion* articles ('Language', 'Food', 'Drink', 'Music', 'Theatre' etc.), and in the Large Glossary. A few foreign words are included. The spellings are taken from those used in the text: they do not, for brevity's sake, include all variants.

ABLE: wealthy
ABROAD: away, out of doors
ACCENT (of speech): the accentuation and the rising and falling of speech in pronunciation
ACCOUNTANT: official accountable for expenditure etc.
ACTION: acting, performance
ACTOR: male or female theatrical performer
ADDES: adze
ADMIRAL SHIP: flagship carrying admiral
ADMIRATION; ADMIRE: wonder, alarm; to wonder at
ADVENTURER: investor, speculator
ADVICE: consideration
AFFECT: to be fond of, to be concerned
AFFECTION: attention
AIR: generic term for all gases
ALPHABET: index, alphabetical list
AMBAGE: deceit, deviousness
AMUSED, AMUZED: bemused, astonished
ANCIENT: elderly, senior

ANGLE: gold coin worth *c.* 10*s.*
ANGELIQUE: small archlute
ANNOY: molest, hurt
ANOTHER GATE'S BUSINESS: different altogether
ANSWERABLE: similar, conformably
ANTIC, ANTIQUE: fantastic
APERN: apron
APPRENSION: apprehension
APPROVE OF: criticise
AQUA FORTIS (FARTIS): nitric acid
ARTICLE: to indict
ARTIST: workman, craftsman, technician, practitioner
ASPECT (astrol.): position of stars as seen from earth
ASTED: Ashtead, Surrey
AYERY: airy, sprightly, stylish

BAGNARD: bagnio, prison, lock-up
BAILEY, BAYLY: bailiff
BAIT, BAYTE: refreshment on journey (for horses or travellers). *Also* v.
BALDWICK: Baldock, Herts.
BALLET: ballad

BAND: neckband

BANDORE: musical instrument resembling guitar

BANQUET: course of fruits, sweets and wine; slight repast

BANQUET-, BANQUETTING-HOUSE: summer-house

BARBE (s.): Arab (Barbary) horse

BARBE (v.): to shave

BARN ELMS: riverside area near Barnes, Surrey

BARRICADOES (naval): fenders

BASE, BASS: bass viol; thorough-bass

BASTE HIS COAT: to beat, chastise

BAVINS: kindling wood, brush-wood

BAYLY: *see* 'Bailey'

BEARD: facial hair, moustache

BEFOREHAND, to get: to have money in hand

BEHALF: to behave

BEHINDHAND: insolvent

BELL: to throb

BELOW: downstream from London Bridge

BELOW STAIRS: part of the Royal Household governed by Lord Steward

BEST HAND, at the: the best bargain

BEVER: beaver, fur hat

BEWPERS: bunting, fabric used for flags

BEZAN, BIZAN (Du. *bezaan*): small yacht

BIGGLESWORTH: Biggleswade, Beds.

BILL: (legal) warrant, writ; bill of exchange; Bill of Mortality (weekly list of burials; *see* iii. 225, n. 2)

BILLANDER (Du. *bijlander*): bilander, small two-masted merchantman

BIRD'S EYE: spotted fabric

BLACK (adj.): brunette, dark in hair or complexion

BLACK(E)WALL: dock on n. shore of Thames below Greenwich used by E. Indiamen

BLANCH (of coins): to silver

BLIND: out of the way, private, obscure

BLOAT HERRING: bloater

BLUR: innuendo; charge

BOATE: boot or luggage compartment on side of coach

BODYS: foundations, basic rules; structure; (of ship) sectional drawings

BOLTHEAD: globular glass vessel with long straight neck

BOMBAIM: Bombay

BORDER: *toupée*

BOTARGO: dried fish-roe

BOTTOMARYNE, BOTTUMARY, BUMMARY: mortgage on ship

BOWPOTT: flower pot

BRAINFORD: Brentford, Mdx

BRAMPTON: village near Huntingdon in which Pepys inherited property

BRANSLE: branle, brawl, group dance in triple measure

BRAVE (adj.): fine, enjoyable

BRAVE (v.): to threaten, challenge

BREAK BULK: to remove part of cargo

BREDHEMSON, BRIGHTHEMSON: Brighton, Sussex

BREW AS SHE HATH BAKED, let her: let her accept the consequences of her own wilful actions

BRIDEWELL-BIRD: jailbird

BRIDGE: usually London Bridge; also jetty, landing stairs

BRIG, BRIGANTINE: small vessel equipped both for sailing and rowing

BROTHER: brother-in-law; colleague

BRUMLY: Bromley, Kent

BRUSH (s.): graze

BUBO: tumour

BULLEN: Boulogne

BULLET: cannon-ball

BURNTWOOD: Brentwood, Essex

BURY (of money): pour in, salt away, invest

BUSSE: two- or three-masted fishing boat

CABALL: inner group of ministers; knot

CABARETT (Fr. *cabaret*): tavern

CAKE WILL BE DOE, all my: all my plans will miscarry

CALES: Cadiz

CALICE, CALLIS: Calais

CALL: to call on/for; to drive

CAMELOTT, CAMLET, CAMLOTT: robust light cloth made from wool or goat hair

CANAILLE, CHANNEL, KENNEL: drainage gutter (in street); canal (in St James's Park)

CANCRE: canker, ulcer, sore

CANNING ST: Cannon St

CANONS: boot-hose tops

CANTON (heraldic): small division of shield

CAPER (ship): privateer

CARBONADO: to grill, broil

CARESSE: to make much of

CARRY (a person): to conduct, escort

CAST OF OFFICE: taste of quality

CATAPLASM: poultice

CATCH: round song; (ship) ketch

CATT-CALL: whistle

CAUDLE: thin gruel

CELLAR: box for bottles

CERE CLOTH: cloth impregnated with wax and medicaments

CESTORNE: cistern

CHAFE: heat, anger

CHALDRON: 1⅓ tons (London measure)

CHAMBER: small piece of ordnance for firing salutes

CHANGE, the: the Royal (Old) Exchange

CHANGELING: idiot

CHANNELL: see 'Canaille'

CHANNELL ROW: Cannon Row, Westminster

CHAPEL, the: usually the Chapel Royal, Whitehall Palace

CHAPTER: usually of Bible

CHARACTER: code, cipher; verbal portrait

CHEAP (s.): bargain

CHEAPEN: to ask the price of, bargain

CHEQUER, the: usually the Exchequer

CHEST, the: the Chatham Chest, the pension fund for seamen

CHILD, with: eager, anxious

CHIMNEY/CHIMNEY-PIECE: structure over and around fireplace

CHIMNEY-PIECE: picture over fireplace

CHINA-ALE: ale flavoured with china root

CHINE: rib (beef), saddle (mutton)

CHOQUE: a choke, an obstruction

CHOUSE: to swindle, trick

CHURCH: after July 1660, usually St Olave's, Hart St

CLAP: gonorrhoea

CLERK OF THE CHEQUE: principal clerical officer of a dockyard

CLOATH (of meat): skin

CLOSE: shutter; (of music) cadence

CLOUTERLY: clumsily

CLOWNE: countryman, clodhopper

CLUB (s.): share of expenses, meeting at which expenses are shared. *Also* v.

CLYSTER, GLISTER, GLYSTER: enema

COACH: captain's state-room in large ship

COCK ALE: ale mixed with minced chicken

COCKPIT(T), the: usually the theatre in the Cockpit buildings, Whitehall Palace; the buildings themselves

COD: small bag; testicle

CODLIN TART: apple (codling) tart

COFFEE: coffee-house

COG: to cheat, banter, wheedle

COLEWORTS: cabbage

COLLAR DAY: day on which knights of chivalric orders wore insignia at court

COLLECT: to deduce

COLLIER: coal merchant; coal ship

COLLOPS: fried bacon or other meat

COLLY-FEAST: feast of collies (cullies, good companions) at which each pays his share

COMEDIAN: actor

COMEDY: play

COMFITURE (Fr. *confiture*): jam, marmalade

COMMEN/COMMON GUARDEN: Covent Garden

COMMONLY: together

COMPLEXION: aspect

COMPOSE: to put music to words. *Also* Composition

CONCEIT (s.): idea, notion

CONCLUDE: to include

CONDITION (s.): disposition; social position, state of wealth

CONDITION (v.): to make conditions

CONDITIONED: having a (specified) disposition or social position

CONGEE: bow at parting

CONJURE: to plead with

CONJUROR: fortune-teller operating by conjuration of spirits

CONSIDERABLE: worthy of consideration

CONSTER: to construe, translate

CONSUMPTION: (any) wasting disease. *Also* Consumptive

CONTENT, by/in: by agreement, without examination, at a rough guess

CONVENIENCE: advantage

CONVENIENT: morally proper

CONVERSATION: demeanour, behaviour; acquaintance, society

COOLE: cowl

CORANT(O): dance involving a running or gliding step

COSEN, COUSIN: almost any collateral relative

COUNT: to reckon, estimate, value

COUNTENANCE: recognition, acknowledgement

COUNTRY: county, district

COURSE: career, way of life

COURSE, in: in sequence

COURSE, of: as usual

COURT-DISH: dish with a cut from every meat

COY: disdainful; quiet

COYING: stroking, caressing

CRADLE: fire-basket

CRAMBO: rhyming game

CRAZY: infirm

CREATURE (of persons): puppet, instrument

CRUMB, get up one's: to improve one's station

CRUSADO: Portuguese coin worth 3s.

CUDDY: room in a large ship in which the officers took their meals

CULLY: dupe; friend

CUNNING: knowledgeable; knowledge

CURIOUS: careful, painstaking, discriminating; fine, delicate

CURRANT: out and about

CUSTOMER: customs officer

CUT (v.): to carve meat

CUTT (s.): an engraving

DAUGHTER-IN-LAW: stepdaughter

DEAD COLOUR: preparatory layer of colour in a painting

DEAD PAYS: sailors or soldiers kept on pay roll after death

DEALS: sawn timber used for decks, etc.

DEDIMUS: writ empowering J.P.

DEFALK: to subtract

DEFEND: to prevent

DEFY (Fr.): to mistrust. *Also* Defyance

DELICATE: pleasant

DELINQUENT: active royalist in Civil War and Interregnum

DEMORAGE: demurrage, compensation from the freighter due to a shipowner for delaying vessel beyond time specified in charter-party

DEPEND: to wait, hang

DEVISE: to decide; discern

DIALECT: jargon

DIALL, double horizontal: instrument telling hour of day

DIRECTION: supervision of making; arrangement

DISCOVER: to disclose, reveal

DISCREET: discerning, judicious

DISGUST: to dislike

DISPENSE: outgoings

DISTASTE (s.): difference, quarrel, offence. *Also* v.

DISTINCT: discerning, discriminating

DISTRINGAS: writ of distraint

DOATE: to nod off to sleep

DOCTOR: clergyman, don

DOE: dough. *See* 'All my cake . . .'

DOGGED: determined

DOLLER: *see* 'Rix Doller'

DORTOIRE: dorter, monastic dormitory

DOTY: darling

DOWNS, the: roadstead off Deal, Kent

DOXY: whore, mistress

DRAWER: tapster, barman

DRESS: to cook, prepare food

DROLL: comic song

DROLLING, DROLLY: comical, comically

DRUDGER: dredger, container for sweetmeats

DRUGGERMAN: dragoman, interpreter

DRY BEATEN: beaten without drawing blood

DRY MONEY: hard cash

DUANA: divan, council

DUCCATON: ducatoon, large silver coin of the Netherlands worth 5s. 9d.

DUCKET(T): ducat, foreign gold coin (here probably Dutch) worth 9s.

DUKE'S [PLAY] HOUSE, the: playhouse in Lincoln's Inn Fields used by the Duke of York's Company from June 1660 until 9 November 1671; often called 'the Opera'. Also known as the Lincoln's Inn Fields Theatre (LIF)

DULL: limp, spiritless

EARTH: earthenware

EASILY AND EASILY: more and more slowly

EAST INDIES: the territory covered by the E. India Company, including the modern sub-continent of India

EAST COUNTRY, EASTLAND: the territory (in Europe) covered by the Eastland Company

EFFEMINACY: love of women

ELABORATORY: laboratory

ELECTUARY: medicinal salve with a honey base

EMERODS: haemorrhoids

ENTENDIMIENTO (Sp.): understanding

ENTER (of horse): to break in

ENTERTAIN: to retain, employ

EPICURE: glutton

ERIFFE: Erith, Kent

ESPINETTE(S): *see* 'Spinet'

ESSAY: to assay

EVEN (adv.): surely

EVEN (of accounts): to balance

EVEN (of the diary): to bring up to date

EXCEPT: to accept

EXPECT: to see, await

FACTION: the government's parliamentary critics

FACTIOUS: able to command a following

FACTOR: mercantile agent

FACTORY: trading station

FAIRING: small present (as from a fair)

FAIRLY: gently, quietly

FALCHON: falchion, curved sword

FAMILY: household (including servants)

FANCY (music): fantasia

FANFARROON: fanfaron, braggart

FASHION (of metal, furniture): design, fashioning

FAT: vat

FATHER: father-in-law (similarly with mother etc.)

FELLET (of trees): a cutting, felling

FELLOW COMMONER: undergraduate paying high fees and enjoying privileges

FENCE: defence

FERRANDIN, FARRINDIN, FARANDINE: cloth of silk mixed with wool or hair

FIDDLE: violin; occ. treble viol

FINE (s.): payment for lease

FINE FOR OFFICE (v.): to avoid office by payment of fine

FIRESHIP: ship filled with combustibles used to ram and set fire to enemy

FITS OF THE MOTHER: hysterics

FLAG, FLAGGMAN: flag officer

FLAGEOLET: end-blown, six-holed instrument

FLESHED: relentless, proud

FLOOD: rising tide

FLOWER: beautiful girl

FLUXED (of the pox): salivated

FLYING ARMY/FLEET: small mobile force

FOND, FONDNESS: foolish; folly

FOND: fund

FORCE OUT: to escape

FORSOOTH: to speak ceremoniously

FORTY: many, scores of

FOXED: intoxicated

FOX HALL: Vauxhall (pleasure gardens)

FOY: departure feast or gift

FREQUENT: to busy oneself

FRIENDS: parents, relatives

FROST-BITE: to invigorate by exposure to cold

FULL: anxious

FULL MOUTH, with: eagerly; openly, loudly

GALL: harass

GALLIOTT: small swift galley

GALLOPER, the: shoal off Essex coast

GAMBO: Gambia, W. Africa

GAMMER: old woman

GENERAL-AT-SEA: naval commander (a post, not a rank)

GENIUS: inborn character, natural ability; mood

GENT: graceful, polite

GENTILELY: obligingly

GEORGE: jewel forming part of insignia of Order of Garter

GERMANY: territory of the Holy Roman Empire

GET WITHOUT BOOK: to memorise

GIBB-CAT: tom-cat

GILDER, GUILDER: Dutch money of account worth 2s.

GIMP: twisted thread of material with wire or cord running through it

GITTERNE: musical instrument of the guitar family

GIVE: to answer

GLASS: telescope

GLEEKE: three-handed card game

GLISTER, GLYSTER: see 'Clyster'

GLOSSE, by a fine: by a plausible pretext

GO(O)D BWYE: God be with ye, goodbye

GODLYMAN: Godalming, Surrey

GOODFELLOW: convivial person, good timer

GOODMAN/GOODWIFE ('Goody'): used of men and women of humble station

GOOD-SPEAKER: one who speaks well of others

GORGET: neckerchief for women

GOSSIP (v.): to act as godparent, to attend a new mother; to chatter. *Also* s.

GOVERNMENT: office or function of governor

GRACIOUS-STREET(E): Gracechurch St

GRAIN (? of gold): sum of money

GRAVE: to engrave

GREEN (of meat): uncured

GRESHAM COLLEGE: meeting-place of Royal Society; the Society itself

GRIEF: bodily pain

GRUDGEING, GRUTCHING: trifling complaint, grumble

GUEST: nominee; friend; stranger

GUIDE: postboy

GUN: flagon of ale; cannon, salute

GUNDALO, GUNDILOW: gondola

GUNFLEET, the: shoal off Essex coast

HACKNEY: workhorse; vehicle

HAIR, against the: against the grain

HALF-A-PIECE: gold coin worth *c.* 10s.

HALF-SHIRT: short shirt

HALFE-WAY-HOUSE: Rotherhithe tavern halfway between London Bridge and Deptford

HALL, the: usually Westminster Hall

HAND: cuff

HANDSEL: to try out, use for first time

HAND-TO-FIST: hastily

HANDYCAPP: handicap, a card game

HANG IN THE HEDGE: to be delayed

HANGER: loop holding a sword; small sword

HANGING JACK: turnspit for roasting meat

HANK: hold, grip

HAPPILY: haply, perchance

HARE: to harry, rebuke

HARPSICHON, HARPSICHORD: keyboard instrument of one or two manuals, with strings plucked by quills or leather jacks, and with stops which vary the tone

HARSLET: haslet, pigmeat (esp. offal)

HAVE A HAND: to have leisure, freedom

HAWSE, thwart their: across their bows

HEAD-PIECE: helmet

HEART: courage

HEAVE AT: to oppose

HECTOR: street-bully, swashbuckler

HERBALL: botanical encyclopaedia; *hortus siccus* (book of dried and pressed plants)

HERE (Du. *heer*): Lord

HIGH: arrogant, proud, high-handed

HINCHINGBROOKE: Sandwich's house near Huntingdon

HOMAGE: jury of presentment at a manorial court

HONEST (of a woman): virtuous

HOOKS, off the: out of humour

HOPE, the: reach of Thames downstream from Tilbury

HOPEFUL: promising

HOUSE: playhouse; parliament; (royal) household or palace building

HOUSE OF OFFICE: latrine

HOY: small passenger and cargo ship, sloop-rigged

HOYSE: to hoist

HUMOUR (s.): mood; character, characteristic; good or ill temper

HUMOUR (v.): to set words suitably to music

HUSBAND: one who gets good/bad value for money; supervisor, steward

HYPOCRAS: hippocras, spiced wine

ILL-TEMPERED: out of sorts, ill-adjusted (to weather etc.; cf. 'Temper')

IMPERTINENCE: irrelevance, garrulity, folly. *Also* Impertinent

IMPOSTUME: abscess

IMPREST: money paid in advance by government to public servant

INDIAN GOWN: loose gown of Indian style, material, or pattern

INGENIOUS, INGENUOUS: clever, intelligent

INGENUITY: wit, intelligence; freedom

INSIPID: stupid, dull

INSTITUCIONS: instructions

INSTRUMENT: agent, clerk

INSULT: to exult over

INTELLIGENCE: information

IRISIPULUS: erysipelas

IRONMONGER: often a large-scale merchant, not necessarily a retailer

JACK(E): flag used as signal or mark of distinction; rogue, knave. *See also* 'Hanging Jack'

JACKANAPES COAT: monkey jacket, sailor's short close-fitting jacket

JACOB(US): gold sovereign coined under James I

JAPAN: lacquer, lacquered

JARR, JARRING: quarrel

JEALOUS: fearful, suspicious, mistrustful. *Also* Jealousy

JERK(E): captious remark

JES(S)IMY: jasmine

JEW'S TRUMP: Jew's harp

JOCKY: horse-dealer

JOLE (of fish): jowl, a cut consisting of the head and shoulders. *See also* 'Pole'

JOYNT-STOOL: stout stool with stretchers, held together by joints

JULIPP: julep, a sweet drink made from syrup

JUMBLE: to take for an airing

JUMP WITH: to agree, harmonise

JUNK (naval): old rope

JURATE (of Cinque Ports): jurat, alderman

JUSTE-AU-CORPS: close-fitting long coat

KATCH: (ship) ketch

KENNEL: *see* 'Canaille'

KERCHER: kerchief, head-covering

KETCH (s.): catch, song in canon

KETCH (v.): to catch

KING'S [PLAY] HOUSE, the: playhouse in Vere St, Clare Market, Lincoln's Inn Fields, used by the King's Company from 8 November 1660 until 7 May 1663; the playhouse in Bridges St, Drury Lane, used by the same company from 7 May 1663 until the fire of 25 January 1672. Also known as the Theatre Royal (TR)

KITLIN: kitling, kitten, cub

KNOT (s.): flower bed; difficulty; clique, band

KNOT (v.): to join, band together

KNOWN: famous

LACE: usually braid made with gold- or silver-thread

LAMB'S-WOOL: hot ale with apples and spice

LAMP-GLASS: magnifying lens used to concentrate lamp-light

LANDS: framing members of ship

LAST: load, measure of tar

LASTOFFE: Lowestoft, Suff.

LATITUDINARIAN: liberal Anglican

LAVER: basin of fountain

LEADS: flat space on roof top, sometimes boarded over

LEAN: to lie down

LEARN: to teach

LEAVE: to end

LECTURE: weekday religious service consisting mostly of a sermon

LESSON: piece of music

LETTERS OF MART: letters of marque

LEVETT: reveille, reveille music

LIBEL(L): leaflet, broadside; (in legal proceedings) written charge

LIE UPON: to press, insist

LIFE: life interest

LIGHT: window

LIGNUM VITAE: hard W. Indian wood with medicinal qualities, often used for drinking vessels

LIMB: to limn, paint

LIME (of dogs): to mate

LINK(E): torch

LINNING: linen

LIPPOCK: Liphook, Hants.

LIST: pleasure, desire

LOCK: waterway between arches of bridge

LOMBRE: *see* 'Ombre'

LONDON: the city of London (to be distinguished from Westminster)

LOOK: to look at/for

LUMBERSTREETE: Lombard St

LUTE: pear-shaped plucked instrument with six courses of gut strings and a turned-back peg-box; made in various sizes, the larger instruments having additional bass strings

LUTESTRING: lustring, a glossy silk

LYRA-VIALL: small bass viol tuned for playing chords

MAD: whimsical, wild, extravagant

MAD (v.): to anger

MADAM(E): prefix used mainly of widows, elderly/foreign ladies

MAIN (adj.): strong, bulky

MAIN (s.): chief purpose or object

MAISTER: expert; professional; sailing master

MAKE (s.): (of fighting cocks) match, pair of opponents

MAKE (v.): to do; to copulate

MAKE LEGS: to bow, curtsey

MAKE SURE TO: to plight troth

MALLOWS: St Malo

MAN OF BUSINESS: executive agent, administrator

MANAGED-HORSE (cf. Fr. *manège*): horse trained in riding school

MANDAMUS: royal mandate under seal

MARGARET, MARGETTS: Margate, Kent

MARGENTING: putting margin-lines on paper

MARK: 13s. 4d.

MARMOTTE (Fr., term of affection): young girl

MARROWBONE: Marylebone, Mdx

MASTY: burly

MATCH: tinderbox and wick

MATHEMATICIAN: mathematical instrument-maker

MEAT: food

MEDIUM: mean, average

METHEGLIN: strong mead flavoured with herbs

MINCHIN-LANE: Mincing Lane

MINE: mien

MINIKIN: thin string or gut used for treble string of lute or viol

MISTRESS (prefix): used of unmarried girls and women as well as of young married women

MISTRESS: sweetheart

MITHRYDATE: drug used as an opiate

MODEST (of women): virtuous

MOHER (Sp. *mujer*): woman, wife

MOIS, MOYS: menstrual periods

MOLD, MOLDE, MOLLE (archit.): mole

MOLEST: to annoy

MOND: orb (royal jewel in form of globe)

MONTEERE, MOUNTEERE: huntsman's cap; close-fitting hood

MONTH'S MIND, to have a: to have a great desire

MOPED: bemused

MORECLACK(E): Mortlake, Surrey

MORENA (Sp.): brunette

MORNING DRAUGHT: drink (sometimes with snack) usually taken mid-morning

MOTHER-IN-LAW: stepmother (similarly with 'father-in-law' etc.)

MOTT: sighting line in an optical tube

MOYRE: moire, watered silk

MUM: strong spiced ale

MURLACE: Morlaix, Brittany

MUSCADINE, MUSCATT: muscatel wine

MUSIC: band, choir, performers

MUSTY: peevish

NAKED BED: without nightclothes/curtains

NARROWLY: anxiously, carefully

NAUGHT, NOUGHT: worthless, bad in condition or quality, sexually wicked

NAVY: Navy Office

NAVY OFFICERS: Principal Officers of the Navy – i.e. the Comptroller, Treasurer, Surveyor, Clerk of the Acts, together with a variable number of Commissioners; members of the Navy Board. Cf. 'Sea-Officers'

NEARLY: deeply

NEAT (adj.): handsome

NEAT (s.): ox, cattle

NEITHER MEDDLE NOR MAKE: to have nothing to do with

NEWSBOOK: newspaper (weekly, octavo)

NICOTIQUES: narcotics, medicines

NIGHTGOWN(E): dressing gown

NOISE: group of musical instruments playing together

NORE, the: anchorage in mouth of Thames

NORTHDOWNE ALE: Margate ale

NOSE: to insult, affront

NOTE: thing deserving of note; note of credit

NOTORIOUS: famous, well-known

OBNOXIOUS: liable to

OBSERVABLE (adj.): noteworthy, notorious

OBSERVABLE (s.): thing or matter worthy of observation

OFFICE DAY: day on which a meeting of the Navy Board was held

OLEO (Sp. *olla*): stew

OMBRE (Sp. *hombre*): card game

ONLY: main, principal, best

OPEN: unsettled

OPERA: spectacular entertainment (involving use of painted scenery and stage machinery), often with music

OPERA, the: the theatre in Lincoln's Inn Fields. *See* 'Duke's House, the'

OPINIASTRE, OPINIASTREMENT (Fr.): stubborn, stubbornly

OPPONE: to oppose, hinder

ORDER: to put in order; to punish

ORDINARY (adj.): established

ORDINARY (s.): eating place serving fixed-price meals; peace-time establishment (of navy, dockyard, etc.)

OUTPORTS: ports other than London

OVERSEEN: omitted, neglected; guilty of oversight

OWE: to own

PADRON (?Sp., ?It. *patrone*): master

PAGEANT: decorated symbolic float in procession

PAINFUL: painstaking

PAIR OF OARS: large river-boat rowed by two watermen, each using a pair of oars. Cf. 'Scull'

PAIR OF ORGANS/VIRGINALS: a single instrument

PALACE: New Palace Yard

PALER: parlour

PARAGON: heavy rich cloth, partly of mohair

PARCEL: share, part; isolated group

PARK, the: normally St James's Park (Hyde Park is usually named)

PARTY: charter-party

PASSION: feeling, mood

PASSIONATE: touching, affecting

PATTEN: overshoe

PAY: to berate, beat

PAY [HIS] COAT: to beat, chastise

PAY SICE: to pay dearly (sixfold)

PENDANCES, PENDENTS: lockets; earrings

PERPLEX: to vex

PERSPECTIVE, PERSPECTIVE GLASSES: binoculars

PESLEMESLE: pall-mall, early form of croquet

PETTY BAG: petty cash

PHILOSOPHY: natural science

PHYSIC: laxative, purge

PHYSICALLY: without sheets, uncovered

PICK: pique

PICK A HOLE IN [HIS] COAT: to pick a quarrel, complain

PICKAROON (Sp. *picarón*): pirate, privateer

PIECE: gold coin worth *c*. 20*s*.

PIECE (PEECE) OF EIGHT: Spanish silver coin worth 4*s*. 6*d*.

PIGEON: coward

PINK(E): small broad-beamed ship; poniard, pointed weapon

PINNER: coif with two long flaps; fill-in above low *décolletage*

PIPE: measure of wine (*c*. 120 galls.)

PIPE (musical): flageolet or recorder

PISTOLE: French gold coin worth 16*s*.

PLACKET: petticoat

PLAIN: unaffected

PLAT(T): plate, plan, chart, map; arrangement; level; [flower] plot

PLATERER: one who works silver plate

PLAY (v.): to play for stakes

POINT, POYNT: piece of lace

POINT DE GESNE: Genoa lace

POLE: head; head-and-shoulder (of fish); poll tax

POLICY: government; cunning; self-interest

POLLARD: cut-back, stunted tree

POMPOUS: ceremonious, dignified

POOR JACK: dried salt cod

POOR WRETCH: poor dear

POSSET: drink made of hot milk, spices, and wine (or beer)

POST (v.): to expose, pillory

POST WARRANT: authority to employ posthorses

POSY: verse or phrase engraved on inside of ring

POWDERED (of meat): salted

PRACTICE: trick

PRAGMATIC, PRAGMATICAL: interfering, conceited, dogmatic

PRATIQUE: ship's licence for port facilities given on presentation of clean bill of health

PRESBYTER JOHN: puritan parson

PRESENT (s.): shot, volley

PRESENT, PRESENTLY: immediate, immediately

PRESS BED: bed folding into or built inside a cupboard

PREST MONEY (milit., naval): earnest money paid in advance

PRETTY (of men): fine, elegant, foppish

PREVENT: to anticipate

PRICK: to write out music; to list

PRICK OUT: to strike out, delete

PRINCE: ruler

PRINCIPLES (of music): natural ability, rudimentary knowledge

PRISE, PRIZE: worth, value, price

PRIVATE: small, secret, quiet

PRIZE FIGHT: fencing match fought for money

PROPRIETY: property, ownership

PROTEST (a bill of exchange): to record non-payment

PROUD (of animals): on heat

PROVOKE: to urge

PULL A CROW: to quarrel

PURCHASE: advantage; profit; booty

PURELY: excellently

PURL(E): hot spiced beer

PUSS: ill-favoured woman

PUT OFF: to sell, dispose of

PYONEER: pioneer (ditch digger, labourer)

QU: cue

QUARREFOUR: crossroads

QUARTER, to keep a: to make a disturbance

QUARTERAGE: any salary or sum paid quarterly

QUEST HOUSE: house used for inquests, parish meetings

QUINBROUGH: Queenborough, Kent

QUINSBOROUGH: Königsberg, E. Prussia

RACE: to rase, destroy

RAKE-SHAMED: disreputable, disgraceful

RARE: fine, splendid

RATE: to berate, scold

RATTLE: to scold

RATTOON: rattan cane

READY: quick, accomplished

REAKE: trick

RECEPI: writ of receipt issued by Chancery

RECITATIVO (stilo r.): the earliest type of recitative singing

RECONCILE: to settle a dispute, to determine the truth

RECORDER: family of end-blown, eight-holed instruments (descant, treble, tenor, bass); P played the treble

RECOVER: to reconcile

RECOVERY (legal): process for re-establishment of ownership

REDRIFFE: Rotherhithe, Surrey

REFERRING: indebted, beholden to

REFORM: to disband

REFORMADO: naval/military officer serving without commission

REFRESH (of a sword): to sharpen

RELIGIOUS: monk, nun

REPLICACION (legal): replication, plaintiff's answer to defendant's plea

RESEMBLE: to represent, figure

RESENT: to receive

RESPECT: to mean, refer to

RESPECTFUL: respectable

REST: wrest, tuning key

RETAIN (a writ): to maintain a court action from term to term

REVOLUTION: sudden change (not necessarily violent)

RHODOMONTADO: boast, brag

RIGHT-HAND MAN: soldier on whom drill manoeuvres turn

RIGHTS, to: immediately, directly

RINGO: eryngo (sea-holly)

RIS (v.): rose, risen

RISE: origin

RIX DOLLER: Dutch or N. German silver coin (*Rijksdaalder, Reichsthaler*) worth *c.* 4s. 9d.

ROCKE: distaff

ROMANTIQUE: having the characteristics of a tale (romance)

ROUNDHOUSE: uppermost cabin in stern of ship

ROYALL THEATRE, the: *see* 'Theatre, the'

RUB(B): check, stop, obstacle

RUFFIAN: pimp, rogue

RUMP: remnant of the Long Parliament

RUMPER: member or supporter of the Rump

RUNLETT: cask

RUNNING: temporary

SACK: white wine from Spain or Canaries

SALT: salt-cellar

SALT-EELE: rope's end or leather belt used for punishment

SALVE UP: to smooth over

SALVO: excuse, explanation

SARCENET: thin taffeta, fine silk cloth

SASSE (Du. *sas*): sluice, lock

SAVE: to be in time for

SAY: fine woollen cloth

SCALE (of music): key; gamut

SCALLOP: scalloped lace collar

SCALLOP-WHISK: *see* 'Whiske'

SCAPE (s.): adventure

SCAPE (v.): to escape

SCARE-FIRE: sudden conflagration

SCHOOL: to scold, rebuke

SCHUIT (Du.): Dutch canal boat, barge

SCONCE: bracket, candlestick

SCOTOSCOPE: portable *camera obscura*

SCOWRE: to beat, punish

SCREW: key, screw-bolt

SCRUPLE: to dispute

SCULL, SCULLER: small river-boat rowed by a single waterman using one pair of oars. Cf. 'Pair of oars'

SEA-CARD: chart

SEA-COAL: coal carried by sea

SEA-OFFICERS: commissioned officers of the navy. Cf. 'Navy Officers'

SECOND MOURNING: half-mourning

SEEL (of a ship): to lurch

SEEM: to pretend

SENNIT: sevennight, a week

SENSIBLY: perceptibly, painfully

SERPENT: variety of firework

SERVANT: suitor, lover

SET: sit

SET UP/OFF ONE'S REST: to be certain, to be content, to make an end, to make one's whole aim

SEWER: stream, ditch

SHAG(G): worsted or silk cloth with a velvet nap on one side

SHEATH (of a ship): to encase the hull as a protection against worm

SHIFT (s.): trial; dressing room

SHIFT (v.): to change clothes; to dodge a round in paying for drinks (or to get rid of the effects of drink)

SHOEMAKER'S STOCKS: new shoes

SHOVE AT: to apply one's energies to

SHROUD: shrewd, astute

SHUFFLEBOARD: shovelboard, shove-ha'penny

SHUTS: shutters

SILLABUB, SULLYBUB, SYLLABUB: milk mixed with wine

SIMPLE: foolish

SIT: to hold a meeting

SIT CLOSE: to hold a meeting from which clerks are excluded

SITHE: sigh

SKELLUM: rascal, thief

SLENDERLY: slightingly

SLICE: flat plate

SLIGHT, SLIGHTLY: contemptuous; slightingly, without ceremony

SLIP A CALF/FILLY: to abort

SLOP(P)S: seamen's ready-made clothes

SLUG(G): slow heavy boat; rough metal projectile

SLUT (not always opprobrious): drudge, wench

SMALL (of drink): light

SNAP(P) (s.): bite, snack, small meal; attack

SNAP (v.): to ambush, cut down/out/off

SNUFF: to speak scornfully

SNUFFE, take/go in: to take offence

SOKER: old hand; pal; toper

SOLD(E)BAY: Solebay, off Southwold, Suff.

SOL(L)ICITOR: agent; one who solicits business

SON: son-in-law (similarly with daughter etc.)

SON-IN-LAW: stepson

SOUND: fish-bladder

SOUND, the: strictly the navigable passage between Denmark and Sweden where tolls were levied, but more generally (and usually in Pepys) the Baltic

SPARROWGRASS: asparagus

SPEAK BROAD: to speak fully, frankly

SPECIALITY: bond under seal

SPECIES (optical): image

SPEED: to succeed

SPIKET: spigot, tap, faucet

SPILT, SPOILT: ruined

SPINET: single-manual wing-shaped keyboard instrument with harpsichord action

SPOIL: to deflower; injure

SPOTS: patches (cosmetic)

SPRANKLE: sparkling remark, *bon mot*

SPUDD: trenching tool

STAIRS: landing stage

STAND IN: to cost

STANDING WATER: between tides

STANDISH: stand for ink, pens, etc.

STATE-DISH: richly decorated dish; dish with a round lid or canopy

STATESMAN: Commonwealth's-man

STATIONER: bookseller (often also publisher)

STEEPLE: tower

STEMPEECE: timber of ship's bow

STICK: blockhead

STILLYARD, the: the Steelyard

STOMACH: courage, pride; appetite

STONE-HORSE: stallion

STOUND: astonishment

STOUT: brave, courageous

STOWAGE: storage, payment for storage

STRAIGHTS, STREIGHTS, the: strictly the Straits of Gibraltar; more usually the Mediterranean

STRANG: strong

STRANGERS: foreigners

STRIKE (nautical): to lower the topsail in salute; (of Exchequer tallies) to make, cut

STRONG WATER: distilled spirits

SUBSIDY MAN: man of substance (liable to pay subsidy-tax)

SUCCESS(E): outcome (good or bad)

SUDDENLY: in a short while

SUPERNUMERARY: seaman extra to ship's complement

SURLY: imperious, lordly

SWINE-POX: chicken-pox

SWOUND: to swoon, faint

SYMPHONY: instrumental introduction, interlude etc., in a vocal composition

TAB(B)Y: watered silk

TABLE: legend attached to a picture

TABLE BOOK: memorandum book

TABLES: backgammon and similar games

TAILLE, TALLE (Fr. *taille*): figure, shape (of person)

TAKE EGGS FOR MONEY: to cut one's losses, to accept something worthless

TAKE OUT: to learn; perform
TAKE UP: to patch up, reform
TAKING (s.): condition
TALE: reckoning, number
TALL: fine, elegant
TALLE: *see* 'Taille'
TALLY: wooden stick used by the Exchequer in accounting
TAMKIN: tampion, wooden gun plug
TANSY, TANZY: egg pudding flavoured with tansy
TARGET: shield
TARPAULIN: 'tar', a sea-bred captain as opposed to a gentleman-captain
TAXOR: financial official of university
TEAR: to rant
TELL: to count
TEMPER (s.): moderation; temperament, mood; physical condition
TEMPER (v.): to moderate, control
TENDER: chary of
TENT: roll of absorbent material used for wounds; (Sp. *tinto*) red wine
TERCE, TIERCE: measure of wine (42 galls.; one-third of a pipe)
TERELLA: terrella, spherical magnet, terrestrial globe containing magnet
TERM(E)S: menstrual periods
THEATRE, the: before May 1663 usually Theatre Royal, Vere St; afterwards usually Theatre Royal, Drury Lane (TR)
THEM: *see* 'Those'
THEORBO: large double-necked tenor lute
THOSE: menstrual periods
THRUSH: inflammation of throat and mouth
TICKELED: annoyed, irritated
TICKET(T): seaman's pay-ticket
TILT: awning over river-boat
TIMBER: wood for the skeleton of a ship (as distinct from plank or deals used for the decks, cabins, gun-platforms etc.)
TIRE: tier
TOKEN, by the same: so, then, and
TONGUE: reputation, fame

TOPS: turnovers of stockings
TOUCHED: annoyed
TOUR, the: coach parade of *beau monde* in Hyde Park
TOWN(E): manor
TOWSE: to tousle/tumble a woman
TOY: small gift
TOYLE: foil, net into which game is driven
TRADE: manufacture, industry
TRANSIRE: warrant allowing goods through customs
TRAPAN, TREPAN: (surg.) to perforate skull; cheat, trick, trap, inveigle
TREASURY, the: the Navy Treasury or the national Treasury
TREAT: to handle (literally)
TREAT, TREATY: negotiate, negotiation
TREBLE: treble viol
TRIANGLE, TRYANGLE: triangular virginals
TRILL(O): vocal ornament consisting of the accelerated repetition of the same note
TRIM: to shave
TRUCKLE/TRUNDLE-BED: low bed on castors which could be put under main bed
TRY A PULL: to have a go
TUITION: guardianship
TUNE: pitch
TURK, the: used of all denizens of the Turkish Empire, but usually here of the Berbers of the N. African coast, especially Algiers
TURKEY WORK: red tapestry in Turkish style
TURKY-STONE: turquoise
TUTTLE FIELDS: Tothill Fields
TWIST: strong thread

UGLY: awkward
UMBLES (of deer): edible entrails, giblets
UNBESPEAK: countermand
UNCOUTH: out of sorts or order, uneasy, at a loss

UNDERSTAND: to conduct oneself properly; (s.) understanding

UNDERTAKER: contractor; parliamentary manager

UNHAPPY, UNHAPPILY: unlucky; unluckily

UNREADY: undressed

UNTRUSS: to undo one's breeches, defecate

UPPER BENCH: name given in Interregnum to King's Bench

USE: usury, interest

USE UPON USE: compound interest

VAPOURING: pretentious, foolish

VAUNT: to vend, sell

VENETIAN CAP: peaked cap as worn by Venetian Doge

VESTS: robes, vestments

VIALL, VIOL: family of fretted, bowed instruments with six gut strings; the bowing hand is held beneath the bow and the instrument held on or between the knees; now mostly superseded by violin family

VIRGINALS: rectangular English keyboard instrument resembling spinet; also generic term for all plectral keyboard instruments

VIRTUOSO: man of wide learning

WAISTCOAT, WASTECOATE: warm undergarment

WAIT, WAYT (at court etc.): to serve a turn of duty (usually a month) as an official

WARDROBE, the: the office of the King's Great Wardrobe, of which Lord Sandwich was Keeper; the building at Puddle Wharf containing the office; a cloak room, dressing room

WARM: comfortable, well-off

WASSAIL, WASSELL: entertainment (e.g. a play)

WASTECLOATH: cloth hung on ship as decoration between quarter-deck and forecastle

WATCH: clock

WATER: strong water, spirits

WAY, in/out of the: accessible/inaccessible; in a suitable/unsuitable condition

WAYTES: waits; municipal musicians

WEATHER-GLASS(E): thermometer (or, less likely, barometer)

WEIGH (of ships): to raise

WELLING: Welwyn, Herts.

WESTERN BARGEMAN (BARGEE): bargee serving western reaches of Thames

WESTMINSTER: the area around Whitehall and the Abbey; not the modern city of Westminster

WHISKE: woman's neckerchief

WHITE-HALL: royal palace, largely burnt down in 1698

WHITSTER: bleacher, launderer

WIGG: wig, cake, bun

WILDE: wile

WIND (s.): wine

WIND LIKE A CHICKEN: to wind round one's little finger

WINDFUCKER: talkative braggart

WIPE: sarcasm, insult

WISTELY: with close attention

WIT, WITTY: cleverness, clever

WONDER: to marvel at

WOODMONGER: fuel merchant

WORD: utterance, phrase

WOREMOODE: wormwood

WORK: needlework. *Also* v.

YARD: penis

YARE: ready, skilful

YILDHALL: Guildhall

YOWELL: Ewell, Surrey